I0024156

JUSTICE IN THE BALANCE

Stanford Studies in Human Rights
Mark Goodale, editor

Justice in the Balance

Democracy, Rule of Law, and
the European Court of Human Rights

Jessica Greenberg

Stanford University Press
Stanford, California

Stanford University Press
Stanford, California

© 2025 by Jessica Greenberg. All rights reserved.

No part of this book may be reproduced or transmitted in any form or by any means, electronic or mechanical, including photocopying and recording, or in any information storage or retrieval system, without the prior written permission of Stanford University Press.

Library of Congress Cataloging-in-Publication Data
Names: Greenberg, Jessica, author.
Title: Justice in the balance : democracy, rule of law, and the European
    Court of Human Rights / Jessica Greenberg.
Other titles: Stanford studies in human rights.
Description: Stanford, California : Stanford University Press, 2025. |
    Series: Stanford studies in human rights | Includes bibliographical
    references and index.
Identifiers: LCCN 2024055986 (print) | LCCN 2024055987 (ebook) | ISBN
    9781503643413 (cloth) | ISBN 9781503643758 (paperback) | ISBN
    9781503643765 (ebook)
Subjects: LCSH: European Court of Human Rights. | International human
    rights courts–Europe. | Human rights–Europe. | Rule of law–Europe. |
    Democracy–Europe.
Classification: LCC KJC5138 .G74 2025 (print) | LCC KJC5138 (ebook) | DDC
    342.2408/50269–dc23/eng/20241122
LC record available at https://lccn.loc.gov/2024055986
LC ebook record available at https://lccn.loc.gov/2024055987

Cover design: Daniel Benneworth-Gray
Cover photograph: Zsófia Vera / Unsplash

The authorized representative in the EU for product safety and compliance is: Mare Nostrum Group B.V. | Mauritskade 21D | 1091 GC Amsterdam | The Netherlands | Email address: gpsr@mare-nostrum.co.uk | KVK chamber of commerce number: 96249943

Contents

Foreword

Jessica Greenberg's much anticipated new book arrives at a moment in which the status of the European Court of Human Rights (ECtHR) has become as tightly bound as ever with the tenuous condition of the vision of European unity. Against this wider background, Greenberg's powerful study offers any number of empirical and theoretical beacons of light for those rightly worried about the future of human rights and the rule of law—in Europe and beyond. And yet, the force of *Justice in the Balance* does not come from a variation on the well-rehearsed argument that human rights and justice-seeking are modes of action and discourse with more lasting vitality than imagined.

Rather, the far-reaching impact of the book is in the way it reveals a different way of understanding the meaning and scope of human rights, the rule of law, and democracy. As Greenberg puts it, these might be rightly understood as social, legal, and discursive achievements worth fighting for, but the struggle over them only partly takes place through the mechanisms of institutions like the ECtHR. Beyond Court judgments and the often-lengthy efforts to execute these judgments, the three horsemen of the modern liberal project also find their expression in everyday practices and leaps of faith, in configurations of human sociality that exist "somewhere between normativity and imagination."

Remarkably, Greenberg traces the contours of these configurations not within the hurly-burly of social activism or across the sweep of political mobilization, or even through her own participation as an engaged anthropologist, but within the august corridors of the Court itself. If a long line of critique has examined the ways in which human rights–based courts—of which the ECtHR is, in a way, a defining paragon—contribute to a pervasive global culture of judicialization—that is, the rendering of social complexity into the constraining logics and languages of law—then *Justice in the Balance* goes some way toward turning this bedrock critique on its head.

Through a landmark institutional ethnography conducted in the "halls, offices, and judicial chambers where human rights and the rule of law are made," Greenberg's research demonstrates that judicialization itself must be understood as a domain of social complexity, one marked by all of the wider contradictions, contingencies, and competing interests that the law is meant to rationalize and bring to heel. As her book examines with such clarity, the various dichotomies that sustain the judicialization critique—and the critique of legal institutions more generally—turn out to be figments, departures from reality that do particular kinds of work, but figments nonetheless.

The ECtHR does not stand apart from Europe's political conflicts; it is infused by them, even if it accounts for them in a language all its own. The Court is not a bastion of reasoned procedure, in opposition to the messiness and disorder of everyday social life; instead, it embodies this messiness, even if it mobilizes all the compromises and institutional sleights of hand that are necessary to soften its destabilizing consequences. And the Court is not a fortress protected by the law's sangfroid, shut off from the manifold crises swirling around Europe's contested borders; on the contrary, the ECtHR, like international law more generally, was born under the sign of crisis, and crises of war and peace, like Russia's invasion of Ukraine, continue to bring the limits of the Court's reach into sharp relief.

But beyond its wide-ranging contributions to debates over the meaning and sustainability of the rule of law, the future of human rights, and the viability of a model of European identity anchored in values like pluralism, tolerance for difference, and collective responsibility, *Justice in the Balance* also speaks to something else, something more fundamental: the reasons that people refuse to abandon legal institutions like the ECtHR, despite its relative impotence in the face of the greatest challenges of our time—the climate crisis, global economic and social inequality, and ecosystemic collapse, among others on a short, but existentially chilling list.

People continue to mobilize for human rights and justice and turn toward courts like the ECtHR despite it all, because, as Greenberg puts it so movingly, they are invested in the best version of these ideals, a version that might be utopian but that has become part of a shared framework for making sense of the world. And if human rights, the rule of law, and democracy—the liberal triumvirate—function in this way, as a lodestar guiding our hopes much more, even as against, our actions, it is because they continue to stand, as Greenberg argues, for a "deep commitment to humanism and the sanctity of the person."

Mark Goodale
Series Editor
Stanford Studies in Human Rights

Preface:
Making Sense of Liberalism and Law

My interest in international law and human rights began in 1996, in Pakrac, Croatia. I spent most of that summer volunteering at a UN-sponsored peace and reconciliation project. The country was ten months out from a military sweep that left the previously ethnically mixed town 70 percent destroyed and still divided. Our group of volunteers spent its days shoveling ash and timber from burned-out houses, chopping wood, hauling water, and listening to the stories of the mostly elderly who remained in town. Chastened by my American naivete about what I had witnessed, I set out to learn more about what kinds of accountability and justice were possible in the wake of violent conflict. These questions sparked and still shape my interest in law and justice.

As it turned out, conversations about post-conflict legal accountability were very much in the air. It was an optimistic moment for democracy and rule of law. The International Criminal Court Preparatory Committee meetings were underway at the United Nations that year. I took an internship at the Coalition for an International Criminal Court and eagerly followed the debates on the draft that would become the Rome Statute. Yet I struggled to make sense of the enormity of wartime violence in comparison to the endless process of legal drafting. My immediate supervisor, a member of the coalition's Women's Caucus, wrote brief after brief and attended meetings at the U.N. The caucus, a group of feminist lawyers, were lobbying to introduce language on gender violence into the statute. One day my boss rushed into the office, breathless and excited. The Prep Comm had just adopted caucus language on gender-based violence. Even as we celebrated the victory, some part of me wondered when and how small revisions to a legal text might ever matter.

The early encounters with the limits of law shaped my professional and research trajectories for the next decade. Unconvinced that liberal legal institutions were the path to social change, I moved into more direct feminist advocacy. When I returned to graduate school, I began a multiyear process researching what became my first book on Serbian student protest movements. Still, law continued to haunt the edges of my research. When I returned to Serbia for follow-up research in 2012, human rights and rule of law dominated visions for social change more than ever. Civil society groups had started to set their sights on the European Court of Human Rights in Strasbourg. I became fascinated by the institution that sought to safeguard human rights for hundreds of millions of people across the continent. Could it achieve the promises that many felt were exhausted by protest and democratic institution building? Would hope and disappointment work in the same way at the so-called center of Europe as they had in "postsocialist margins"?

In Strasbourg, I once again found I had to reconcile the paradoxes of law and justice. I tracked the ping-ponging between technical rules and procedures and the Court's lofty role as the "conscience of Europe." This was never clearer than in winter 2022, when Russia's invasion of Ukraine shook the legal communities I had been studying. After years of building democracy, rule of law and human rights, a Council of Europe member state had violated every norm on which that community was based. The war in Ukraine highlighted people's investment in the rule of law and its profound limits. As I discuss in the conclusion to this book, the links between justice and law, and the lines between complicity and institutional compromise had never seemed so fraught.

The war in Ukraine crystallized the vulnerabilities of rule-of-law institutions in the face of overwhelming state violence. But it was not the only instance that brought the fragile nature of international law to the fore. Less than two years later, the Hamas militia-led killing and capture of civilians in Israel on October 7 shocked the world. Israel's invasion of Gaza and the subsequent scale and brutality of the violence generated worldwide calls for justice and accountability. International legal institutions, from the International Court of Justice to the International Criminal Court, took center stage. They put states on notice that the world was watching. But they also failed to stop the violence.

People expressed their frustration and grief about the failures of international law in countless news columns, social media posts, classrooms, and more importantly on the streets. As one institution after another seemed to fail—international courts, the "international community," and the liberal university—young people did not wait for courts and politicians to deliver a better world. Like other movements grounded in nonliberal forms of mutual aid and self-organization, these vernacular approaches to care and social solidarity exceeded the boundaries of existing institutions (Brković 2024; Channell-Justice 2022). The scenes of student protest across North America, tent camps, impromptu libraries, Muslim and Jewish interfaith celebrations, and public education contrasted with videos of police beatings and arrests. The discrepancy prompted Belgrade-based journalist Lily Lynch to post, "Western liberals spent the four years of the Trump presidency yammering on about the 'authoritarian playbook' which they have clearly embraced themselves as an instruction manual."[1] The tension between the role of universities to safeguard academic freedom and democratic deliberation and the repression by those selfsame institutions was on full display. Indeed, it hadn't been so clear for generations.

Yet, even as existing institutions failed to deliver justice, people continued to imagine better futures through the language of legal accountability and human rights. Many people I spoke with—students, human rights activists, scholars—asked themselves what might come after this moment of new lateral solidarities, citizen volunteerism, and organizing. How could new political energies be harnessed to reshape the university, our governments, our institutions, the world? This has been an enduring question in anthropology and political and social theory: under what conditions do the contingent, energetic, and powerful moments of resistance and solidarity endure? After the revolution, what comes next? This question is not about how we theorize and how we act. It is about the necessary connection between the two.

In this, my second book, I no am no longer grappling with what happens after a revolution. Instead, I try to ask what might happen after the slow decline of its antithesis: liberalism. The reasons why people value international rule of law are clearest when these norms fail to work. It is in the breach that we can track why and how people experiment with the affordances of liberal institutions and rework them in new, transformative ways. And it is in moments of failure that we can also see how people struggle to reinvent forms and networks to coordinate social change at difference scales and across time and space. It may seem strange to ask what happens after liberalism through a granular analysis of one of its most exemplary forms: the international human rights court. But where better to understand the production of liberal commitments and their global export than from the everyday sites in which they are generated, as particular, contingent, and contested (Fedirko 2021, Candea 2021).

I made the choice to imagine "post-liberalism" within liberal institutions for three reasons (Zenker 2021, Mazzarella 2019). The first is contextual. As I note in the introduction, the judicialization of politics has emerged as the late twentieth and early twenty-first century language of post-revolutionary social change. Understanding that transition from an ethnographic, experiential, affective, and practice-based perspective is critical to understanding why liberalism gained such a deep global hold in the first place. This book is a story of why and how people come to be invested in the liberal imaginary and the sense of agency and efficacy it makes possible.

The second reason is pragmatic. In understanding why people are drawn in and hold fast to liberal imaginaries, we can better understand what work institutions do in the world. To ask this question is to force us to contend with the deeply contradictory and often painful histories of liberal institutions and liberal forms: their role in systems of domination and white supremacy and the unequal wages of the status quo (Ahmed 2012; Berlant 2016; Mills 1999). But it also provides empirical and ethnographic purchase on the role of actually existing institutions to create conditions for coordination and collaboration, experiences of efficacy and agency, and the expression of self-constituted ethical communities.

My third reason for focusing on existing liberal institutions is anthropological. As with all forms of social life, our analysis is always improved by grappling with the messy and infinitely rich lifeworlds of the people and places that we study. Anthropological complexity need not be a descriptive reiteration of how humans make meaning. It can also be a pathway to identifying strategies for moving the world forward. We are all deeply contradictory beings, and our institutions are no less so. As a teacher used to caution us in our early years of graduate school, we all have to balance our ideological checkbooks. Indeed, liberalism is nothing if not the balancing of an ideological checkbook—economistic metaphor intended. But it is precisely the act of balancing—and the movement it generates—that is important. That movement is defined by coordinates and terms not of our choosing, to be sure. But the fact of movement indicates that worlds of possibility beyond those terms are possible.

This book tries to track liberal European social, ideological, and cultural forms as they are made, contested, and (re)consolidated. I analyze what ethical stances the rule of law enables. What forms of agency do human rights shape and foster? What conversations does the language of law and human rights open and foreclose? This book foregrounds the lessons that we might take from human rights and rule-of-law institutions about communicating across conflict and difference, about defining and then stretching the scope of inclusion.

Not everyone will agree that existing institutional forms can or should be redeemed. I appreciate that some institutions are beyond saving and that we ought to be wary of reformism (Burton 2023; Luxemburg 1900). But I am not yet convinced international law and legal institutions are beyond repair. Histories of worldmaking (Getachew 2019) and the longue durée of Third World approaches to international law (Anghie 2023) provide indications that legal frameworks can be mobilized in the service of the otherwise. On-the-ground movements echo and rework liberal, constitutional forms and rule of law procedures from democratic people's plenums (Kurtović and Hromadžić 2017) to constituent assemblies and referenda (Muehlebach 2023). People mobilize mass movements through legal institutions like the European Court of Human Rights in unexpected and transformative ways—even in contexts of rising authoritarianism (Kubal 2023). These innovative uses of law help us see the importance of organizational questions in social change movements: How do we make decisions? Who should be involved? How do we sustain knowledge and relationships over time? In looking to both the old and emergent, we find pragmatic models to work through questions about the possibilities of human sociality and justice at scale.

Critically, postliberalism is not illiberalism. Reworking the fabric of institutions in the name of inclusion and social justice enhances our democracies, while illiberalism and "autocratic legalism" (Scheppele 2018) undermine them from within. If we are to move to whatever form of justice comes after liberalism, we might ask what we want to hold on to and what lessons we can take away about the possible connections among democracy, rule of law, and human rights. The analysis of actually existing rule-of-law institutions allows us to explore the lived, affective, and granular lifeworlds of the "grammars" (Fedirko et al. 2021) of "actually existing liberalism" (see Hindess 2008; Dzenovska 2018). If existing institutions have a relationship to postliberal futures, we need to interrogate how they work now. This is small step to building forms of social coordination and communication that might be more just than what came before.

Acknowledgments

This book has been a very long time in the making. Along the way I have relied on the guidance, wisdom, and support of many old friends. And I have had the pleasure and good fortune to learn from many new ones. These acknowledgments are only a partial and likely inadequate record of the gratitude I feel and the intellectual debts I owe. Thanks go first and foremost to my home department of Anthropology at the University of Illinois. I am lucky to have amazing colleagues who keep work interesting, meaningful, and fun. Thanks in particular to Kate Bishop, Jenny Davis, Jen Delfino, Brenda Farnell, Cris Hughes, Elise Kramer, Kora Maldonado, Ellen Moodie, Andy Orta, Gilberto Rosas, and Krystal Smalls. The U of I community is a warm, vibrant place, and I have especially benefitted from friendship and conversations over the years with Ikuko Asaka, Jake Bowers, Eric Calderwood, Kim Curtis, Liv T. Davila, Jerry Davila, Marc Hertzman, Jamie Jones, Lilya Kaganovsky, Brett Kaplan, Craig Koslofsky, Michelle Koven, Soo Ah Kwon, Justine Murison, Dana Rabin, John Randolph, Manuel Rota, Gisela Sin, and Cara Wong. Jackie Ross, Colleen Murphy, Margareth Etienne, and Lesley Wexler were particularly helpful in helping me ease my way into law school and providing guidance and inspiration while there and since. Antoinette Burton created a wonderful space for inquiry and community at the Humanities Research Institute, and I am particularly grateful to her, Nancy Castro, and my cohort of Humanities Research Institute Fellows for a year of lively conversation as well as time to write and think. I have always learned as much from my students as I've taught them. Gratitude goes especially to Dilara Çalışkan, Ezgi Güner, and Ben Krupp for fruitful conversations and collaborations on this and other work. I am also thankful to Tuba Akin, who provided invaluable assistance in finalizing this book manuscript. Here in Champaign-Urbana, community is of course much wider than work. A special shout-out to the kids and parents (and animals) of Carle Park, Urbana: we couldn't have come through the pandemic quite so well without your warmth, humor, and many, many afternoons under the trees.

I was lucky enough to have time, space, and support to experiment and explore over the course of this project. A University of Illinois Study in a Second Discipline Fellowship made it possible for me to enroll at the College of Law and earn a one-year master's degree. Funding for this research project also came from a National Science Foundation Law and Science Fellowship, and time in Strasbourg was supported by a Fulbright Grand-Est Fellowship. That said, the findings, conclusions, and opinions in this book are mine alone and do not necessarily represent the views of these funding agencies. I am also grateful for funding support from the UIUC Campus Research Board in the Office for the Vice Chancellor for Research (OVCR). In all these endeavors the OVCR team, led by the incomparable Maria Gillombardo, provided invaluable feedback. That team continues to keep nurturing the spirit of generosity and critical conversation inspired by our much missed colleague Nancy Abelmann.

I am in awe of and so thankful to so many friends and colleagues from whom I have learned over the years. Several of you have done more than your fair share of reading and commenting on my work, particularly Anya Bernstein, Courtney Handman, Sarah Muir, and Alejandro Paz. I have been so lucky to have Susan Gal as a mentor and a role model for many years. Inspiration has come from reading and talking with Jens Adam, Hayal Akarsu, Gretchen Bakke, Amahl Bishara, Čarna Brković, Erica Bornstein, Heath Cabot, Summerson Carr, Jillian Cavanaugh, Frank Cody, Susan Coutin, Jane Cowan, Hilary Dick, Ela Drążkiewicz, Elizabeth Dunn, Dace Dzenovska, Taras Fedirko, Sandhya Fuchs, Ilana Gershon, Andrew Gilbert, Radhika Govindrajan, Andrew Graan, Sarah Green, Elissa Helms, David Henig, Douglas Holmes, Azra Hromadžić, Larisa Kurtović, Jonathan Larson, Paul Manning, Agathe Mora, Andrea Muehlebach, Arzoo Osanloo, Aga Pasieka, Ivan Rajković, Jonathan Rosa, Natalie Rothman, Justin Richland, Natalia Roudakova, Shalini Shankar, James Slotta, Larissa Vetters, and Jessica Winegar. I am so very grateful to be in conversation with you.

When I began this project, I knew alarmingly little about the European

Court of Human Rights. Marie Benedicte Dembour was an invaluable resource, advocate, and friend. I am also grateful to a vibrant and exciting community of experts on the Court and Council of Europe, from whom I have learned so much: Jill Alpes, Karen Alter, Basak Çalı, Rachel Cichowski, Andrew Drzemczewski, Corina Heri, Elisabeth Lambert, Philip Leach, Mikael Madsen, Alice Margaria, and Anne Katrin Speck. In Strasbourg, I deeply benefitted from the wisdom and experience of Jeremy McBride and Tatiana Termacic. But I am most grateful for their warmth and friendship. Thanks to Katya Malareva and Rita Patrício for always-illuminating conversations. Thanks also to Thi Mai and Alex Bernemann for helping us create a home away from home. I am also deeply appreciative of space to write while in Strasbourg, as a guest of the SAGE (Sociétés, Acteurs, Gouvernement en Europe) Lab at the University of Strasbourg. None of this work would have been possible without the time, generosity, and patience of many interlocutors at the European Court of Human Rights (ECtHR) and the Council of Europe and the many strategic litigators and advocates who shared their experiences and insight with me. I hope to have done justice to your commitments and efforts in the pages of this book. I am especially grateful to the folks at the European Implementation Network, especially George Stafford and Ioana Iliescu for welcoming me into their work whenever they could and teaching me so much about implementation.

It has been a pleasure to work with Stanford University Press. Special thanks to Dylan Kyung-lim White for his enthusiasm and steady hand with the publication process. I am appreciative of the time and engagement of the two anonymous reviewers for this manuscript, and the guidance of series editor, Mark Goodale. Thanks also to Lori Allen (as Allen Key Edits) for a keen editorial eye and feedback.

As always, my family gives meaning and joy to all the work I do. For my wonderful and always supportive in-laws, Rita and Joe Doussard, I have boundless gratitude. Donald and Maxine Greenberg have always modeled curiosity, deep empathy, attunement to the human experience, and a healthy dose of cynicism. Thank you for that and for your sustained love and support since the very beginning. Joshua Greenberg, you would have been endlessly amused to know that I went to law school. I think of you every day and wonder what conversations we might have had and tort jokes we might have made. Gabriel and Julian Doussard, loving you both keeps me going. Seeing the world through your eyes makes it possible for me to hold on to curiosity, humor, joy, and hope, even in dark and difficult times. Finally, it is a miraculous thing when you build a life so intertwined with another that it is not clear where one mind ends and another begins. Any words seem utterly inadequate to express the depth of one's feelings in such a situation. But with that caveat in mind, thanks also go to Marc Doussard.

JUSTICE IN THE BALANCE

Locating the European Court of Human Rights

THE EUROPEAN COURT OF HUMAN RIGHTS (ECtHR) sits alongside the Ill River in Strasbourg, France. The city is a designated "European capital" renowned for its stunning cathedral and picturesque network of canals. Once one of the world's most contested frontiers, today you can take a leisurely bike ride across the open border with Germany or picnic on the banks of the Rhine. The city's Quartier Européen (European Quarter) is home to the Court and the Council of Europe, the continent's largest interstate nongovernmental organization, with forty-six member states. It is also home to one of two seats of the European Parliament, a European Union governance body distinct from the Council. The Quartier is marked by the weight of the region's contested history. The surrounding streets bear monuments to the statesmen that breathed life into the vision for an integrated post-WWII Europe. This they grounded in shared literary, philosophical, and scientific traditions echoing across the centuries and the city's street names. These streets mark an alternate historical imaginary of shared European origins to the bloody story of war and nationalism.

It is thus fitting that the main artery, the Avenue of Europe, transforms into the Street of Human Rights as it crosses the canal in front of the Court. After all, human rights, alongside democracy and the rule of law, is one of three pillars on which Council founders tried to secure a lasting peace. In the aftermath of World War II and amidst a growing commitment to international law, these politicians asked for the previously unthinkable: that sovereign nation states cede power to an international system based on consensus and compromise, but with binding commitments to interstate supervision. Whether the initial willingness to participate was based in cynicism or utopian thinking, progressive or conservative politics is still a matter of debate (Bates 2011; Duranti 2017). The analysis that follows will demonstrate the difficulty in disentangling the two. But the role that international legal institutions have played in shaping contemporary Europe is undeniable (Alter 2001; Stone Sweet 2004; Pavone 2022). Seventy-five years later, the resulting European Convention on Human Rights (ECHR) system has been called "the most effective system of international protection of human rights in existence" (Bates 2011, 2). It has been a leading institution among international courts and tribunals, increasingly a feature of the twentieth- and twenty-first-century legal and geopolitical landscape.

It is worth pausing to appreciate the sizable leap of faith these early legal institutions required in the wake of violence and the specter of totalitarianism in Europe. Then, as now, it is not intuitive that a consensus-based international system set up by states would be an effective mechanism to ensure rule of law, human rights, and democracy. Neither is it self-evident what "effective" would mean for a court tasked with ensuring state compliance with human rights norms for over 700 million people. Philip Leach and Alice Donald have characterized the ECHR system as "a complex web of interaction and interdependence between institutional actors, each of which has different functions, expertise, competence, and claims to legitimacy—and none of which can secure the objective of the Convention alone" (2016, 303). Analyzing and assessing the efficacy of this complex web is inseparable from asking how different stakeholders access and mobilize it (Cichowski 2007; Sundstrom et al. 2019), on what ideological grounds it rests (Dembour 2006), and who is included and excluded in the process (Dembour 2015; Baumgärtel 2019).

Other scholars of the Court have analyzed the formal mechanisms, case law, and high-level diplomatic negotiations that define the system. It is through these that the Court tries to "manage the 'dilemma of effectiveness' it confronts daily" (Stone Sweet et al. 2022, 247). This dilemma means raising standards of rights protection in Europe, while retaining the support of those on whom the Court most depends for its success. In this book, I take a different approach. I start with this "dilemma" not as a problem to be solved by technical means. I approach it as a framework through which multiple legal actors negotiate what it means to be effective in the first place. Answering any normative question about the ECHR system (Is its case law consistent? Is its doctrine well developed? Are member states adequately complying with its decisions?) depends on whom you are talking with and what is at stake. As with other transnational legal and governance networks, the answer depends on one's political and social location (Riles 2000; Cowan 2013; Muller 2013; Niezen and Sapignoli 2017). This book embraces the analytic purchase of that messiness. Multiple conflicting perspectives are not an obstacle to understanding the Court and ECHR system. They are central to understanding how international legal institutions operate and why people increasingly engage with them.

In approaching the ECHR system from this ethnographic perspective, I show that international human rights and rule-of-law institutions constitute "epistemic communities" that are grounded in but not exhausted by their formal institutional norms and goal (Haas 1992). Issuing judicial rulings and generating doctrine or norm-based codes of legal interpretation are a key part of what international legal institutions do. But they also make forms of sociality possible beyond the law. The meaning of human rights in practice sits between the norms that shape it as a prescriptive legal system and a culturally salient lifeworld (Cowan et al. 2001; Merry 2006a). In turn, legitimacy is embedded in the affects, histories, and senses that mark legality as a unique form of socially situated performance (Allen 2009, 2013; Niezen 2010; Cooper 2018; Clarke 2019; Osanloo 2020; Bens 2022).

The social legitimacy of law is always tied to its communicative properties and persuasive effects (Constable 2014; Valverde 2015). Like other forms of international governance that rely on "strategic publicity" (Graan 2016), people perform legality in relationship to differently situated audiences and publics (Cody 2023). And like other international legal institutions, the ECtHR's authority is tied to that publicity via legal spectatorship and spectacle (Eltringham 2012). Yet while the rule of law is oriented toward a "transnational public" (Rajah 2015, 350), its persuasive effect starts with everyday practices. It is this layered aspect of performance that helps us understand international law and human rights not only as an outward facing project. It is also an intimate and densely woven set of interactions that shapes legal institutions recursively "from the inside out" (Riles 2000). The commitment to enacting law cannot be separated from the relationships, professional identities, and ethical commitments it fosters. In tracking these interactions, I put the dynamic qualities of human rights at the center of an analysis of international legal institutions.

At stake is understanding why people commit to work within the constraints of law, despite its exclusions and frustrations.

Asking what nonnormative work international legal institutions *do* leads to answers to another pressing question: why are people across the world increasingly turning to legal institutions to secure collective political futures? Scholars have named this growing intersection of law, governance, and social change the juridification or judicialization of politics (Hirschl 2004; Huneeus et al. 2010; Eckert et al. 2012). As an ideological project, it is defined by people's "startingly persistent faith in 'the law' and the growing recourse to legal means to envision social and political change (Eckert et al. 2012, 3). This wasn't always the case, particularly when international legal institutions first came on the scene. For much of the twentieth century, human rights law played second fiddle to contentious street politics, solidarity movements, and armed resistance (Moyn 2010). In Strasbourg, it took the court until 1968 to even issue its first ruling—a far cry from the thousands of cases it hears now.

This began to change in the waning days of the Cold War. The 1990s were a veritable age of rule of law and donor-led democratization efforts (Guilhot 2005). The proliferation of legal institutions included international criminal courts and tribunals, regional human rights courts, people's tribunals, and transitional justice mechanisms across the globe (Alter et al. 2018; Wilson 2001, 2011; Clarke 2009; Teitel 2014, 2011; Chowra and Shafafi 2019). These have arisen alongside or been fueled by the expansion of a global industry in rule of law, democracy promotion, and constitutional reform movements (Carothers 2006; Shaffer et al. 2019).

At the same time, the rise of international human rights has been a key factor in displacing revolution with legal technocracy (Goodale 2019). And it is not only left, progressive, or liberal social movements that are judicializing politics. We are seeing the results of increased judicialization in conservative strategic litigation and organizing as well (Ziegler 2020). It is a move best encapsulated by the shift from an age of revolutions (Skocpol 1979) to the "bureaucratization of utopia" through international governance and law (Billaud and Cowan 2020).

What accounts for this turn to judicial solutions for complex social and political problems? And why would people turn to law when legal advocacy often raises as many questions as it resolves (Marshall and Hale 2014)? Thirty-plus years have revealed the limits of legal and judicial reform efforts in democratization. In some cases, constitutional reform has been central to what Kim

Lane Scheppele has termed "autocratic legalism:" a form of lawfare or abuse of legal mechanisms for anti-democratic means (2018). Critiques of human rights from both theoretical and empirical grounds are exhaustive (Langford 2018). International legal institutions have perpetuated racism, colonial legacies, and even plunder (Achiume and Bali 2021; Anghie 2005; Clarke 2019; Mattei and Nader 2008).

Yet activists and engaged legal scholars continue to invest hope in the idea that international law and human rights can do better (Sikkink 2018). Social change agents build and mobilize international legal framework to create transnational legal normativities from below (Canfield et al. 2021). Some of these efforts are driven by strategic actors taking advantage of new institutional opportunities—particularly in the context of European integration. Strategic litigators and cause lawyers (Pavone 2022; Sarat and Scheingold 2001), NGOs (Hodson 2011), and a rising transnational lawyer class have driven the turn to courts out of professional interests (Dezalay and Garth 2012; Vauchez 2012). But this does not alone explain the pervasiveness of the turn to law among both elite and grassroots actors across the ideological spectrum. Nor does it explain the dramatic and often emotional tone of policymakers, lawyers, activists, or scholars. For many, law is a bulwark against authoritarianism, populism, and other crises of democracy (Lacey 2019). Human rights law can spark feelings of urgency, hope, frustration, compromise, and even boredom or despair (Langford 2018). The rule of law sparks passion from lawyers, media personalities, politicians, and street protestors. It even has the ability "to hurt feelings" (Buyse et al. 2021, 2).

This book speaks to why judicialization is such a compelling form of sociality for those who practice and participate in it. We rarely look to liberal, proceduralist institutions themselves to ask why they compel loyalty even, or especially, in times of institutional vulnerability or perceived crisis. Drawing on my research across the ECHR system, I show that investments in international legal-institution building are not only a strategic endeavor. These investments exceed formal boundaries between law and politics, rationality and emotion despite (and sometimes through) maintenance and projection of those distinctions and categories. Everyday practices of judicialization are a means of responding to the limits of human agency in an impossibly complex and often violent world. Engaging with legal and human rights institutions allows diverse social actors to focus sustained attention, create shared frameworks, and build relationships over time. It is in this sense that judicialization is its own kind of worldmaking and political imagination channeled through the logics and language of law. Understanding this begins in the halls, offices, and judicial chambers where human rights and rule of law are made, from the ground up. It requires asking how international legal institutions become institutions in the first place.

What Is the ECHR System and What Does It Do?

What is the European Convention on Human Rights? And how does a seventy-year-old, sixty-two-page document support the weight of forty-six member countries, six hundred registry staff, seven hundred million people subject to Court jurisdiction, and tens of thousands of judgments, case documents, and domestic legal systems? How does one build from the fragile basis of soft diplomatic power and moral authority to a European constitutional order? (Stone Sweet 2009). Answering these questions starts with the ways that the Council of Europe translates democracy, human rights, and rule of law from ideas to practice and from paper to material infrastructure.

These three pillars refer to the system's core values. They are also reflected in the Council's organization. Democracy is enacted through deliberation that recalls but cannot substitute for that of its democratic state membership. The Secretary General, elected by the Council's Parliamentary Assembly, provides leadership and sets the strategic plan and budget. The Committee of Ministers, composed of member-state foreign secretaries or permanent diplomatic representatives, has the power to draft treaties, which must be signed by member states to take effect. It also oversees execution of the European Court's judgments. The Parliamentary Assembly is composed of 306 members of Parliament from member states that deliberate twice a year. It is responsible for electing the Secretary General, Human Rights Commissioner, and judges (one from each member state) for nine-year terms to the Court. The system's commitment to democratic participation allows for formal mechanisms for civil society participation. These include the Congress of International Non-Governmental Organizations and local electoral representation via the Congress of Local and Regional Authorities. The Human Rights Commissioner is tasked with independent oversight of human rights compliance.

The ECtHR, the largest binding human rights court in Europe, is the crown jewel of this system. The Court oversees compliance with the ECHR. The Convention includes rights of freedom from torture and slavery, criminal and civil procedural guarantees, and freedom of conscience, religion, and expression, to name a few. Although the Council of Europe has produced many treaties, the ECHR is the most extensive. Accession to the Convention is required for all Council members. This brings them into the Court's binding jurisdiction. One of the system's most unique features is that it grants the right of individual petition. Unlike most apex, or high, courts, individual applicants can bring cases to the ECtHR for state violations of their Convention rights. The system offers human rights protections to over 700 million people, citizen or not, if they are on member state territory or territory within a member's effective control.[1] This comprehensive jurisdiction and individual petition translates into a Court mailroom flooded with thousands of ink-and-paper appeals from applicants across the continent every year. The tension between individual application and the massive administrative apparatus that it requires is often expressed through two competing characterizations of the ECHR system: the conscience of Europe or a bureaucratic machine.

The Court itself is an impressive glass and steel building. Beyond the gates, up the stairs, and past a security desk and metal detectors is a large atrium. It is an open, light-filled space enclosed by floor-to-ceiling windows. The atrium contains a large upright display case filled with copies of the ECHR translated into the languages of the Council member states. Beyond this is another set of doors leading to a warren of offices that stretch back a full city block. It is here that over six hundred staff, including lawyers and administrative support, and forty-six judges process applications, prepare and translate files, communicate Court findings to the public, and decide on cases.

Lawyers and administrative and translation staff form the registry. They are tasked with providing legal and technical support for the Court's judicial functions. Alongside judges, drafting lawyers compose judgments once cases have been decided. Depending on their legal complexity, these decisions are taken by different judicial formations. These can consist of one, three, seven, or seventeen judges. Seven-judge formations are organized into sections. They issue rulings, known as Chamber judgments. States and applicants can appeal these Chamber judgments. If they win the right to appeal, the case moves to a seventeen-judge formation known as the Grand Chamber, which may uphold or overturn the initial ruling.

When the Court determines that a state has violated the Convention, responsibility for overseeing the implementation process moves from the legal arm of the ECHR system to its diplomatic one. Council staff working to implement judgments are housed across the street. Court judgments are legal decisions about whether a state violated the rights outlined in the Convention. If a violation is found, the Court will outline an individual measure, often in the form of monetary compensation. But a violation can also result in policy or legal changes within national systems. The process of supervising these individual and general measures falls to the Committee of Ministers (CM), composed of members of national diplomatic corps. They are supported by the Department for the Execution of Judgments, which is staffed by lawyers. The CM meets four times a year to review judgments being executed. These Committee of Ministers' Human Rights (CMDH) meetings are confidential and allow diplomatic representatives to negotiate over judgments, oversee the execution, and engage in persuasion, diplomatic negotiation, and information sharing. Although the meetings are closed, civil society groups have formal channels to submit information to the CM for consideration.

With jurisdiction over forty-six member states and the right of individual petition, judges would never be able to rule on all cases that flood the mailroom. The Court has strict admissibility rules that dictate whether it will hear an applicant's case.[2] There are practical, legal, and geopolitical reasons for these limitations. From a pragmatic perspective, the Court does not have the staff or funding to hear every case from every applicant. Admissibility criteria weed out cases that are not covered by the Convention, are not filed within the Court's four-month timeline, or have not met other procedural criteria. A case may be rejected without review on the merits or the substance of its claims. Most cases are rejected for failure to comply with procedural criteria. Of these, the most significant is whether applicants have exhausted all available domestic remedies in their home jurisdictions. Applicants must take their case all the way to highest possible court in their national legal system that has jurisdiction and can provide an effective remedy.

Exhaustion speaks to the Court's role as a guarantor of shared human rights values among a group of sovereign nation states. The ECtHR is not meant to substitute for domestic legal systems and remedies already in place. It is only if those systems do not functionally uphold Convention principles that the Court has jurisdiction. But exhaustion also has another important role to play. It generates the materials that ultimately make it into a file on which the Strasbourg Court can base its ruling. The Court does not review the facts of a case. In technical terms, it is not a Court of "fourth instance." It instead reviews whether a domestic judicial system was in compliance with

ECHR principles in its investigation and review. Records of these domestic judicial proceedings are central to ECtHR review.

Exhaustion also reflects the system's commitment to subsidiarity. Subsidiarity is a theory of power sharing and rule of law based on European institutions' respect for the democratic sovereignty and cultural and political norms of the member states. At the same time, the Court's role in "European supervision" and subsidiarity are always in play. This interplay shapes judicial interpretation. Judges and drafting lawyers must balance case law, the Convention, the domestic legal record and national judges' reasoning, and the details of an applicant's case. Ultimately, the goal of the system is to harmonize and integrate ECHR principles into domestic systems. This would mean that national legal and legislative systems have so thoroughly integrated ECHR principles and procedures that there is no need for a European-level human rights court at all. It is a vision of European unity achieved through the force of law.

Within this Court and Council structure there are clear institutional competencies for ensuring that member states uphold the three pillars of democracy, human rights, and rule of law. But while these commitments are the system's raison d'être, what they mean in practice is more elusive. The ECHR outlines human rights obligations and their limits. The Court's judgments form an extensive archive of interpretation and guidelines for realizing these rights in specific cases. This body of knowledge is known as case law. Judges balance Convention rights and past Court decisions within the bounds of interpretative frameworks, or doctrines. Achieving the balance between democratic and international legal sources of institutional authority produces the third of the Council's core pillars: the rule of law. The rule of law is a principle by which public powers are subject to legal constraints. In theory, the legal nature of these constraints is paramount. That no one is above the law is ensured through regular and transparent application of procedures that apply to even the most powerful. It is a means of "tempering power" (Krygier 2019, 2016). As the law checks political power, political institutions—grounded in democratic will via representative processes—limit judicial power.

The rule of law requires balancing political and legal forms within democratic systems of representation and governance. By managing this balance, judges, policymakers, and state representatives carve out domains for the legitimate exercise of power. The balance is also premised on a normative distinction between domains of law and of politics. But as with most ideological distinctions, things are a little more complicated in practice. In the words of a senior official at the Council of Europe, an expert in human rights and constitutional law, the rule of law is "a process" and "not a definition." There is no *fixed* relationship between law and politics, he explained, nor between an international human rights court and democratic, sovereign nation-states. The rule of law requires "balancing" the irresolvable flux among institutional values and norms. It is a process that is always embedded in concrete relations of power and the histories, contexts, and meanings that shape interpretation in practice (Çalı 2007). At heart then, studying the ECtHR begins with analyzing the stakes, participants, and means of this careful and constant balancing act.

Methods for Studying International Legal Institutions

One of this book's central epistemological commitments is to analyze global systems by locating them socially and historically. But how does one study socially situated processes across a vast international legal network? I begin from the premise that the ECHR system is fundamentally shaped by the interpretative and communicative frameworks it generates and the interactions those frameworks make possible. Transnational legal networks are always realized in the communicative forms through which people activate and navigate them (Canfield 2022; Babul 2017; Merry 2006b). Attuning to such "communicative infrastructures" (Handman 2025: 8) is a way of tracking the social life of categories and concepts that often seem too diffuse or abstract to be subject to granular analysis.

It is for this reason that I focus not only on what my interlocutors say but on the production and maintenance of institutional channels through which those communications flow (Handman 2025). I examine how certain relationships come to "count" as legitimate "communicative pathways" and the social and ideological work that goes into creating and policing the boundaries around them (Handman 2025: 18). In a legal context like a court, people are often quite reflexive about the intertextual links and the genres through which people are authorized to speak in legally consequential ways (Cabatingan 2023; Richland 2021). This reflexivity constitutes the distinction between what (and who) is inside and outside the law. In turn, advocates, litigators, and applicants work to move ideas, texts, and people across those boundaries in order to rework legal accessibility and recognition from within (Greenberg 2024). In this way, we can view the ECHR system and the

Court as an ideological, material, and epistemological conjuncture in which certain ways of seeing the world, posing questions, and generating solutions come to make sense. They are what David Scott (2004) has called a "problem space"—a framework through which people channel collective questions through shared, if contested ways of posing and answering questions about the world. As a problem space the ECHR system works to cohere and delimit "a context of argument and, therefore, one of *intervention*" (Scott, 4; italics in original). Asking and answering questions through the language of human rights shapes "an ensemble of questions and answers around which a horizon of identifiable stakes . . . hangs. That is to say, what defines this discursive context are not only the particular problems that get posed as problems as such . . . but the particular questions that seem worth asking and the kinds of answers that seem worth having" (Scott 2004, 4). Not everyone is equally positioned to speak or be listened to. In this sense, problem spaces enable and they limit. They endure and they change. But they form the communicative warp and woof that makes institutional action possible and sensical. Conducting an ethnography of a global problem space forced me to make some unique methodological choices. I started with the anthropological insight that all international legal systems begin and end with ordinary people and their everyday practices. Using inductive field-based methods, my early interviews focused on people's experiences of working in the Court or the Council or in litigating cases in Strasbourg. Over time, I identified common ways of talking about the ECHR system, as well as shared concerns. For example, the question of backlog of unprocessed cases came up early and often. This keyed me into tensions within the institution that I address throughout the book. Strategic litigators often spoke to me about the time that cases took, something that inspired the analysis of chapter 5. In this way, I developed an analytic framework through which I could navigate a vast research site through conversational give and take. It was a process highly dependent on the time, generosity, and insight of the many people I spoke to.

My participant selection was likewise broad. I conducted about 100 formal interviews, engaged in participant observation and many informal conversations. I tried to account for a range of different professional and personal roles through which people engage the ECHR system. I used snowball-sampling methods, relying on interviewees to refer me to other colleagues and acquaintances who would be willing to talk. This expanded my reach across several different networks. It was especially important in a context in which confidentiality and professional ties are important for vetting trustworthiness. This method also allowed me to trace social and conversational links through which ideas, texts, and negotiations flowed. These included repeat players in litigation, advocacy networks, and relationships among judges and registry staff with long-standing ties to Strasbourg and each other.

Of course, individual perspectives were important and often revelatory. I include these where I can. However, given the demands of confidentiality, I often cite to people when their comments are exemplary of larger debates. Rather than quote exhaustively, I put different voices and perspectives in conversation to draw out resonances across them. I listened for evidence of the world that different people, often strangers to each other, co-created through shared genres and reference points. This process helped me identify thematic nexus points: instances of disagreement and agreement through the shared terms that people use to diagnose problems and invest meaning in the ECHR system.

Because I did my research over several years (2016–2024), the character and context of these conversations changed. They often focused on the concerns of the day, including prominent cases or salient political and legal events. But I was also able to see how the maintenance of networks and connections created a sense of institutional continuity. Any ethnography is only a snapshot of a particular moment in time. But by comparing the narratives, key terms, and driving questions that interlocutors shared at one moment in time with those of other periods, I was able to track how my interlocutors created a sense of institutional continuity and discontinuity. In turn, I was able to analyze concretely what people counted as "crisis" or a destabilizing threat to the rule of law and what they held onto as enduring features of the system, such as proceduralism or case law consistency. Of course, what counted as crisis, threat, or resource also shifted over time and from different perspectives, as I discuss throughout the book. This is especially clear in chapter 4 on the use and meaning of numbers. I also sampled for interviewees across generations and periods of Court history: former and sitting judges; senior, middle rank, and junior registry lawyers; newer and more experienced litigators and advocates. This intergenerational focus alongside case law and archival documents helped me track patterns and shifts in how people expressed hopes, aspirations, and frustrations with the ECHR system.

People's sense of the institution was also impacted by how the Court and Council function as a workplace. I spoke to people formally and informally about their workplace experiences, including the administrative assistants, librarians, and translators who also make the Court what it is. These professionals are not only critical participants in the often-invisible labor of Court administration and functioning. They also have firsthand contact with the practical limits of human rights law as a bureaucratic apparatus—from dealing with translating paper applications and judgments across languages and workable digital formats to managing the pace of workflow and communication systems.[3] Along the way, I was able to get a sense of the rhythms of work life, the movement of texts, and affective and embodied experiences at the Court. I followed these aspects of law as labor through interviews, office observation, and group interactional settings at conferences, presentations, and workshops. I supplemented these observations with analysis of cases and case law guides, Grand Chamber hearings, and other recordings of conferences, speeches, and events, all available online.

At times, my interlocuters were careful about what they shared with me. Given the importance of confidentiality in the system, I tried hard to respect those boundaries (see chapters 2 and 3). I use pseudonyms throughout the book, except when referring to published work by Council staff or judges.[4] Readers may find it frustrating that I do not give more explicit details. And indeed, at times knowing people's specific country of origin and other background material would make the analysis richer. But because the ECHR system is relatively small and people might be easily identified by specifics such as country, age, gender, or position (especially if used in combination), I usually omit these details. Instead, I give a sense of who people are institutionally within the broader conversations I outline.

These methodological choices centered the interactional and reflexive dynamics at the heart of legal institutions. I actively included my own voice and perspectives in how I framed questions or offered comments in conversation. This helped me connect with people on a more substantive level, clarify what I didn't understand, and be more transparent about my research goals. As part of this project, I earned a master's in law at my home institution in 2016–2017. My goal was to better understand the legal field and learn important content and legal writing skills (including comparative international and human rights law and common law legal interpretative approaches).[5] My goal was also to experience and embody the law from a practitioner perspective, as much as possible. I came to this project with extensive training in critical legal and social theory and felt confident in my ability to engage from this perspective. But I was interested in being able to think and act from *within* law's normative constraints. It was not easy to reconcile the two. I had to learn to wear different hats in different conversations—for example, when sitting exams or later teaching graduate and undergraduate courses in the anthropology of law. But it was an experience that I discovered resonated with many of my interlocutors. They also constantly balanced their observations, convictions, and nonlegal critical perspectives with their commitment to working within legal constraints and logics.

When discussing these tensions, I found that people were open to critique and engaged in it productively themselves. In one of my first interviews with a senior lawyer at the Court, he urged me to be critical, noting it was good for the system to have outside perspectives. At the same time, most people were protective of the Court, an institution that inspired both occasional doubts and deep commitment. I have tried to honor the spirit of critique with care that I saw mirrored in my conversations over the years. As I discuss below, critique with care is particularly important in an international legal institution that rests on consensus. This is not only an ethical question. It also speaks to the ways in which the rule of law is always a situated performance. Attending to these interactive aspects of legal legitimacy and its simultaneously enduring and fragile qualities is a central contribution of this book.

Vernacularizing the Global: Human Rights and the Anthropology of Europe

I built an analytic framework through which to track the institutional and legal contexts central to my object of study through the ethnographic approach outlined above. From an anthropological perspective, these institutional contexts are necessary but not sufficient for getting at the social life of law. The next step in my analysis was to embed categories of practice in the social and cultural contexts of the ECtHR as a uniquely European institution. As Sally Merry has noted in analyzing the circulation of human rights across different contexts, the "things we call global are often circulating locals" (2006b, 40). What she terms "venacularization of human rights" is not only a process of translating from cosmopolitan ideas to "local" contexts. The global "center" is likewise composed of its own particularities. How and why people believe in local norms as universally binding requires empirical attention to Europe as a place and a project, shaped by what Michel-Rolph Trouillot (2002) has called "North Atlantic universals." Such universalizing norms are words that project the North Atlantic experience on a universal scale that they themselves helped to create. North Atlantic universals are particulars that have gained a degree of universality, chunks of human history that have become historical standards. They do not describe the world; they offer visions of the world. They appear to refer to things as they exist, but because they are rooted in a particular history, they evoke multiple layers of sensibilities, persuasions, cultural assumptions, and ideological choices tied to that localized history. (847)

It is this combination of situated practice and institutionally backed abstraction that creates the universal as such.

Vernacularizing the global means placing the ECtHR in relationship to its "provincial" European histories, concerns, and ideologies (Chakrabarty 2000). Scholars of the ECtHR have situated it within Cold War politics and colonial legacies, European integration, nationalism, and the rise of liberal institutionalism (Madsen 2018, 2007; Duranti 2017; Moyn 2014; Moor and Simpson 2005). It is not surprising then that debates about the scope and reach of the Court would fall along these historical fault lines and the visions of sovereignty and rights that they underwrote. I examine these historical contexts as they shape core notions of European belonging (chapters 1 and 2) and how far rights can address these ongoing issues of structural exclusion and violence (chapter 6; see also Greenberg 2021a).

Many of the same tensions and historical legacies chronicled by anthropologists of Europe find their way into the halls of Strasbourg (Asad et al. 1997). These include ongoing erasures of minority populations within ethnically defined national polities (Karakasidou 1997), the contradictions of secularism (Fernando 2014; Ozyurek 2006), and the tension between racialized bordering practices and ideals of mobility and tolerance (Silverstein 2005; Cabot 2014; De Genova 2017). Granular analysis of everyday practices demonstrates the way that supposedly enduring social formations like the state and the nation are in fact contingent social achievements often shaped through the language of law (Navaro-Yashin 2012; Bryant and Hatay 2020). Likewise, the ECHR system is also shaped by the violent and more mundane ways in which North Atlantic universals are maintained through erasure and the production of "white innocence" (Wekker 2016), and the impact of European racial formations in defining and accessing human rights (Bruce-Jones 2016).

Legal and human rights categories also bear the traces of Cold War geopolitical divisions, including key categories of legal and political personhood, media expression, property, labor, and market transition central to rights claims (Mora 2023; Fedirko 2021; Mattioli 2020; Dunn 2004; Verdery 2003). Seemingly unshakable world historical categories such as capitalism and communism were always tenuous local achievements (Verdery 1996; Gal and Kligman 2000). As scholars chronicling European integration have shown, the contemporary institutions of the EU and the Council are deeply shaped by these histories (Gille 2016; Myslinska 2024; Holmes 2001), as are concepts of liberal European tolerance, democratic capacity, and the rule of law (Krastev and Holmes 2019; Dzenovska 2018). These perspectives are critical to understanding how putatively "universal" or even "European" rights are always shot through with histories that are inseparable from the social life of rights and their overt and implicit persuasive and communicative force.

Crisis and Law in Europe

The idea of Europe and the European Court system as *in crisis* is another key context for understanding the situated concerns of legal actors in Strasbourg (Heri 2024). From 2016 until 2024 when I conducted research, the Council system contended with Brexit, an attempted coup and subsequent government crackdowns on civil society in Turkey, EU sanctioning of Poland and Hungary for threats to judicial independence, the meteoric electoral rise of Euroskeptic right-wing populists across Europe, and Russia's invasion of Ukraine. The urgency and foreboding shadowed almost every encounter I had with people reflecting on the ECHR system in this context. People often spoke of the rule of law as a social contract that relied on rational commitments and strategic interests. But in practice, the rule of law emerged from the effect of people continuously binding themselves to texts and to others in a leap of faith. It is a strange kind of faith to be sure. It is one that is routinized through technocratic language, legal argumentation, and strict jurisdictional scope. The notion of crisis then is both experientially disconcerting and highly productive in shaping people's commitment to legal institutions.

In the context of crisis real or perceived, Court authority requires constant maintenance through everyday practice and performance. Such authority is always "partial, variable, and highly dependent on a range of different audiences and contexts" (Alter et al. 2018, 4). It is "intersubjective and co-constitutive: it must be both asserted by International Courts and recognized by audiences who are independent of each other" (13). The chapters that follow track the institutional labor that goes into maintaining and projecting authority. They demonstrate that the legitimacy of the system is not only an end but a means through which people feel bound to the institution. Institutional legitimacy is an ethos that drives engagement, interactions, and recommitments to the system again and again over time. In this way failures and critiques are as important to people's investment in human rights law as its success. It is through these commitments to work with and improve human rights that people build thickly woven relationships to legal norms and other institutional actors.

Learning to Speak and Listen: The ECHR System as a Communicative Field of Practice

As an ethnographer, these approaches to framing ECHR through its interactions, questions, and relationships came from the cues and clues I took from my interlocutors. Many interviewees talked about navigating different audiences, crafting compelling arguments, and anticipating reactions. This is not surprising for a field like law, which is defined by shared forms and beliefs about what counts as persuasive talk (Mertz 2007). But although people spoke explicitly about the power of well-reasoned legal arguments, their narratives of engaging in the ECHR system frequently centered on all the extralegal work they did to make those arguments land. Persuasion was as much about figuring out how to be recognized and heard as an authorized social subject as the content of one's speech. This meant learning how to embed technical aspects of negotiation and argumentation in social interactions. It necessitated learning how and who could speak with the weight of institutional authority.

This was particularly clear in a civil society workshop that I attended in summer of 2018. As part of my research, I had the privilege to observe trainings and seminars among human rights lawyers and advocates. These frequently focused on how to effectively use the system to advocate for their clients and for better human rights standards in their home countries. In this workshop, the speaker, Matej, a human rights lawyer, demonstrated that learning to mobilize the persuasive force of legal language was not only a technical exercise. It was about the social relationships that shape why some kinds of arguments are more convincing than others. In the process, human rights advocates cultivate "listening subjects" (Inoue 2006), those who might hear their messages and take them up to generate legally and diplomatically consequential effects.

Matej shared how he first encountered the ECtHR and learned to navigate it. He first engaged the ECHR system from afar, as a strategic litigator. This is a process of building a case domestically as a step toward eventual litigation in

Strasbourg with the goal of shaping the Court's case law. His NGO was based in a large Eastern European country, and the stakes of the cases were high. Their clients were bringing Article 2 and 3 violations, the right to life and protection from inhumane and degrading treatment. These involved forced disappearances and systematic state violence. While the applicants had already suffered irreparable loss of loved ones, family members of the disappeared sought some kind of justice. This was not only monetary compensation for life lost. They wanted state acknowledgment of violence or effective investigation into crimes that had been committed. This meant that Matej's group needed to not only win a judgment of a violation. They had to follow those judgments through an execution process in which the Committee of Ministers would advocate for structural change or legal accountability on the ground. Matej and his colleagues had spent years learning how to manage communication and persuasion across both the legal and diplomatic branches of the ECHR system to try to achieve these effects.

Matej's presentation spoke to much more than the technical issues of bringing a case or following up to ensure meaningful implementation. His very personal and often humorous story was about how relationships formed through the institution were key to successful advocacy. His first steps were not unlike my own early ethnographic forays: sending emails, snowballing introductions and meetings, and learning the geography of the city and the social relations that gave it life and dynamism. For Matej and his NGO, the process of getting a foot in the door took about a year and a half. He detailed how his organization's early outreach efforts, cold-calling, and emails eventually turned into enough responses to set up appointments in person. Only then did he swap virtual space for actual meetings in offices across Strasbourg's European quarter.

Being in the city and navigating its streets and offices were key steps in learning how to operate the Convention system. Some days he went to five or six meetings a day, drinking five or six cups of coffee to be polite. As a result, he joked with the training participants, he quickly learned the location of the city's public bathrooms. But, he explained, effective participation in the human rights conversation required more than mapping streets in Strasbourg, finding a couch on which to crash, keeping track of bathrooms, or gaining access to the offices. It was about speaking through the modes of address that would make one's claims intelligible and persuasive. He had to learn specific genres of legal and diplomatic talk. But those were useless without understanding the social context and connections through which that speech would be impactful. Persuasion meant his arguments would continue to circulate in meaningful ways. This could be achieved if he convinced others to speak about his cases, using his organization's framing.

Persuasive advocacy required actively using legal channels to move case documents from one point to another and framing those texts in ways that would advance his clients' interests. As a litigator he anticipated how original court proceedings and arguments might be taken up by Strasbourg judges, then become a legally binding judgment, and finally move to closed-door diplomatic contexts. These arguments and information only took on another persuasive life when he learned how to "draw [diplomats' and lawyers'] attention" to certain ways of framing a case. This required building partnerships and allies across the NGO, Council staff, and diplomatic spheres. These social relations produced that access that allowed his NGO to, in his words, "knock on Strasbourg's door."

The metaphor of knocking on a door reminds us that human rights advocacy includes an embodied stance (at the threshold of an institution) and the social ties that must be in place for that knock to be heard and answered. A great deal goes into making that knock possible. A judgment is part of a long-term advocacy process. Lawyers try to anticipate how a case will wind its way through domestic legal channels before getting to Strasbourg. This includes creating a case that makes sense for one audience, such as a domestic court, while anticipating how those texts might be received and picked up by different audiences in the future—for example, judges or a drafting lawyer in Strasbourg. Even before the judgment, many human rights organizations engage in years of planning. They work to create a legal case that will later be admissible and convincing to the Court. As I noted earlier, to be admissible to the European Court of Human Rights, an applicant must exhaust all possible domestic remedies in their home judicial system or convincingly prove that no such remedies were available. For those with an eye toward Strasbourg, lawyers first appeal to domestic legal systems while incorporating human rights framing that could be taken up later by the Court. This is a process that involved, in Matej's words, "pushing cases" through a country's "legal machinery." Taking cases through the domestic system and building a file made knocking at the door possible down the road. Linking texts in one locale to texts in another is a key part of what people can use institutional networks to do. And these linkages rely on building relationships that can serve as relay points for moving arguments, texts, and language from one point in the system to another.

Being listened to in any context is a complicated social interaction that takes time and work (Slotta 2023). But it is especially complicated when mo-bilizing an argument for different audiences who hold different roles and positions in a system. In his presentation, Matej explained the relay among different kinds of evidence and communication across legal, political, and diplomatic points in the system. Translating across these domains is what cre-ated his experience of being heard and impactful. After getting a judgment at Court, the next step is execution, a process that activates a different arm of the ECHR convention system. Matej explained to the group that to shift from judgment to implementation required finding allies by learning "the dynamic in Strasbourg." By this he meant understanding the geopolitics within and among member states: Which representatives might have interests or stakes in human rights improvements in their major trading partners, neighbors, or other relationships, for example? Who was willing to speak out on a par-ticular set of human rights issues? Who would be less likely to be critical of a key ally or of a human rights issue that their own domestic system was also inadequately addressing? If no one would be comfortable being out in front of an issue, this process might include building a critical mass of other diplo-mats, so that people weren't lone voices on a sensitive topic. He advised that it was helpful to understand who is "in the political map" in relationship to an advocate's own country. This could refer to finding a particular diplomatic representative that might agree to speak on behalf of the applicant's case. Sometimes this included getting the right kinds of information and framing into people's hands. It could even mean helping to get certain questions into the "mouths of deputies." Advocates might also have to simplify and summa-rize respondent-state counterarguments, both anticipating and reframing re-actions and counterreactions in a language understandable to and actionable for foreign diplomats.

Finally, knocking at Strasbourg's door was not only a technical or profes-sional exercise. It also included deeply embodied and affective orientations required to knit together applicants' experiences of suffering and loss and with the technical bureaucratic apparatus of human rights (Chua 2018). In an interview with Matej and a colleague after the training, this affective di-mension was evident. I asked him which case stuck with him the most, which one he carried to Strasbourg when he knocked on the door, and he related the details with a shaking voice and tears in his eyes. This deep connection with the sorrow and the pain of the applicants was also something he carried with him and wove into the communicative frame. In this way, strategic litigators and human rights activists are also tasked with translating human experience into the language of law and diplomacy.

Performing the Rule of Law

As Matej's example shows, human rights work when people learn to build the social conditions for reception of their arguments. And it is these communicative features of rights that allow differently positioned people—activists, judges, lawyers, diplomats—to translate legal language for different audiences and across different scales of action. This is true not only for advocates standing "outside" or at Strasbourg's door. I heard similar stories of learning and mobilizing the communicative cultures of Strasbourg from judges, registry lawyers, Council staff, and diplomatic legal attachés. To engage the system, then, requires people to situate themselves simultaneously in relationship to case law, institutional categories, and social relationships that can at times be contradictory and are always complex.

It is in navigating this relationality that the ECHR system endures as a problem space. Its flexibility allows for coordination through disagreement and norm generation without total closure. Over time, these repeated interactions in relationship to formal rules and norms shape the conditions for commonsense ways of ordering the world. These interactions are also part of why institutions come to feel enduring, real, and even inflexible, despite their roots in contingent and practice-dependent building blocks. To participate in such institutionally mediated conversations is to necessarily build on and express goals and actions within particular forms of persuasive speech. This is so even when not everyone agrees on what counts as a persuasive or meaningful interpretation. For example, the notion of justice is surprisingly fluid within a human rights court. In one interview, a senior registry official even gently chided me for even bringing justice into the equation. He instead argued that a commitment to rule-of-law and case-law consistency was at the heart of the Court's legitimacy. Some judges characterized themselves as true believers in human rights or the project of European belonging. Others described themselves as black-letter lawyers, interested in the challenge of the job but hardly devotees of human rights law for its own sake. Figuring out how to persuade a black-letter law judge just doing her job is no less central to enacting human rights than to catch the attention of the committed believer. And not everyone with influence in the system is inspired to enact change at all. As one diplomatic attaché reminded me in an interview, many were there to serve the interests of their home states as much as to preserve human rights.

But regardless of individual intentionality, those who participate in the system are drawn into it in some way or another. People participate in shaping the meaning and scope of human rights and rule of law by drafting and circulating texts that become building blocks down the road. Their arguments and ideas and their cases and advocacy approaches are resources or hindrances for others who engage or reframe the institution in turn. Whether lofty or mundane, strategic or resolutely technical, everyday interactions do not exist in a vacuum. People are aware of the framings that came before. And they anticipate and respond to these different framings when they launch their own interventions into the legal and diplomatic conversation. Anticipation is part of a recursive feedback loop that shapes actions and interactions over time. Arguments win and lose, as do applicants and advocacy attempts. But participation in the conversation is what builds the system across a multitude of loosely coordinated interactions.

It is through this recursive feedback loop that people generate the system's legitimacy, intentionally or not. In this sense, legal authority is never about singular moves in a field of play. It is grounded in the act of being in the conversation and watching others committing to that shared conversation again and again. And it is in this sense that persuasion and publicity also matter for a range of audiences, not all of whom have the same ideas or commitments to international human rights law. The ECHR and the Court have inspired countless commentaries from scholars, policy observers, and human rights advocates. Beyond this vast literature, the ECHR system lives in media coverage, domestic political disputes, and law programs across Europe. The Court occasionally plays a starring role in nationalist, populist screeds against European integration. In the lead-up to Brexit, the Leave campaign cited the overreach of the Court, even though it is not an EU institution. In response to *Hirst v. UK* (2005), the infamous prisoner voting rights case that secured franchise for a violent offender, British Prime Minister David Cameron famously and publicly noted that complying with the judgment would make him feel "physically ill."

It is not possible to separate this engagement and critique from the work of the institution itself. Many working in the system feel pressure to convey its legitimacy and defend its methods. For some, this means creating the most efficient institution possible, at the expense of transparency or easier access for individual applicants. For others, legitimacy comes from robust judicial constraints on state sovereignty. Still others frame the system's relevance through its ability to respond to emerging human rights challenges such as online speech rights, women's reproductive health, or climate change. Despite this heterogeneity, almost everyone I spoke with was invested in building the institutional image in the name of human rights and the rule of law. Whether cynical or idealist, strategic or myopic, this is a shared framework that animates the performance of legality and shapes its persuasive effect. Yet the public performance of legal legitimacy is a double-edged sword. In watching and being watched, legal actors engaging the ECHR system always also open themselves up to critique in uncertain times.

Legal Certainty in Uncertain Times:
Global Contexts of Judicialization

If the ECHR system is built out of densely woven interactions, they are nonetheless woven around a shared core of uncertainty. The ECHR system, while "binding" based on the Convention, is at the end of the day unenforceable outside the soft power, moral persuasion, strategic connections, relationships, and publicity around which people have built the system. The system works insofar as people act "as if" it is real and binding (Wedeen 1998). This means it is particularly destabilizing when people begin to ask themselves and others, "What if?" What if a sovereign nation-state simply doesn't comply with a ruling? What if people lose faith in the institution? From the perspective of those that defend it, it is most at risk when that negotiated quality and its contingency become evident.

It is not new for proponents of international law to oscillate between proclaiming its crisis-ridden vulnerability and its necessity and institutional durability. As with many socially meaningful ethical systems, the rule of law is simultaneously a taken-for-granted social fact and prone to doubt and reflexive critique (Robbins 2004). This is certainly evident in the language of the preparatory documents penned by the founders of the ECHR system. As I detail in chapter 1, their debates were characterized by both an optimism and deep anxiety about compliance with soft legal norms. It was often in the same breath that people passionate about the ECHR system would speak of its fragility and endurance.

Exemplary is an interview I conducted with a long-time human rights scholar and strategic litigator, whom I'll call Theodore. Having argued before the Court, analyzed it, and contributed volumes to international human rights scholarship over a long career, Theodore told me people had always spoken of the Court in crisis. And indeed, this notion of crisis predated the Court. Comparing the situation of rising fascism and authoritarianism in the 1930s to the sense that "crisis is again on the horizon," he noted that we are better off than we had ever been. The difference between now and then was that there was no UN, no ICC, no ECHR in the pre-war period: "These institutions were built for this crisis." He concluded by saying that the ECtHR " is a great court. . . . As a judicial body it's the best thing we have on the planet."

In recent years, failures and limits of the rule of law have been met with calls for more law. This is not (only) naïve liberal certainty. It is an outcome of a process in which international institutions have been central to liberal worldmaking as mechanism for generating accountability in the post–Cold War era (Teitel 2011). But it is also in part evidence of the productive fiction behind all forms of human sociality at scale—that they are necessarily hegemonic projects that must be nurtured and maintained—making them subject to transformation but also collapse. It is not only the lawyers, judges, applicants, or human rights advocates who engage in this leap of faith. Their struggle and efforts shed light on a much broader interplay of certainty and anxiety in contemporary liberal imaginaries at the dawn of the twenty-first century. As I write, South Africa has taken Israel to the International Court of Justice for the crime of genocide in Gaza. Leading legal scholars have called for a new forum to try Russia for the crime of aggression in Ukraine (Hathaway 2022; Wolfson 2022). The faith in and crisis of rule of law is a shared global condition that connects places, institutions, and people.

This enduring sense of threat and renewal characterizes international legal institutions as in a state of "routine crisis" (Muir 2021). Analyzing the persistent and commonplace narratives among her middle-class Argentinian interlocutors, anthropologist Sarah Muir argues that discourses of political and economic crisis were "a mode of engagement as much practical and logistical as intellectual and theoretical. These critical practices allowed people to comprehend [political and economic transformation and instability] not simply as disorder, but as meaningful disorder" (16). In turn, the daily repetition and routinization of these daily engagements through the lens of crisis produced both a sense of enduring social and national order and deep uncertainty. Similarly, my interlocutors' persistent discourses of rule-of-law crisis oscillated between arguing for the necessity of rule-of-law institutions, representing idealized visions of normative stability, and enumerating external threats to social and legal orders. But as a mode of engagement, the language of crisis or threat was a constant source for renewing the investment in and necessity of legal norms and institutional practices. In this sense, the legitimacy of international rule of law is never fully in crisis *or* robust and necessary. It is simultaneously both. This insight helps move our analysis beyond the ping-ponging sense that international and human rights law are alternately "not enough" and that they might save us all from our own worst selves (Moyn 2018; Sikkink 2018). Obscured in this polarizing debate is the fact that crises and hope are two sides of the same coin: both are features of what international law is and does as complex network of relationships, commitments, and social worlds. A normative commitment to rule of law structures social relationships in the name of liberal ideals of progress, the distinction between law and politics, and the deference to and constraints of state sovereignty in an international order. The routinization of crisis is also a set of taken-for-granted institutional practices that organize people's commitment and recommitment to nurture and maintain the rule of law not despite but because of its seeming fragility.

The paradox here is that the very means of producing and enacting legitimacy can produce conditions for its opposite: critique, frustration, and experiences of injustice. Contradictions aren't exogenous to how and why international law works as a flexible resource for worldmaking. They are intrinsic to how these systems knit together epistemic communities across diverse locales and with wide-ranging commitments. It is in bringing different approaches together in the same frame that people create room to maneuver through advocacy, persuasion, and creative interpretation of what the law is and should be. Figuring out how far you can stretch normative commitments while retaining their binding social and institutional heft is part of the ideology and practice of balancing so central to the ECHR system in all its interpretative and practice-based meanings.

An ethnography of an international human rights court can also address this seemingly paradoxical relationship between international law as feeling really real and really fragile. International legal institutions frequently exist at this breaking point and the ever-present threat that states or powerful individuals might opt out and that people lose faith in institutions.[6] It is this balance between fragility and necessity that drives people's intense, continued investment in institutions. International law works as a leap of faith that is both ephemeral and grounded in everyday practice. It works when relationships and commitments become goals in themselves. In this sense, legitimacy is not an effect of how an institution works; it is what drives engagement in the first place. While fragile and uncertain, it also generates relationships that can feel enduring, even authoritatively binding. And it can feel like a will-o'-the-wisp when it fails to deliver justice and accountability.

The Role of Critique in International Human Rights Scholarship

Given this, the analyst of rule of law and human rights is as much a part of a field of social and epistemological practice as an objective observer. She also shapes the legitimacy of legal institutions by virtue of participation in the conversation about them. This fact forces legal anthropologists to always think alongside our interlocutors, rather than merely "about" them (Nader 1972, 2011). Writing about the institution quickly becomes part of the problem space that is the object of study itself.

Thus, even within a nonnormative analytic approach to international legal institutions, one cannot avoid taking a normative stand on how they *ought* to work. Nick Cheesman (2018) has argued that ethnographers of the rule of law should approach their object of study critically and be clear and open about their own and others' positions. Rule of law ethnography "calls for certain commitments but remains open to alternatives. . . . The passionately humble advocate for ethnographically informed inquiry into the rule of law enters into a cautious but engaged dialogue with research subjects and the idea of the rule of law itself" (178). It is my hope that in analyzing how human rights institutions like the ECHR system work through the generation of collective commitments and norms, we can better identify the levers that make them subject to collective critique, intervention, and organizing.

Legal institutions will always police the boundaries of who can and cannot speak in the name of the law, often in highly gendered, classed, and racialized ways (Fuchs 2024; Hlavka and Mulla 2021; Baxi 2014). But these conditions of legal intelligibility (Prasse-Freeman 2023) are also subject to advocacy through normative pressure points, coalition building, and the strategic deployment of communicative frameworks. I agree with Theodore, who I quoted above, that the world is a better place for having the ECtHR in it. This is in large part because of the passion, hard work, and dedication of the many people I chronicle here. Human rights and the rule of law are not fixed principles—certainly not ones that can be exported around the globe or consistently applied with some technocratic tinkering (Carothers 2006; Cheesman 2018). They are cosmologies of worldmaking grounded in a willful commitment to generate enduring sociality out of the discursive materials of human interrelationships: consensus, commitment, persuasion, and power. In analyzing the social life of international legal institutions, we might yet expand and redirect the judicialization of the political toward more just ends.

These commitments also hinge on ethnography and law as parallel approaches to knowledge-making that describe and intervene in the world (Nader 2011). It is not always easy to identify where and how they might enter into productive conversation, if at all (Vetters and Margaria 2024; Coutin and Yngvesson 2008; Riles 2006; Goodale 2006).[7] Ethnographic theory helps us understand how people navigate and meaningfully act in and on the world. Legal theory is likewise an approach to empirical analysis but backed by normative commitments to compel and not only analyze action. Legal philosopher Samantha Besson (2017) has argued for a practice-based focus on human rights to bridge the gap between epistemologically different accounts of human rights. Theorizing from practice requires "taking the legality of human rights seriously" (330). Besson suggests that human rights is a uniquely legal way of intervening in and theorizing the world and cannot be collapsed solely into political, moral, or ethical questions: "The law amounts to a practice where abstract moral ideas meet social facts and where both are in mutual tension. This makes human rights law (as legal practice) an interesting case for the human rights practice in human rights theory, and, in turn, legal theory an attractive resource for human rights theory to account for that object" (331).

I take Besson's charge to take law seriously on its own terms. Doing so requires talking across the epistemological divides that often separate doctrinal and critical social scientific analysis in legal studies. But the benefit of thinking across these domains of analysis is manifold. It lets us see how the combination of normative architecture and creative experimentation is central to what people do with human rights as a form of praxis. Legal and institutional infrastructures allow people to "select, experiment, and adjust . . . tools and techniques, rather than create a wheel wholly anew" (Cabatingan 2023, 12). Legal actors can use institutional affordances, goals, and spaces to work and rework human rights for different collective projects. Within their worlds of experience, people engaging in and through institutional norms are often quite reflexive about inhabiting and reproducing these norms. And it is at these sites of reflexivity and learning that norms are also subject to being reshaped and changed through the nonnormative, interactional, social, and discursive aspects of institutionalization.

It is thus under conditions of creativity within institutional contraints that people become attached to judicialization as a form of sociality. Or in the words of one long-time, high-ranking Council lawyer, the legitimacy of the ECHR system rests on convincing member states that "it is better to be in the system than out of it."

Chapter Outline and Plan of the Book

The chapters in this book demonstrate how the ECHR as a normative legal system is grounded in concrete social contexts, ideologies and historical compromises. They track the shared dilemmas, paradoxes, anxieties and hopes that define the Court as an institution in practice: a material-affective-semiotic apparatus for generating ways of talking about, and experiencing, and enacting social change through legal means. And they show how people project these grounded, vernacular approaches to human rights out to different audiences and publics. In the process differently positioned legal actors both perform and challenge the legitimacy and authority of the rule of law. Working through the affordances of legal institutions produces a sense of judicialized agency: the experience of being effective in the world by binding oneself to the constraints of institutional rules of engagement. And yet the competing claims and goals of the system shape a widespread sense that human rights, rule of law, and the European project are always deeply fragile. This dual sense of efficacy and crisis is central to understanding people's increasing attachment to rule of law institutions at precisely the moment when it seems law has failed again and again.

Chapter 1 explores the idea of European belonging, and the constitutive tensions at its heart. I ask how the ECHR system works back and forth between different definitions of culture to define an "us" of European community and a "we" of sovereign nation states. This dual mandate to enact European supervision *and* deference to sovereign nation states forms the axes of the ECtHR's impossible jurisdiction. Within these axes, legal actors plot narratives and pinpoint coordinates through case law and doctrine to advance legally persuasive and socially resonant claims. Chapter 2 continues to look at how definitions of "us," "them," and "we" shape case law and practice following the Cold War and Council expansion in the 1990s. Expansion profoundly changed the meanings of rule of law and human rights in practice, even as it entrenched long-standing relationships of geopolitical power in the shadow of the Cold War. Chapters 3 and 4 move from historical context to explore more everyday life and work at the Court and Council. Chapter 3 examines four discrete communicative modalities through which people enact and perform the rule of law: efficiency, consistency, transparency, and confidentiality. Chapter 4 examines the role of numbers in representing and legitimating the work of the Court and execution of judgments. At times, these different modalities work in unison. At other times they come into conflict. Both chapters show that clashes among repertoires and perspectives are not about failures of the system to function. They are expressions of the competing understandings of what and who the ECHR system is *for* and what success and justice look like in practice. Chapters 5 and 6 introduce new voices into the conversation about what and who rights are for. These chapters turn to civil society and strategic litigators and the networks in and through which people shape the ECHR system beyond the four walls of the Court. Chapter 5 focuses on strategic litigators who bring cases to Strasbourg with the goal of shaping case law and doctrine over time. I track how litigators frame the meaning of human rights cases litigation through the language of time: what a case means, how long it ought to take, and through what temporal frameworks it ought to be judged as effective. Such competing experiences of time have sparked new advocacy strategies, ethical commitments, and litigator subjectivities. Chapter 6 explores this process by following a single case as it moved from litigation to execution. I analyze *D.H. and Others v. Czech Republic*, a highly influential case on structural racism in the education system. The case points to the discursive labor through which people turn structural violence into a justiciable human rights problem. And the almost twenty-year story of execution points to the work required to retranslate legal problems back into institutionally meaningful responses to that problem. Finally, the Conclusion takes up the painful and still timely question of the fragility of human rights and rule of law institutions. Beginning with Russia's expulsion from the Council of Europe following the 2022 invasion of Ukraine, the Conclusion asks how far an international legal system can accommodate compromise before it becomes complicit in state violence.

ONE

Defining "Us"

Culture and the Court

NATZWEILER-STRUTHOF, fifty kilometers from Strasbourg as the crow flies, was the Nazi regime's westernmost death camp. An old ski resort nestled in the Vosges, the idyllic mountains and pungent pine forests formed a backdrop to unspeakable violence. Although not as well-known as other camps, Struthof is exemplary of the deep ties between European human rights and the Second World War. The comparatively small population of prisoners was incredibly diverse—so much so that they spoke a camp creole to communicate across language barriers. A sign in the camp, which is now an outdoor museum, quotes French resistance fighter and political prisoner Robert Salomon: "It was in the concentration camps that our solidarity of free men was born, our European common brotherhood beyond our languages, our nationalities, our faiths, our beliefs or our borders. . . . Long Live France, Long Live Europe, Long Live Freedom and Long Live Peace."

While exemplary of the most optimistic visions for an integrated, peaceful Europe, Salomon's vision also foreshadows the compromises of the community that followed. The judicial and diplomatic institutions meant to secure this vision relied on an ideal of common European belonging, to be sure. But they also never truly moved beyond languages, nationalism, or borders. And while a solidarity among free men emerged at the camps, the political and social organizations they went on to build pitted individual rights against state power. It was along these two axes that the tensions of European integration unfolded as a series of compromises: a common European framework among distinct national entities and differently rights-bearing individuals subject to sovereign control over the terms of social belonging.

These tensions continue to shape the European Court of Human Rights in case law, doctrine, and everyday practice. Cases on migration exemplify the contradictions between a borderless brotherhood and the reality of "Fortress Europe," a space of violent policing and exclusionary citizenship regimes (Greenberg 2021a; De Genova 2017; Baumgärtel 2019). Cases on freedom of expression, conscience, or family rights put the terms of culture and state and of individual and society in constant play. In these domains, states have leeway, or a "margin of appreciation," to circumscribe individual rights on the grounds of security and protection of society and morals as might be "necessary in a democratic society."[1] As a former Court president explained to me in a 2017 interview, "The doctrine of margin of appreciation . . . means that the court accepts that human rights are not necessarily protected in the same way across the forty-seven countries. . . . There are geographical differences, economic differences, cultural [differences]. . . . The Convention applies from Lisbon to Vladivostok in Siberia. . . . A certain degree of difference is not only tolerated, but maybe encouraged."

Yet despite this heterogeneity, the Court is also tasked with judging cases in terms of shared European legal trends and changing social mores. Such a "European consensus" represents the common grounds for human rights: modernity, tolerance, and progress. It is this sensitivity to changing *European* norms that makes the Court "a living instrument." This means, in the words of a senior registry official, that "the law must be stable" but it cannot "stand still." It does this by being "attentive to . . . legal development in the states."

These axes of judicial authority—European supervision versus deference to sovereign nation states— form the crux of what I call the ECtHR's impossible jurisdiction. Crosscutting this tension is the need to harmonize and balance forty-six highly diverse national, political, cultural, legal, and linguistic contexts. Cultural difference is thus both a problem to be managed and the means of enacting shared European human rights commitments. It is a source of legal and doctrinal authority through which applicants, state representatives, and judges define the Court's jurisdiction in practice.

Culture, Sovereignty, and Rights

In this chapter, I demonstrate how ECtHR judges, lawyers, applicants, and state respondents generate interpretative power by working the ambiguities and historical resonances of "culture" and its cognates. Talking about civilization, society, morality, and European belonging is one way to keep the ECHR system flexible and workable through (rather than despite) its constitutive tensions. I build on the insights of law and language scholars into the ways in which language practices are a site for enacting sovereignty and carving out zones of jurisdiction (Cabatingan 2023; Richland 2021; Kahn 2019). Operating as a "strategically deployable shifter" (Urciuoli 2008), culture points to a shared context of European norms and values but is ambiguous enough to refer to different ideological genealogies and the political and legal grounds they authorize. Thus culture can be mobilized in the name of shared rights commitments, thereby justifying court supervision. And it can be used to safeguard national difference as the exclusive domain for sovereign state power.

The tension between universal rights and cultural specificity is something that defines most international human rights regimes. Cowan, Dembour, and Wilson (2001) have identified four major approaches to understanding the nexus of rights and culture. The first two, "rights *versus* culture and rights *to* culture," concern "conversations about the legal and political status which 'a culture' does or does not have." The third conjunction, "rights *as* culture," introduces legal processes as their own social field that intersects with but is not reducible to other sociohistorical dynamics and practices. And the fourth is "culture as a *means* of analysing and better understanding the particular ways that rights processes operate as situated social action" (4).

To this I add culture as a legal pivot: a socially resonant category that can both link and turn on related or contradictory meanings to support different modes of argumentation and legal authority. Culture works this way most clearly as a flexible doctrinal category that gives legal actors *interpretative room for maneuver*. The interpretive work of cultural difference is most explicit in cases that raise "difficult moral issues," in the words of one judge. A common example is Article 8, the right to respect for privacy, family life, and home. Unlike cases of core rights (like prohibition of torture or rights to life or liberty) that leave little room for balancing, these "moral issues" require weighting state sovereignty, social norms, democracy, tolerance, and minority rights. Such cases may include issues as diverse as privacy or reputation rights, assisted suicide, gay marriage and adoption, or the role of technology in fertility or family planning. By linking culture, demos, and political will, contracting state representatives argue for Court deference to national decisionmaking. And by linking culture, European belonging, tolerance and social progress, applicants argue for human rights protections in terms of evolving European norms. This justifies international supervision that supersedes exclusively national, social, and political contexts. These seemingly contradictory arguments about the legal significance of culture hinge on long-standing European ideologies of personhood, sovereignty, and law. At the same time, notions of culture and civilization also form a resonant way to talk about Europe as an ideological and social project—one grounded in notions of progress, tolerance, and the cultivation of modern dispositions. In both cases, culture (and cultural difference) also serves as a means of delimiting political and legal rights—a process grounded in but not exclusive to Europe's long colonial history. In this way, "culture talk" provides a repertoire of ways to talk about specific legal and jurisdictional relationships. It is also used to delimit who is protected by and from state violence, and under what conditions individuals deserve rights.

Culture, National Difference, and the Idea of Europe in Postwar International Law

In the immediate post-WWII period, the drafters of the ECHR faced a seemingly insurmountable problem. They had to generate a collective system for the supervision and enforcement of rights. But it needed to be grounded in the heterogenous legal systems of sovereign nation-states. That system had to both encompass and supersede national difference. It required building legitimacy as a community of shared values that was enforceable through diplomatic power and rule of law norms. There were few models in international law that attempted such a balancing act. Existing international legal frameworks and customary law were based on a nearly unshakeable deference to national sovereignty and a right to self-defense. While the trials at Nuremberg and Tokyo foreshadowed international criminal courts of a later era, their binding force was grounded in the stick of military defeat and the carrot of international aid (Bass 2000). In 1948 the United Nations had promulgated the Declaration of Human Rights. While a moral and diplomatic victory to be sure, the Declaration lacked an enforcement mechanism—a limitation of which the ECHR drafters were very much aware.

It was with both optimism and caution that the newly founded Council of Europe launched an initiative to draft a European convention on human rights. In grounding sovereignty in a territorial logic, the ECHR founders reasserted human rights law as a mechanism for ordering the world into nation-states (Wheatley 2023). They also linked jurisdiction to territory in ways that excluded colonial and administrative holdings from the rights and benefits of that legal order (Moor and Simpson 2005). Yet they nonetheless challenged territorial sovereignty by proposing binding international legal obligations to which all democratic European nations would be bound (and bound together). The trick in so doing was to turn disparate national instances of "us" into a collective European "we."

Between 1949 and 1950 a consultative assembly of the Council of Europe drafted a proposal for the ECHR. The early texts were drafted by members of the European Movement and later debated and revised by the Consultative Assembly. These proceedings, formed the basis for the Convention, finalized by the Council's Committee of Ministers. As historian Edward Bates has noted, the European Convention on Human Rights was "an ambivalent instrument" from the beginning (2011, 8). For some, it only needed to guarantee a baseline for protection against totalitarianism and fascism. For others, like European Movement representative and passionate Convention advocate Pierre-Henri Teitgen, it held the potential for a true and evolutive European bill of rights (8, 45). Teitgen, the former French minister of justice, drafted the initial European Movement draft proposal with Sir David Maxwell-Fyfe, former deputy chief prosecutor at Nuremburg and British home secretary, and Fernando Delhousse, a renowned Belgian jurist. As a group, the men represented very different positions with regard to the scope of the Convention. Teitgen's ambition for the system balanced Fyfe's far more sovereignty-shy approach as a British representative. The resulting draft was destined to be a document marked by compromise. Given the range of disputes, it was miraculous that the group produced consensus at all. This came at the cost of creating anything more than a minimalist legal framework that guaranteed a baseline set of standards for protection of European democracy (Bates 2011, 53).

The resulting system did eventually operate as a binding guarantee of individual human rights adjudicated by a court with full jurisdiction over member states. But that process took decades. The early decades of the ECHR system were defined by heated debate among a handful of legal thinkers but little attention within a broader public. Among early drafters, some imagined the ECHR as the basis for a European constitutional order grounded in a bill of rights. Others sought to ensure that the Convention was a mere floor for rights protections that safeguarded sovereignty above all else (Bates 2011). It was the colonial states—namely France and the United Kingdom—that pushed back against compulsory jurisdiction, fearing that the ECHR system would implicate them in the midst of decolonial struggle (Madsen 2018; Madsen 2004). This early period was defined by "the legal-diplomatic nature of the Convention system" in which "the Court and Commission had to strike a fine balance between developing the Convention and simultaneously persuading reluctant governments of the institutions' sensitivities to complex domestic sociopolitical contexts" (Madsen 2018, 249).

As a result of optional jurisdiction and right to individual petition, the early system produced little attention and no case law. This began to change in the 1970s. The softening of Cold War divisions and eventual decolonization removed some states' initial reluctance to be bound by Court rulings (Madsen 2018, 251). A handful of states began to accept both Court jurisdiction and the right of individual petition. As a result, domestic judges and politicians were required to consider the Convention as a binding legal framework (Bates 2011, 11). Seeking new forums for European-level litigation and advocacy, an emerging cohort of lawyers turned an eye toward Strasbourg.[2] In 1968 the Court issued its first violation in the Belgian Linguistics case concerning access to French language education in non-majority-French-speaking districts. It was not, however, until the mid-1970s that the Court issued a handful of influential decisions and began to develop a more significant legal profile. This period of case law was pivotal in laying down interpretative frameworks, or doctrine, that have remained influential to this day (Bates 2011, 16). As Bates notes (17–18), this early case law addressed minor deficiencies in existing legal standards within the long-standing democracies that formed the early membership of the Council. These cases were remarkable in that they socialized European judicial review for sovereign democratic states. But they were fairly uncontroversial in limiting oversight to violations that "concerned the types of civil liberty issues that might be adjudicated upon by constitutional supreme courts in political democracies" (18). Rather than serving only as a human rights bulwark against totalitarian violence, the Court found improvements at the margins of existing democratic constitutional orders.

By the early 1970s the Commission was ready to exercise its power of referral to the Court more often. Suddenly (or so it may have seemed), member states were regularly found in violation of the Convention (Bates 2011, 18). Through the 1970s and 1980s, the scope and type of cases began to grow and shift. Madsen notes that in this period, jurisprudence shifted from the more politicized and intractable issue of interstate complaints to social issues that allowed for the development of jurisprudence (2018, 253). Moving into the 1990s, the Court began to take on repetitive cases linked to underlying structural-rights violations in zones of conflict. Exemplary are the Southeast Turkish cases that dealt with state violence against Kurdish populations. The Court was reluctant to make the systematic and patterned nature of those violations explicit (Kurban 2020), although these earlier cases anticipated later reforms at the Court to deal with ongoing, repetitive and structural problems.

With more cases, there was an increasing push for reform of the system. By the early 1990s there was pressure to deal with this growing caseload and the variety of cases coming to Strasbourg. The Council of Europe was expanding rapidly during this period. Eastern European countries sought membership as part of a larger democratization process and transition from state socialism. The system was moving into a dual role in relationship to different kinds of rights: egregious and often violent rights violations in situations of conflict, structural issues related to transition from socialism to democracy, and the continued "refinement" of democratic constitutional orders in Europe's so-called mature democracies. With Council membership as a spur to judicial, political, and economic reform, ECtHR case law became a key part of European integration. Expansion also spurred one of the most significant reforms in the Convention system: the signing of Protocol 11. Protocol 11 established a permanent Court in lieu of the Commission referral system. It made Court jurisdiction binding on all Council member states and established the right of individual petition for anyone on Council member-state territory.

From the beginning, advocates and critics of the system debated the foundational tensions at the heart of the system: sovereignty versus supervision and individual rights balanced against state authority to shape social and collective life. Those interpreting the convention in turn translated these debates into legal frameworks via doctrine and case law. It was through these mechanisms—judicial interpretation, legal argumentation, and concrete cases—that foundational questions of individual rights, jurisdiction, and sovereignty became consequential, without ever being definitively resolved.

Indeed they couldn't be, precisely because the ECHR had cohered competing approaches to culture and rights into its very framework. Invoking notions of culture spoke to the dual grounds of the system: an integrated European "us" versus the irreducible specificity that was the grounds of nation-state sovereignty. It is to this history that I now turn.

"Culture," "Civilization," and Europe in Drafting the Convention

Nineteenth- and twentieth-century theories of state sovereignty linked political legitimacy to land, soil, blood, and language, often calqued as "culture" (Gellner 1983). Yet, the idea of European modernity was also grounded in civilizational exceptionalism that positioned Western Christendom as a source of universal values: rationality, progress, and other "North Atlantic universals"(Trouillot 2003, 2002). Abstract categories of citizenship, or socially contracting "possessive individuals," sat in tension with visions of collective cultural belonging (Macpherson 1962). Ideologies of political modernity rested on reconciling the two through discrete spheres specific to the liberal state, the production of rational publics, and a strict separation of market, state, and private domains (Habermas 1992). In this tradition, "culture" was a civilizing force for shaping political and social consensus, overcoming and flattening the specific different ethnonational belonging and class interests (Lloyd and Thomas 1998). Because *culture* can stand in for the cultivation of modern political sensibilities and essentialized, autochthonous social belonging, it served as a highly productive term with which to ground often contradictory political and legal claims. Whether *culture* refers to civilization in an abstract mood or primordial belonging comes down to the interpretative frames and intertextual relationships through which it is figured (Bauman and Briggs 2003). These tensions, long embodied in the hyphen between *nation* and *state*, are present in debates about international legal sovereignty as well. National culture was a framework for postimperial state sovereignty and a problem to be managed and organized through legal frameworks (Wheatley 2023). This ideological trace is clear in the ways that original preparatory text drafters mobilized different notions of culture to create consensus. They did so by playing with the ambiguity of its intellectual and political legacies.

These shared but multivalent coordinates formed the basis for human rights as a mode of argumentation for a particular vision of state, society, and individual. Within this, culture served as a repertoire that allowed the ECHR framers political cover to achieve the seemingly impossible, as they debated and drafted a new system. They had to convince nation-states, for whom blood, soil, territory, and sovereignty were entangled, to yield that sovereignty to an international institution. The framework of shared European values allowed skeptical participants and ECHR optimists to come together around a document that deferred resolution of some of the stickiest issues: jurisdiction, relationship to colonial holdings, the binding nature of the Convention system and its institutional design, and the right of individual petition (Bates 2011; Duranti 2016; Moyn 2010). In the process, drafters reframed that which was "foreign" or external to national sovereignty as an expression of "us" all along: our shared values, our culture, our Convention. Rather than resolve the underlying tension of international legal authority and national sovereignty, they built it into the system as a flexible, and underdetermined, legal pivot.

The trace of this initial balancing act is evident in the opening paragraph of the European Convention and its invocation of "European countries which are like-minded and have a common heritage of political traditions, ideals, freedom and the rule of law" bound together "in accordance with the principle of subsidiarity" and who enjoy both "a margin of appreciation" and are "subject to the supervisory jurisdiction of the European Court of Human Rights established by this Convention." Which countries were included in this bundle of "like-minded" states has changed over time. This fact alone is evidence of how flexible and productive definitions of shared cultural belonging can be. I will return to those issues in chapter 2. For now, I turn to the convention-drafting process itself to analyze the way in which it locked a constitutive tension into the founding text of the ECHR system. I then turn to the contemporary legacies and iterations of that process in doctrine and case law.

The convention drafting process was a long, negotiated process, first initiated by members of the European Movement. This was a postwar platform for coordinating those committed to European integration and institution building. Members of the group drafted the earliest proposals for the Convention. The Consultative Assembly of the Council of Europe, composed of ten European states, debated and revised the proposal. It was then sent to the Committee of Ministers, alongside a committee of legal experts, for final drafting. The Preparatory Works at the Consultative Assembly remain the richest source for analyzing the drafting process and the surrounding debates. This archive reveals key controversies that shaped the subsequent draft and indeed the Convention system's development over time.

The drafting committee for the Convention faced several thorny issues at the outset. Most challenging was the scope of the Convention's jurisdiction and the basis of its authority. How could the ECHR be both grounded in domestic legal orders and supersede domestic difference through a binding international system? This required the drafters to translate specific national systems into a common community. The terms *civilization* or *civilized nations* created that common framework, while papering over the debates, differences, and disagreements unfolding in the drafting room itself.

For example, the rhetorical work of culture is clear in one of the central debates that faced the Consultative Assembly. There were two options for defining rights. The ECHR could offer a full and comprehensive definition of rights. Or it could be a more minimalist document that provided flexibility for interpretation over time (see Council of Europe 1976 [vol. 3], 12). Those in favor of comprehensive definitions sought to limit the scope of future interpretations. It was members of the English delegation that most forcefully argued this position. They advanced arguments based on rule-of-law principles: a defined list of rights meant that states knew the scope and limits of rights to which they would be held to account. Definitions were thus an argument not only about the scope of law. They stood in for the balance between an international legal order and domestic sovereignty. This balance also spoke to the relationship between law and politics within a newly integrating European system, still reeling from the experience of fascism. After all, it was still a fresh memory that fascist leaders could co-opt democratic institutions to build a violent, authoritarian state. Many states' delegates had no desire to yield the democratic sovereignty they had just defended with their lives. At the same time, these states had little appetite for an international authority to question the sovereignty they held over colonial territories.

That these debates center on the French and English delegations is not a surprise given their central role in defining postwar European rights as a legal and social field (Madsen 2004). And as one can see in the debate, there are two very different understandings of rights at play. The French drew "on a tradition of seeing human rights as a mixture of socio-political struggle and graduated legalization of these accomplishments" (Madsen 2004, 59) while the British approached rights with "a 'closed circuit' of the legal system," which produced "an archaic jungle of documents, principles and conventions" and left rights much less "at the centre of the public discourse on the transformation of the postwar state" (60). Thus the debate over definitions of rights was not only about which country would win the day on establishing itself as the author of European rights. It was also about different visions—proceduralist and narrow or socially embedded and capacious—of rights.

From the British perspective, it was particularly urgent that definitions would be "certain, and sufficiently detailed to be the subject of application by judges who act in accordance with a certain law, and not as politicians who act in accordance with a political discretion" (Council of Europe 1975 [vol. 1], 80).[3] These pro-definition representatives argued that "in the absence of clear and precise definitions, States party to the Convention might be in great doubt as to whether they were in a position to accede to the Convention; how could a country feel sure that its laws were consistent with the obligations it would assume on accession if it did not know precisely what were the obligations involved?" (Council of Europe 1976 [vol. 3], 255–256). This included not only the definition of those rights, but their limits (Council of Europe 1976, 255–256). The scope of definitions and limitations implied that a signatory would have control over those areas that the ECHR did not outline comprehensively.

The counterargument, exemplified by French representatives (and joined by Italian and Belgian voices), was that the ECHR should enumerate general principles that would be broad and flexible. This would allow for rights to develop in scope over time. Advocates of this general approach also presented pragmatic arguments: definitions would be a time-consuming task that would delay drafting and ratification. It would be impossible to "agree on all details regarding the definition of every human right" and the details of their limitations (Council of Europe 1976 [vol. 3], 256). This "would therefore threaten to delay the setting up of European institutions and bodies" (256). The time frame necessary for definitions was a frequent refrain in proceedings, echoed by Teitgen himself. He noted drafting comprehensive rights definitions would "mean the indefinite postponement of our aim," making it "necessary to hand the task on to the next generation. . . . That would be the best means of achieving nothing" (Council of Europe 1975 [vol. 1], 274).[4] The representatives of the European Movement also used the preparatory drafting process to argue against the need for strict and precise definition of rights. They noted that "it is true that the Draft Convention does not attempt to define with legal precision the human rights which it seeks to guarantee. To do so would involve the negotiation of a massive and extremely complicated legal document. Apart from the time and effort that such a work would involve . . . it is not at all certain that it would, in the end, achieve the legal clarity desired." Such comments anticipated pragmatic arguments against precise definitions as impracticable or too time consuming, which appear throughout the debates and speeches in the official Preparatory Works. In addition, a system would only be effective if it didn't have gaps and loopholes through which member states could evade protections. The advocates of enumeration understood that the more precisely rights were defined, the less authority the system would have. In this way, enumeration was not only timely. It was also a more comprehensively ethical system.

At its heart, the debate hinged on a deeper disagreement over the very meaning of *European community*. Was it a set of formal, legal obligations grounded in a kind of contractual "club," or "joint trusteeship" in the words of one United Kingdom representative? Or was it an expression of shared values, norms, and cultural presuppositions expressed as law? In this view, the basis of community was not a negotiated contract—social or otherwise. It was an organic expression of already existing and shared values among "civilized nations." Contractual membership and cultural belonging were two ways of authorizing the grounds of rights across a system of democratic nation-states. Here they served as competing ways to justify international law and manage the relationship to sovereign power.

The European Movement's arguments illustrate the claim that definitions were unnecessary because Europe was an already constituted progressive, democratic community of common political and social values. Given this, precise definitions would not necessarily expand existing liberties, and the process of negotiation of precise definitions might even limit or lower the standards for collectively agreed-on rights. Its members were already part of the same European cultural and civilizational community. We are, in short, already us.

This logic was echoed in Teitgen's opening address to the drafting committee. In it, he turns national legal specificity into evidence for common European belonging. He notes:

> These are the principles and legal rules which, since they are formulated and sanctioned by the internal law of all civilised nations at any given moment, can therefore be regarded as constituting a principle of general common law, applicable throughout the whole of international society. From the moment when judicial law, English law, Swedish law, French law, Norwegian law, American law, lay down a sanction, or an identical or similar rule, it is possible to say that it forms part of the common heritage of civilised nations, and to deduce that, in each internal law, it is the expression of a principle valid for the whole of international society. (Council of Europe 1975 [vol. 1], 280)

In another instance, Mr. Teitgen argued against including specific definitions in the following way:

> Life does not always follow the rules of logic. . . . One cannot say, one fine
> morning, with any chance of success: "we will now make a code of European
> freedoms." In France, the Emperor Napoleon did draw up some codes, but
> these codes were in effect but a formulation of three hundred years of custom
> and jurisprudence. . . . The Napoleonic code was simply an ordered transcrip-
> tion of all that had already been confirmed by courts, jurisprudence, experi-
> ence, custom and popular consent. . . . It is in the same in the international
> field. . . . Experience shows that the Court comes first. (Council of Europe 1975
> [vol. 1], 274–276)

Here Teitgen counters the call for definitions with pragmatic arguments
and a moral commitment to what the drafters owe to the next generation. He
appeals to a circular form of reason: the civilized nation is self-evident and
will naturally produce civilized laws. In analogizing to the Napoleonic code,
he suggests that legitimate legal institutions draw on existing culture, custom,
and practice that form the basis for a system grounded in popular consent. It is
an argument about the suturing of legal legitimacy to the foundational terms
of nation-state authority and, by extension, the role of custom and community
as the basis for international law.

Drafters also invoked common heritage and shared civilizational values to
anticipate persuading broader European publics of the necessity of a shared
human rights framework that would unite (and perhaps supersede) national
belonging. The Court and Convention failed to attain widespread public recognition for decades. But the drafters used tropes of a European demos, figured
throughout the preparatory works as "European public opinion," to whom
they were beholden. This contributed to arguments for the urgency of the Convention project. It was to this public—the figure of European demos—that the
drafting committee ought to be beholden on the grounds of democratic will.
As I argue in chapter 3, the idea of a legal public, an audience uniquely attuned
to and engaged by arguments made in and through the language and practice
of the rule of law, was always part of the persuasive architecture of arguments
for the Convention system. Regardless of the broader uptake, the idea that
legitimacy and publicity were intertwined supported numerous other kinds of
arguments about why and how the Convention should be drafted in a broader,
more accessible and timely manner. Thus, a French representative noted that
if the drafting committee failed to produce a workable document, "European

public opinion would be deeply disappointed" (Council of Europe 1976 [vol. 3], 306). The idea of common European heritage and the figure of the "European public" are taken up in specifically doctrinal ways, as I discuss in the next section. This public would recognize the value of human rights precisely because they were already part of European civilized values.

Ultimately, the drafting committee came to a compromise position, combining draft versions that offered some definitions of human rights but less comprehensively detailed than some had hoped. The resulting draft kept some definitions, which according to Lord Layton from the United Kingdom included "a short list which . . . contained matters on which we could accept one another's intervention." The goal, he explained, was to "lay down the rules of club, so we drew up this Convention as a symbolic, clear declaration which marks us as free Western Europe" (Council of Europe 1977, 67). While the delegates who favored more detailed enumeration of rights still objected to the "legal formalism" over general principles (Council of Europe 1977, 68), they accepted definitions with a backstop. Teitgen noted:

> We should be prepared to accept their [the UK's] definitions, but we should add—and this seems essential to me—that these definitions propounded to us shall be interested in the light of the general principles of law obtaining among civilized nations. If we act in this way, whatever obscurities and lacunae may subsist in these definitions would be removed. (Council of Europe 1977, 69)

The backstop here is slight in language but transformative in perspective. It reiterates a recursive logic wherein precise definitions are grounded in assumptions of cultural and civilizational belonging at the heart of international customary law. It is thus, to return to another of Teitgen's formulations quoted at length above, that "English law, Swedish law, French law, Norwegian law, American law, lay down a sanction, or an identical or similar rule . . . that . . . forms part of the common heritage of civilised nations" (Council of Europe 1975 [vol. 1], 280). Europe is reflected in the Convention as an expression of common principle. How then could it be an incursion on national sovereignty? The ECHR is thus "a fusion, so to speak." When it was "interpreted here necessarily in light of general principles of law recognized by civilized nations," that community "need not be afraid there will be any further gaps" (Council of Europe 1977, p. 69).

The compromise and the resulting language framing the ECHR itself are evidence of the way that culture concepts provided flexibility through underdetermination. Notions of common culture filled in the gaps and resolved the tensions of sovereignty and European law. In the absence of defining rights comprehensively, the drafting committee opted for a mobile and recursive logic that allowed subsequent jurists to move back and forth between the particular and the universal, the sovereign and the European. The travaux and the system itself rest not on specificity of human rights but on the movement between instances of specific rights, expressed in their breach, within the constraints of "general principles."

The Convention as a Living Instrument: Culture in Doctrine

From the beginning, cultural and legal pluralism posed a challenge to the Court and Convention system. Shifting understandings of culture helped create conditions for compromise in the drafting process. But that process also locked ambiguity into the system as a central building block. Culture talk became a resource for managing, rather than resolving, the system's foundational tensions over European and national legal authority. The ECtHR is not alone in facing the conundrum. Legal systems derive legitimacy from the application of principles to specific cases. But the fact of cultural and social difference challenges the very logic of abstract principles themselves (Gershon 2011). This challenge is particularly difficult for a regional human rights court whose jurisdictional authority always rests on a tenuous balance between pluralism and harmonization.

It is thus no surprise that this legal pivot between national difference and shared European norms came up in many interviews I conducted. One judge noted in a 2016 interview, "It's one thing for a national court like the U.S. Supreme Court [to decide cases within a Federal system]. . . . [They might say,] 'We have federal constitution, we are a nation state.' We have, we're supposed to have common cultural values. The problem is I come from [a small northern European country]; my judgments have to be implemented in Azerbaijan, Armenia, Russia." And yet, as much as he was deeply committed to subsidiarity from a judicial perspective, he noted in the same interview that in adjudicating cases, "context is everything." He elaborated that was why "we have an incredibly strong tradition in this court of comparative analysis of laws, of trying to get the overall picture of a particular social phenomenon in all of the forty-seven member states. That is why we have developed the notion of a European consensus as being a very strong indicator of when we can use and develop a living instrument."[5]

It was through case law and doctrine, or interpretative legal frameworks that people created workable strategies for this balance. Different notions of "culture" formed the backbone of key doctrinal frameworks: margin of appreciation, European consensus, and the Convention as a "living instrument." Alongside these case-by-case interpretative moves, the Council also implemented policies and new protocols that tipped the balance between deference and intervention. The judge quoted above reminded me that the history of the Court was "an ebb and flow in relation to the environment in which it is situated in any given moment." The time of our interview was a period many referred to as the age of subsidiarity, a phrase taken from an influential 2014 law review article by Icelandic judge, and later Court president Robert Spano. In it he argued for a stronger emphasis on domestic incorporation of human rights principles that would bring the ECHR "back home" to states. The piece and Spano's presidency marked an epoch that many characterized as a move toward margin of appreciation within Court case law. Many judges and lawyers that I interviewed between 2016 and 2018 were supportive of this more sovereignty-shy approach. But not everyone was convinced. In response to my questions about margin of appreciation, one longtime (now retired) and highly respected Eastern European judge raised an eyebrow and told me sardonically, "Europe is in a nation-state mood." He saw the growing trend toward margin of appreciation as a kind of "deferentialism" to state sovereignty, beyond its original doctrinal intention.

The age of subsidiarity was ushered in by a series of high-level diplomatic conferences and the passing of new protocols. These served as binding amendments to the Convention. For example, Protocol 15, first proposed in 2013 and ratified in 2021, amended the Convention preamble to include references to subsidiarity and margin of appreciation. Nonetheless, as with all acts of balancing, there was room for negotiation in practice. Interpretative flexibility rests not in particular terms but in the complex and contested histories of interpretation, institutional power, and ideology that give rise to these terms in the first place. Countervailing margin of appreciation were other doctrinal frameworks—in particular, European consensus and the notion of the ECHR as a living instrument. Both these frameworks also relied on notions of culture, civilization, and norms to define a European us. Shared European norms materialized through comparing, sketching out, and arguing for an emerging picture of a particular social phenomenon across member states.

Projecting this other "us" was often an effect of legal research and comparative international perspectives. Many interviewees, particularly registry lawyers, spoke of the importance of comparative law in work at the Court. Comparison helped lawyers and judges to understand not only what issues were shared across countries. It also revealed where gaps in legal clarity required more directed legal and judicial interpretation to define emerging areas of law. As one highly experienced legal researcher in the registry explained to me in a 2018 interview, putting country systems into comparison revealed the underlying human rights problem in a given case. Sometimes that difference or problem required a "judicial response that harmonizes the law or system," and sometimes it required deference through subsidiarity for "sensitive matters." Sometimes, those gaps stood in for areas where the Court ought to pull back and defer to the fact of specificity and difference as a basis for a wide margin. At other times, a matter of European human rights principle might well be on the line, and despite a lack of consensus, the Court ought nonetheless to step in. The Court's authority rests in establishing which version of a European "us" has primacy: a collective community of legal norms or a discrete community of individual states. The answer is always both, in theory. But practice requires an emphasis on one or another version of which "us" is in play. This shapes what perspectives doctrinal and case law comparisons judges use for interpreting the convention.

Comparison thus allowed judges to turn difference into an argument for legal authority or for legal deference—making culture a resource rather than a problem from a legal perspective (Sarat and Berkowitz 1998). Cultural difference might call for the tempering of Court authority, as in margin of appreciation. And it can be the means for subsuming contextual specificity in the name of shared values (for example, tolerance and broad-mindedness). The Court balances the rights of applicants against the needs of a state to safeguard democracy or ensure the safety and well-being of a population. The conditions under which a state can justify such violations depend on whether the right can be qualified or on the degree of "derogability" of a right (Çalı 2007). State violations of rights such as freedom of expression or freedom of conscience may be deemed necessary to the maintenance of social order or democracy (as defined in limiting clauses spelled out in the Convention). These qualified rights rest on "an underlying assumption that factual and empirical circumstances matter in interpreting, delineating, and implementing the proper scope of the operation of the right" (Çalı 2007, 256). It is into this space that a flexible notion of culture enters as a critical interpretative pivot for enacting and managing sovereignty. It is to these doctrinal moves that I now turn.

The Work of Culture in Margin of Appreciation and European Consensus

The doctrinal framework for balancing individual rights against social norms and what is "necessary in a democratic society" is the "margin of appreciation" afforded to member states. Margin of appreciation rests in the idea that only domestic political and legal actors truly know a social and political context well enough to determine the necessity of state intervention. It follows from the idea that the ECHR system operates as subsidiary to national domestic legal systems. Practically speaking, when cases touch on sensitive social or religious norms, the Court tends to defer to national political and legal representatives, who are better positioned to understand cultural contexts. But it also must balance these perspectives with shared rights principles, particularly when there is a larger "European consensus," or evidence that standards and norms are changing across member states.

The best example is also the most precedentially important: the case in which the margin of appreciation doctrine was first explicitly articulated, *Handyside v. The United Kingdom* (1976). *Handyside* rested on whether the UK had violated the rights of a publisher by imposing fines and destroying copies of a translation of a popular Danish book that the British authorities deemed obscene. The *Little Red Schoolbook*, a frank and at times explicit handbook, introduced adolescents to issues that ranged from drug use to relations with parents and to sex and sexuality. The English courts held that the book violated English obscenity law. The applicant was the publisher, who claimed a violation of his Article 10 freedom of expression rights. The UK argued in Strasbourg that the fines, seizure, and destruction of the text were necessary in a democratic society. The ECtHR ultimately found no violation of the Convention.

In *Handyside*, the Court reiterated that its supervisory role needs to be balanced with respect for domestic legal systems and the sovereignty of participating member states. The case also established the principle that offensive speech should receive special protection in matters of freedom of expression. It thus both affirmed the importance of freedom of expression in the name of democracy and curtailed those rights in the name of democracy. The case drew on the two paradoxical understandings of the European democratic order discussed above: protection for individual rights in the framework of tolerance and the right of sovereign nation-states to define the meaning of democracy in their national (and cultural) context. As I argue at length elsewhere (Greenberg 2021b), the Court tacked back and forth between the content of the offensive speech and its context. In so doing, it both codified a principle of tolerance and broad-mindedness for speech that might offend but limited that right by deferring to national culture.

The Court's argument in finding no violation did not rest in an assessment of the quality of the speech itself (that would be beyond the scope of the Court, which does not judge the facts of a case). It lay in whether the procedural relationships between domestic courts and applicants were handled in light of Convention principles. The Court assessed whether the domestic English courts fully understood and considered the rights of the applicant in the specific context in which the *Little Red Schoolbook* would be read and circulated. The judgment focuses on how well the domestic court read the offensive speech in context, in terms of local cultural norms and in terms of principles of democracy more generally. The judgment notes:

> The [ECtHR] attaches particular importance to a factor to which the judgment of 29 October 1971 did not fail to draw attention, that is, the intended readership of the schoolbook. . . . In these circumstances, despite the variety and the constant evolution in the United Kingdom of views on ethics and education, the competent English judges were entitled . . . to think at the relevant time that the Schoolbook would have pernicious effects on the morals of many of the children and adolescents who would read it. (*Handyside* § 52)

In this passage, obscene speech is grounded in local cultural norms and contexts. The judgment is characterized by these references to cultural specificity, triggering an outer limit of the ECtHR's competency (and hence jurisdictional authority) to understand "culture." These serve as a limit to European supervision and trigger deference from the European Court. The European Court notes:

> It is not possible to find in the domestic law of the various Contracting States a uniform European conception of morals. . . . By reason of their direct and continuous contact with the *vital forces of their countries*, State authorities are in principle in a better position than the international judge to give an opinion on the exact content of these requirements. (*Handyside* § 48; emphasis added)

The *Handyside* decision speaks to the role that culture plays in mediating the tension between sovereignty and international supervision. As linguistic anthropologists have argued, legal actors and others often figure socially mediated struggles over authority through metaphors of space and time (Carr and Lempert 2016). The judgment links the Court's authority to intervene (or not) to how it imagines different groups of people will read and be impacted by the book in different contexts. Potential young readers will be affected differently than national authorities, and international judges. The question of obscenity can be resolved by relying on a doctrinal commitment to the authority of local (and state) communities to decide what is best for these young readers in their particular social context. In this way, European norms are superseded by national authority's supposed proximity to "vital forces," a "direct and continuous" relationship figured through the language of locality, place, and culture.

Within Convention law, freedom of expression triggers two competing understandings of democracy. Both are related to the question of who determines the cultural impact of speech. Should it be a shared European perspective? Or should it be determined via a culturally specific expression of local norms? *Handyside* takes up the essential problem of who has (and who ought to have) the last word for reading and judging text in context. Across these cases, contradictory relationships to text map onto and are argued in terms of more fundamental jurisdictional questions that link locality to sovereignty. And indeed, subsequent use of the *Handyside* doctrine, via margin of appreciation, is precisely to adjudicate this tension between super-state European supervision through collective norms and domestic sovereignty through deference to unique cultural and historical contexts.[6]

More recent examples of margin of appreciation cases demonstrate the continued entanglement of notions of culture, state sovereignty, and the limits on Court intervention. For example, in the 2014 Grand Chamber case *S.A.S. v. France*, margin of appreciation operates by bundling social and cultural norms (the idea of living together or *vivre ensemble*) with expressions of political will (democracy). *S.A.S. v. France* was decided in 2014 at the Grand Chamber, the highest level of the Court. It became a judicial referendum for the both the controversy of the French 2010 ban on the full-face veil and the lively debates on the issue of tolerance in multiple European countries. The applicant was a French national and devout Muslim who wears the burqa and niqab (*S.A.S.* para. 11). She brought the case as a challenge to the French 2010 legislation prohibiting the concealment of the face in public places. Although the language of the legislation is broad, third-party civic groups and scholars have interpreted it as an attack on full-face veiling. The law itself cites several reasons for the ban, which include public safety and security, the defense of public order, the breach of the dignity of veiled women and equality between the sexes, and a violation of the "requirements of 'living together'" in French society.

The Court has a troubled history in relationship to the question of freedom of religion with respect to pious Muslim women's veiling practice (Brems 2021). Its early case law upheld national bans on veiling by relying on the figure of the pious Muslim woman as being without agency and in need of protection by the Court. Such a figure is familiar from both colonial and more recent liberal democratic treatments of Muslim women's subjectivity (Fernando 2014).

The logic of argumentation in *S.A.S.* is striking precisely because it departs from previous cases. The *S.A.S.* judgment consistently asserts the applicant's individual choice and conscious commitment to the full-face veil and resoundingly rejects the paternalistic gender equality arguments of the earlier decisions. Yet *S.A.S.* still finds that the French state is within its margin-of-appreciation rights to sanction the wearing of full-face veil coverings—a position that re-entrenches French secularist assumptions through notions of "culture" and its relationship to French democratic and republican logics (Fernando 2014). As in the analysis of *Handyside*, the relationship between culture, locality, and sovereignty forms the limit to Court jurisdiction through the framework of margin of appreciation.

A judge on the Court at the time of the case who I interviewed expressed some frustration and critique of the Court's reasoning about the notion of "living together." As in *Handyside*, arguments about cultural specificity—including "vital forces" in *Handyside* and "living together" in *S.A.S.*—bundled notions of cultural specificity and political authority. This generated the conditions for ECtHR deference. The judge noted:

> It's a question of legal culture and quite often you are confronted with well-structured, comprehensive reasoning when you see that all different arguments are weighed . . . and that can be in the legislative process. If you take the question of the burqa, and you look at what the French have discussed, and you look at the legislation process, and you look at the year that they have really tried to look at these different issues. That is something that you think, . . . now, what's my role, where they have already discussed everything? Whereas in other countries the legal culture is different and you see a law adopted unanimously, or you see no argumentation, or you see a judgment and it is extremely superficial, or very positivist—just applying the law without looking at it. . . . Of course, you think procedure does matter. . . . When you see a procedure when everyone is involved, you must ask: can an international judge ask for more?

When I spoke with this judge, I was interested in some of the judicial thinking behind a decision that seemed to (a) contradict previous legal reason and (b) to produce the same exclusionary effect. The form of argumentation in *S.A.S.* was new, but the result was the same: a gendered and racialized exception to human rights norms governing religious expression. Why did the French state receive judicial deference for a legislative action that clearly produced discriminatory effects? I broached this question by discussing the standard of scrutiny appropriate to that legislative reason. The judge responded, "I found the argumentation of the majority wrong. . . . It was not so much the religious, but the general approach. I couldn't really see how the way people dress . . . it's not aggressive toward others. It's just different. And why not accept difference?" Even though the judge did not agree with the Court's argumentation, that fusion of procedure and notions of culture made it difficult to justify a Court intervention. The judge noted, "As I said, I found that the procedure of elaborating the laws was very profound. It was clear that there was a huge majority. I also understood that this was culturally very important for French society."

In this case, when culture meets procedure, it was difficult for the Court to assert its supervisory role. The French government representatives argued an essential link between particular kinds of embodied practice (face-to-face contact) as the root of French sociality (living together) and democracy. Thus, safeguarding cultural norms equated to safeguarding democracy itself. In bundling notions of culture, locality or proximity, and political representation in terms like "vital forces," margin of appreciation builds on the long-standing tradition that links place-based definitions of belonging to unbreachable sovereignty. From this perspective, courts, and an international quasi-constitutional human rights court in particular, do not have the democratic legitimacy to intervene. Rather, the authority of the court stems from the indirect relationship between the rule of law—as a system in which clear, predictable rules and constraints govern actions and behaviors—and democracy as an expression of collective will, embodied in shared principles. Thus, invoking notions of "society" and "vital forces," or what is deemed "necessary in a democratic society," are doctrinal expressions of this fusion between localized expressions of cultural specificity and democratic will.

European Consensus and Living-Instrument Doctrine

Given this strong deference to national cultural context and subsidiarity, it might be surprising that the Court ever finds violations in such sensitive matters as expression, family and privacy rights, conscience, or religion. Yet it is precisely notions of culture and its relationship to democracy that also ground and authorize international legal authority. If margin of appreciation fuses locality, culture, and sovereignty as a bulwark against Court supervision, the notion of European consensus and the Convention as a living instrument often support the opposite effect. This sense of "collective, European values" (culture in the second sense) is alive in a countervailing doctrine of European consensus. It invokes another tradition of minority rights protections, and tolerance etched into shared visions of postwar progress. Practically speaking, if a respondent state argues that curtailing an individual's rights is necessary in a democratic society, that argument will be weighed against a comparative approach to laws and policies among member states. If there is an absence of consensus or clearly emerging norms (for example, in policies regarding medical ethics), a respondent state has a wider margin of appreciation. Deference is due to country-specific ways to manage social issues according to local notions of culture and society. Yet if there are emerging trends within the European community, judges can take these into consideration. Likewise, if there are principles or values like tolerance or broad-mindedness that harken back to conceptions of European democracy or modernity, these too might come into play as a comparative interpretative framework.

The ECHR as a living instrument means that cases must be interpreted in light of present-day conditions (*Tyrer v. UK* 1978). Since the landmark *Tyrer* decision, the notion of a living instrument has been central to the Court's adaptive creativity to changing contexts (Mowbray 2005). It takes the form of different interpretive frameworks or doctrines that judges use to read concrete facts and details of cases against past case law, Convention principles, and new protocol rights and frameworks. Talking about the Convention and linking it to other texts—applications, judgments, domestic and international law, policy documents, and doctrine—is part of what makes communication and coordination possible across the ECHR system's sprawling institutional network. This intertextuality forms the basis of a system flexible enough to respond to the pressures of the Cold War, post–Cold War European integration, and emerging challenges like new technology, climate disaster, mass migration, and war. At the same time, judges and registry lawyers carefully police the boundaries of Convention interpretation so as to project the sense of continuity and consistency across the years. It is this dual dynamic of interpretative flexibility and endurance that shapes the living-instrument idea in practice.

This is particularly clear in the Court's case law on issues pertaining to sexuality, gender orientation, and LGBTQ+ rights.[7] This case law has developed rapidly over a relatively short period of time and has thus been an area of experimentation in the balance of margin of appreciation and evolving norms and rights standards. The combination of strong human rights advocacy and use of strategic litigation means these cases are often well-chosen to push case law forward and build precedent and new interpretive principles over time.[8] As a result, these cases have been touchstones in developing case law on the Convention as a living instrument and on the evidential strategies for establishing European consensus.

A case contemporary with *Handyside, Dudgeon v. The United Kingdom* (1981) is exemplary. The landmark case of *Dudgeon* dealt with the criminalization of male same-sex sexual acts in Northern Ireland. The judgment invoked the same bundle of nationally specific social mores that was the basis for deference in *Handyside*, and indeed leaned on it heavily. But in this instance, the Court found a violation in part by asserting the importance of tolerance and broad-mindedness as a foundational commitment.

In *Dudgeon*, the Court established that there was a clear breach of the applicant's right to respect for his private life. At issue was whether the laws in Northern Ireland were necessary in a democratic society for the protection of morals and the protection of the rights of others (construed here as youth and those who might be offended by homosexual sexual practices). The Court balanced the context of Northern Irish "moral ethos" and "moral standards of society as a whole" (para. 47) against a general legislative environment in Europe in which there "is legislation on the matter in all the member States of the Council of Europe" (para. 49). And while it found that "it is for the national authorities to make the initial assessment of the pressing social need of each case" with an extensive margin of appreciation "where the protection of morals is in issue" (para. 57), the decision was nonetheless "subject to review by the Court" (para. 52). The judgment in this context reaffirms that "the notion of 'necessity' is linked to that of a 'democratic society,' . . . two hallmarks of which are tolerance and broadmindedness" (para. 53) and must be proportionate to a legitimate aim. As in *Handyside*, the balance of legal restrictions were grounded in locally salient notions of culture and the "moral fabric of society." The Court weighed "the moral climate in Northern Ireland in sexual matters" (para. 57) is against tolerance as a shared feature of democracy.

While Northern Ireland was not alone in Europe in same-sex legal restrictions, and while there was variation in these approaches, the Court backgrounded both the lack of European consensus and the strong cultural, religious, and moral component of this legislative field. The judgment notes:

> As compared with the era when [the legislation] was enacted, there is now a better understanding, and in consequence an increased tolerance, of homosexual behavior to the extent that in the great majority of the member States of the Council of Europe it is no longer considered to be necessary or appropriate to treat homosexual practices of the kind now in question as in themselves a matter to which the sanctions of the criminal law should be applied. The Court cannot overlook the marked changes which have occurred in this regard in the domestic law of the member States. (*Dudgeon*, para. 60)

Dudgeon is a case in which the interpretative wiggle room created between margin of appreciation, European consensus (or lack thereof), and a notion of tolerance as a shared, essential aspect of European democratic culture is evident. It is also evidence of the ways in which LGBTQ+ rights have been squeezed between different doctrinal frameworks. This has both paved the way for an expansion of rights in this area and constrained forms of legally recognizable personhood in others (see Johnson 2013). Yet over time, and across cases, advances have followed as one notion of culture (as tolerance) displaced another (as local moral and social order). In 1986, the Court found no violation in *Rees v. The United Kingdom* in which a transgender applicant alleged a violation of Article 8's right to private life on the grounds of the state's refusal to legally register the applicant's status as a woman. While finding no violation, however, the Court put states on notice that it would track changing social norms in future cases. In the landmark 2002 transgender rights case *Christine Goodwin v. UK*, the judgment acknowledged a sea change in European social norms that supported a violation of Article 8. With *Christine Goodwin*, the judgment establishes a thorough review of the legal landscape in and outside Europe. In balancing "the general interests of the community and the interests of the individual" (*Goodwin*, para. 72), the Court "proposes to look at the situation within and outside the Contracting State to assess 'in the light of present day conditions' . . . the appropriate interpretation and application of the Convention" (*Goodwin*, para. 75). Here the "us" of the national context is subsumed by the "us" of a legally mediated European one. In *Rees* in 1986, there was "little common ground [that] existed between States," and the law "seemed to be in a state of transition" (para. 85, *Goodwin* citing to *Rees*). In *Christine Goodwin*, the judgment still notes a lack of European approach; it finds "clear and uncontested evidence of a continuing international trend in favour not only of increased social acceptance of transsexuals but of legal recognition of the new sexual identity of post-operative transsexuals" (para. 85). Given that "in the twenty-first century the right of transsexuals to personal development and to physical and moral security the full sense enjoyed by others in society cannot be regarded as a matter of controversy requiring the lapse of time to cast clearer light on the issues involved" (para. 90). Given this, the contracting state no longer enjoyed a wide margin of appreciation in this area (para. 93).

Between *Handyside, Dudgeon, Rees*, and *Christine Goodwin*, tolerance emerges as a line along which Court jurisdictional authority runs. It is the balance of one notion of culture as toleration and one as an expression of localized, vital forces that makes the interpretative difference.[9] In speaking about the emergence of European consensus, a longtime Council lawyer pointed me to precisely this moment in the Court's history. My interviewee, Gunther, was a senior lawyer in the Department for the Execution of Judgments but had been at the Court or the Council for decades. He was an astute observer of the politics and culture of the Council and was well positioned to speak to shifts in the doctrinal concepts and their application over the longue durée.

He explained to me that consensus was as much an interpretive process as a decision about when to push or not push member states. Rather than existing as a pregiven fact, the Court builds case law "on a very casuistic basis." Consensus thus emerges slowly over time, as he noted: "At some stage you have 70–80 percent of the Council of Europe who is along a certain line and then the last come [along]. We forced you to join." If in *Rees*, the Court reasoned by lack of consensus and the strength of a particular notion of social and cultural specificity, the judgment, he explained, nonetheless charged states to "keep this area under close scrutiny to see if the situation should not be changed. And over time of course it has changed." And yet, it was also the case, in *Dudgeon* and other early gender and sexuality rights cases that this slow and cautious approach existing alongside more concerted decisions to act. Thus "when you had the first British cases, I think Britain was certainly not alone in Europe [in criminalizing homosexual sex] and still the court said no, this is a question of principle. We find a violation."

Consensus was thus both a strategy and an interpretive field of play. One longtime LGBTI human rights advocate captured both the time, effort, and guesswork that went into building a consensus and the hope that the Court accepted it as dispositive. He noted, "All you can do is keep pushing forward" to build a case for an evolving consensus. Of course, he added, "Consensus is . . . a judicial practice, which they sometimes use—they sometimes don't use. They use it in different ways; they do whatever they want. . . . They are inconsistent, and no one ever knows when is it evolving? When is it achieved? How far did it go? Why here and not there?" Achieving or establishing consensus was thus a process of trial and error. It emerged from a combination of new cases, strategic litigation, and broader advocacy and awareness campaigns about changing social norms and rights across Europe and in national contexts. Evidence of on-the-ground trends could be linked to doctrinal categories, legal research, and judicial strategies, like the use of comparative European and international law. What tipped the balance toward one doctrinal frame or another, however, was which version of cultural norms—and the European "us" associated with them—was persuasive. If margin of appreciation was rooted in a notion of deep, long-standing cultural continuity, and judicial deference to local norms, then consensus put ideas of European tolerance in play by a shared, modernizing European "us."

Thus, alongside tolerance, consensus also introduced a notion of modernity, which was also reflected in living-instrument doctrine. Many interviewees believed the Court needed to keep pace with cutting issues to maintain legitimacy as a leading European institution. A senior registry lawyer, a longtime observer of the Court, pointed to the necessity to keep up with research and reasoning on cutting-edge issues like technology, surveillance, or reproductive or health technologies. The key was not to identify what the Court's perspective ought to be per se but whether it was fairly representing the legal trends or perspectives of its constituent member states. My interlocutor explained the process:

> [There is a] general approach that the court has for these cutting-edge issues. It will often carry out research in what the law is in the 47 countries—[for example,] what is the law on same-sex marriage or adoption for a single mother. And in many cases it sees that there's an emerging trend. And if we follow that trend, then [formalize it], that's one way in which new principles can

develop. .... After those sorts of legal studies are carried out, [judges] identify a principle which they can live with.

He added, although maybe "there are some who love to criticize [the consensus notion and] the application of that notion willy-nilly," when it comes to "issues relating to modern technologies or issues related to private life, it plays a big role."

While technically, European consensus or living-instrument doctrine do not have an inherently rights-friendly meaning, they are resonant with long-standing assumptions about liberal progress. Regardless of the normative impact, consensus is a temporal envelope that weds notions of place (Europe) to notions of time, embodying the Court's "evolutive" nature as a living instrument (Dzehtsiarou 2019). Mapping the ECHR along a linear timeline counterposes national time (Anderson 1983) with its emphasis on cyclical notions of cultural transmission within the framework of legal and sovereign continuity so central to ideologies of European nations and nationalism (Wheatley 2023). And these values are tied to historical evolution and development—a temporal framework born in the European Enlightenment that links European belonging to particular movements of time and progress (Koselleck 2004). This weights evidence of shared European values, on the policy and legal level, against an individual state's claim that violations are necessary to society or democracy. Culture as a concept in this tradition is fundamentally pedagogical: it rests in the critical function that institutions play in shaping modern European citizens (Lloyd and Thomas 1998).

The Afterlives of Defining Rights: When "Them" Has Been "Us" All Along

The tension between state sovereignty and shared European belonging has been a constant throughline in the history of the European Court. Culture has been a productively ambiguous concept that takes on continued salience in ECHR's language, drafting history, and doctrine. As with all shifting, ideologically resonant, and underdetermined terms, *culture* takes on continued meaning in everyday practice.

Yet what I have hoped to show in this chapter is that while the balance of this debate shifts, the mechanisms for working it out in practice remain remarkably consistent. The tension between national sovereignty and European ideals, like the tension between democracy and law, is not resolvable. It is baked into the very structure of European governance if the nation-state is the dominant organizing political and social unit. While there are alternative and likely more just solutions to this problem, such as the abolition of nation-state borders, that is not in the cards for the ECHR system and other governance and rights structures. For now, engaging with democracy, human rights, and rule of law is a process of weighting the balance and rewriting the terms of who counts as "us" in the protection of fundamental rights.

As with all aspects of the Court, however, this balancing does not take place in a vacuum. In addition to applicants, nation-states, policymakers, and curious academics, there is a broader audience for arguments about who counts as a national or European "we." I close with one example of how *culture* talk shapes the broader processes of publicity and persuasion in which the Court is embedded.

While I was conducting field research, perhaps no conflict exemplified the continuities and variations of these debates more than that of Brexit. Despite not being EU institutions, the European Convention on Human Rights and the Strasbourg Court were drawn into these debates. Strasbourg became a pro-leave punching bag in the UK. This was in part due to a controversial and highly publicized case, *Hirst v. The United Kingdom*, known infamously as the prisoners voting rights case. It was a case that received a great deal of negative press in the English media and became synonymous with international regulatory overreach. At the height of the Brexit Leave campaign in 2016, Theresa May (then UK home secretary) argued that Britain ought to pull out of the European Convention on Human Rights. The Convention is not an EU institution, so it was not directly threatened by Brexit. But ECtHR and the Convention system had become a flash-point symbol of foreign interference with British sovereignty and security.[10] May argued that England was better off and more secure without it.

This was a proposition with serious consequences. Withdrawal from the Convention would take access to the Court off the table for those on British soil. But there were other long-term repercussions. In 1998, the UK signed the Human Rights Act integrating the European Convention directly into British law. In turn, the Good Friday Agreement, which formed the basis for peace in Northern Ireland, rested on that 1998 Human Rights Act. The Convention was thus directly linked to the rights framework at the heart of the accords. It was a moment celebrated as a true maturation of the ECHR system and an achievement of the goals of the system working themselves out through domestic law and policy. Quietly but centrally, European human rights integration became a condition of possibility for peace in one of Europe's most entrenched conflicts.

In response, a group of actors pulled together a four-minute skit hosted on the *Guardian* newspaper's website.[11] The well-known actor Sir Patrick Stewart played a politician who was furious at European incursions on British heritage and sovereignty. As the scene opens, Stewart angrily asked, "What has the European Convention on Human Rights ever done for us?" His political advisors vigorously agree. Stewart launches into an anti-Europe diatribe. But as the video progresses, the advisors begin to take the question seriously. What has the ECHR ever done for us? What began as a rhetorical critique ends with a concrete list of benefits of the ECHR: freedom from torture and degrading treatment, freedom from slavery, and peace in Northern Ireland. Faced with overwhelming arguments, Stewart's character reluctantly agrees that the Convention has had its uses. But then why, if it was such a great idea, he asks, didn't the English come up with it themselves.

> STEWART: Look here. I'm not against human rights, of course not, but I say we don't need lectures from the Frogs and the Krauts. This is Britain, the land of Magna Carta, we invented human rights, for G-d's sake. We should be writing our own bill of rights and foist it on the Europeans (ha ha ha). Let's see how they how they like it then.
>
> (*GROUP LAUGHTER*)
>
> POLITICAL ADVISOR: Uh, we've already done that, actually.
>
> STEWART: What?!
>
> POLITICAL ADVISOR: Well, after we won the war, British legal experts did draft a bill of human rights to help Europe sort itself out, you know to protect people from abuses of state power, and that kind of thing.
>
> STEWART: Really?
>
> POLITICAL ADVISOR: Oh, yeah.
>
> STEWART: Are you sure?
>
> POLITICAL ADVISOR: Oh yes.
>
> STEWART: Ah. Well, that's good. What's it called?
>
> POLITICAL ADVISOR: The European Convention on Human Rights.
>
> (*LONG AWKWARD PAUSE*)
>
> STEWART: Oh, fuck off!

We can't know the full impact of the skit, although it received 1.2 million views on YouTube, the last I checked. But the rhetorical trick it employs is exemplary of how people have used notions of culture to mediate the tension between international legal authority and national sovereignty. Rather than put "our culture" in opposition to "their international law," the skit skillfully inverted the foreignness of the Convention by reframing every argument against as an argument for its essential Englishness. It raised the question of how we can be against something that is and has always "us" all along. And it answered that from the Magna Carta to the post-WWII architecture for peace, European human rights were always already English human rights.

Whether they were aware of it or not, the comedy players were drawing on a long-standing framework that was central to the ECHR's early adoption and later success. As with many international legal institutions, the question is how to balance systems of democratic representation grounded in national popular will with supranational authority that safeguards individual human rights. With the founding of the permanent Court, this question gained urgency as a question of what gives the Court its *democratic* authority vis-à-vis culturally specific legal and social norms.

In this chapter, I analyzed how this generative tension plays out in practice through the strategic deployment of shifting notions of culture (Urciuloi 2009). In tracking the uses and meanings of culture in different domains across the Court, we can understand how the tension of sovereignty, jurisdiction, and international human rights creates a set of coordinates to turn irresolvable tensions into a productive nexus of legal authority. The foundational contradictions of the European nation-state, the tension between abstract liberal individualism, and the jealous guarding of national notions of belonging continue to define human rights as an ideological project in specific and institutionally significant ways.

TWO

Bringing the Outside In

Council of Europe Expansion after the Cold War

AS CHAPTER 1 DEMONSTRATED, the ECHR founders achieved consensus by drawing a sharp division between Western democracies, the fascist past, and communism in Eastern Europe. This divide continued to shape Council and Court staff's understanding of the rule of law and the scope of human rights throughout the Cold War (Madsen 2007). But beginning in 1990, the Council faced a new challenge. How would it integrate postsocialist Eastern European states after the Cold War and the dissolution of the Soviet Union? If the 1990s was widely seen as a period of "transition" to democracy, what role would the Council play?

The Council of Europe added twenty-five new member states between 1990 and 2007, with Montenegro the last to join. This almost doubled state membership and afforded Convention rights to millions more people. But the rapid expansion of Europe to include the formerly communist states sparked profound questions for Council and Court staff. Many wondered what would happen to democracy, human rights, and rule of law with the accession of the newly democratizing Eastern states. Some feared accepting these new members would undermine the legitimacy of a system built on European values that had been explicitly defined against communism (Moyn 2014). But to not accept these states threatened the legitimacy of a system whose reason for being was to integrate Europe through those selfsame values.

In this chapter I explore the impact that the Council of Europe's expansion had on the ECHR system. I analyze how people reconceptualized the meaning of rule of law and human rights in light of this shift. And I argue that rather than resolving or reconciling this tension, judges, lawyers, and diplomats developed ways to manage and sustain difference within the ECHR system itself. In place of a minimalist system that rarely issued judgments against its democratic member states, the Council and Court implemented a more self-consciously hierarchical and pedagogical approach. The more "mature" democracies would teach new member states how to become democratic. Court staff and leadership facilitated these shifts through new administrative and policy procedures. This included new admissibility criteria, new ways to rank importance of cases, and entirely new areas of Convention case law.

An anthropological analysis of administrative and doctrinal changes in the post-expansion period reveals two key insights. First, administrative, policy, and doctrinal responses were inseparable from the social and cultural categories through which people made sense of the post–Cold War transformations. The second and related insight is that for rule of law to remain salient and persuasive, its terms and expressions must be flexible, situational, and subject to change over time (Cheesman 2018). As with any rule-of-law institution, the ECHR system works not as a top-down imposition of power. Rather, it functions because it has an extensive and persuasive world view that people have adopted and translated into meaningful forms of legal and diplomatic practice. Had the Council and Court remained divided at an overtly ideological level, neither could have functioned as long or as effectively as they have. Critical to expansion was that the institution maintain and project a balance of interests. A sense of fairness was key for the legitimacy of an institution promoting democracy and equality before the law. And yet not all states and the kinds of cases applicants might bring would or could be treated the same.

This meant that *difference* within the system was a social fact of everyday life and work. Most people with whom I spoke acknowledged that ideals of equality before the law necessitated nuance and compromise in practice. At times, people treated this as a matter of fact and value-neutral proposition. After all, not all cases were the same in weight, significance, or interest. But at other times, the fact of difference and differentiation could be a source of tension, particularly when it mapped on long-standing distinctions and hierarchies among states.

The result was the emergence of pathways and pressure valves through which the judges, lawyers, and other staff made sense of difference and incorporated it into the system itself. New administrative procedures for processing cases, such as single- or three-judge formations, and new registry categories for bundling applicants, such as well-established case law or pilot procedures, were examples of concrete institutional responses to geopolitical shifts. And in both cases, these new administrative procedures facilitated processing an influx of new kinds of applications. This led to people making associations and naturalizing links among *kinds of legal issues* and particular places. In this way, alternative pathways meant to facilitate expansion also created internal modes of differentiation within the ambit of law. These distinctions built on and reanimated distinctions of East and West, old and new member states, and mature and immature democracies—civilizational hierarchies that have long been at the heart of international and European law (Anderson 2023; Anghie 2023).

As a result, expansion both changed the meanings of rule of law and human rights in practice and re-entrenched long-standing relationships of power. Rather than pose a challenge to the system, this contradiction reveals the flexibility of the ECHR system as a social and discursive field. A once defining external boundary became an internal mechanism for differentiation *within the institution*. This process shored up the importance of the Council and ECHR system in an integrating but still divided European legal and political geography.

Bringing the Outside In: Council of Europe Expansion

For early member states notions of "culture" and "civilization" operated as vague but powerful categories to define shared European belonging (see chapter 1). But just as often, the drafters defined this European community by what and whom it excluded. The presumption of shared cultural and political norms shaped a great deal of early Convention practice, including the long delay in ratifying the Court's binding jurisdiction. It also led to a great deal of deference to nation-states for the first few decades.

In part, this belonging was premised on the idea that member states had relatively similar and functioning human rights mechanisms and norms in place. Prior to expansion, the earliest cases of repetitive and systematic violations had been from Italy. A large share of these cases related to criminal and civil procedural rights and the length of judicial proceedings (Haider 2013). But most other case law stemmed from individual cases that dealt with improving already democratic systems at the margins—at least according to many Council staff with whom I spoke. Gunther, a longtime Council staff member who witnessed accession firsthand, attributed the initial rarity of cases to a general trust in national systems to handle human rights issues domestically: "What was necessary in democratic society was pretty much respected among the member States in the old pre-1989 configuration." It was perhaps for this reason, he noted, that the Commission didn't send many cases on to be heard by the full Court to issue binding judgments. His explanation was that the Commission felt these were national questions that were being "dealt with pretty decently in [member] countries."

With the end of the Cold War, the accession of formerly communist Eastern European states was a fundamental challenge to these ideas of shared cultural and political values. Western policymakers across Europe were explicit that the newly democratic, newly independent states needed guided transition that would root out the legacies of state socialism.[1] For the Council, this took the form of concerns about the maturity of domestic legal and political systems to resolve human rights issues. But it also posed practical questions about how to deal with rising caseloads and new areas of Convention violations.

Until 1998, with the signing of Protocol 11 and the establishment of a permanent Court, the ECHR was overseen by the European Commission. This diplomatic body rarely referred cases on to judges. Protocol 11 was a 1994 amendment to the Convention that accomplished a number of reforms. It shifted all tasks formerly divided between the European Commission and the ECtHR to the Court, including filtering and processing of applications, determining admissibility, negotiating friendly settlements, and fact-finding (Haider 2013, 4). At the same time, Protocol 11 reaffirmed the right of individual application as a core principle of the Convention system, introducing Strasbourg as an avenue of last resort for millions of Europeans.

Between 1959 and 1998, the Court delivered 859 judgments in total.[2] Between 1999 and 2020, that number was over 20,000, clustered around a few high-count states (figure 2.1).[3] Alongside this process, the origins of applications and the kinds of human rights being breached also changed. Many of these violations clustered around human rights violations pertaining to property rights, prison conditions, fair trial rights, deprivation of liberty, torture, and degrading treatment (figure 2.2).

Expansion thus posed practical issues, including quantities of applications unseen in the system's history. Human rights violations of a totally different type and order piled up. These applications also changed the character of case law

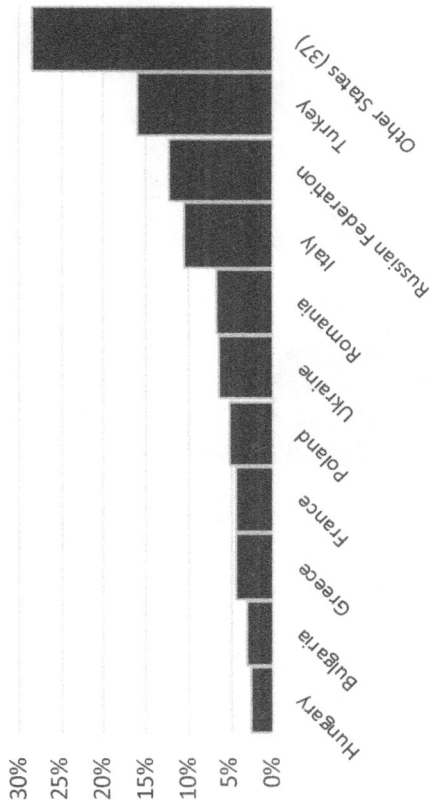

FIGURE 2.1. Judgments delivered by state (% of total), 1959–2020.
Between 1959 and 2020, the Court delivered 23,406 judgments.
Source: Council of Europe, *ECtHR Overview 1959–2020, 3*, https://
www.echr.coe.int/documents/d/echr/Overview_19592020_ENG.

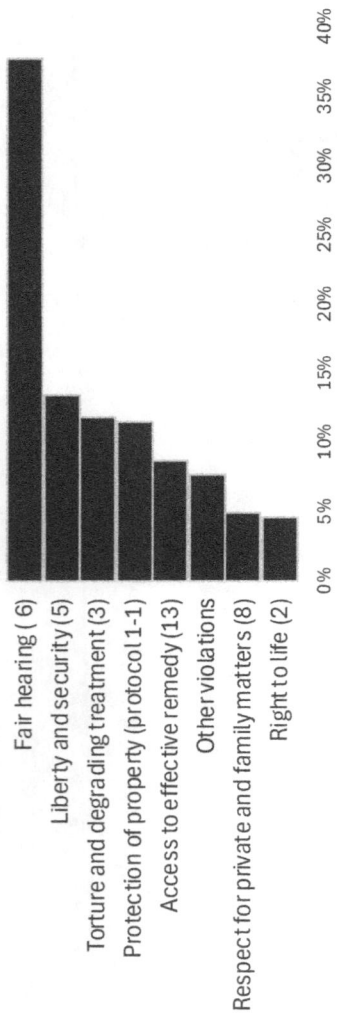

FIGURE 2.2. Subject matter of Court's violations judgments, 1959–2020. Source: Council of Europe, *ECtHR Overview 1959–2020*, 6, https://www.echr.coe.int/documents/d/echr/Overview_19592020_ENG.

and the ECHR conventions being brought before the Court. New kinds of cases included prison conditions, property restitution, media and free speech codes, and cases of torture and degrading treatment. With Eastern European accession, the Court had to address not only new but more legally and legislatively complex issues of a structural nature—for example, post-communist property restitution.[4] These kinds of cases could include tens or even hundreds of applicants. Expansion was thus not only a moment in which people confronted integration of former communist states in abstract ways. It required dealing with an onslaught of more and new kinds of applications in everyday practice.

Accession and expansion took on a unique legal character. This led people to make patterned associations between types of human rights violations and types of places and state systems. In describing this period, Gunther noted, "When we started to have the cases against the former communist countries, horrible situations came up where everyone said this is not possible. [We dealt with] plenty of situations. . . . which we had never seen before. People [would] be in detention under such conditions that we didn't even imagine." These new cases posed pragmatic, political, and ethical dilemmas for Council staff. Gunther, in recounting this, spoke of the "shock" he and others experienced when their understanding of human rights hit a "new reality which forced the convention organs to develop jurisprudence in plenty of areas [that had] not been necessary in the ancient European world." These were violations that had been previously "unimaginable in Europe." Gunther was not the only person I heard speak of encountering these new kinds of violations in terms of shock. Where one stood with respect of such violations—and whether one could or could not imagine them—was a way to narrate legal expertise and ethical personhood within a post–Cold War political and social geography.

At the same time, expansion also brought new perspectives on human rights for even longtime staff members, lawyers, and judges. As Gunther explained to me, it even shook people's confidence in their own democratically "mature" systems. Post-expansion, people within the system began to recognize that human rights violations might be structural in nature, even in their home states. Lawyers from original member states turned a critical lens back toward what many had assumed to be unproblematic democratic orders without underlying structural human rights issues. As Gunther explained,

the old states . . . started to question their own systems [and looked] a bit more carefully at "have I done things rightly?" And even the Commission and the Court started . . . to be more critical to each other. This gentleman's club where you trusted each other disappeared a little bit . . . and the Court and the Commission started to apply what they had to be credible in the essence of law. We have a nondiscriminatory approach. . . . [When] they had started to see problems in some Eastern European States because the situation was horrendous, [they realized these] principles had to be applied in the old states.

From their perspective, he noted, the old states realized that "I also have problems here somehow, and I can improve."

Expansion challenged the system's underlying sense of confidence and the taken-for-granted assumptions about national states as always reliable partners in protecting human rights. In addition, expansion revealed an always existing but often unspoken aspect of the rule of law: it was clearly contextual, negotiated, and often tenuous. It required diplomacy and negotiation to function. This meant human rights were simultaneously binding and unenforceable in any absolute way. The fact that the system needed to and could accommodate such variation was both a strength and a potential weakness. It raised these questions: How different is too different, and how violent is too violent to be contained within the rule of law? And who gets to determine when and how such a limit has been breached? For the system to maintain relevance, it would have to be flexible enough to redefine European belonging in the post–Cold War period.

From Consensus to Persuasion: Making Sense of East-West Relations during Expansion

The tensions and subtle inequalities of integrating newly democratic countries into European governance structures and systems of audit and surveillance were not specific to the Council (Gille 2016). But the criteria for membership posed a uniquely thorny issue for an institution that presented itself as "the conscience of Europe." Council expansion was controversial, even divisive, among leadership and staff. Those who supported bringing new members in argued that it was the best means of facilitating democratic transition. From this perspective, the Council was the institution best positioned to provide incentives in the form of diplomatic access, expertise, institutional support, and some modest funding. It could also serve as a watchdog overseeing the transition process. Opponents took the position that the formerly communist Eastern European states were not ready or able to commit to the core pillars of democracy, human rights, and rule of law. Bringing in new democracies would at best water down the system. At worst it would undermine its moral and political integrity.

Insider accounts of Council expansion point to these tensions. In a 2017 article on expansion, longtime Council of Europe staff member Andrew Drzemczewski detailed the challenges of including formerly socialist countries that many Council members believed were "not fully ready for democracy" (135):

> When countries, principally from Central and Eastern Europe, the so-called "new democracies," indicated their desire to join the Council of Europe, the decision to include them could not be refused. Were these decisions taken too precipitously? . . . As staff member[s] of the Council of Europe . . . we were of the view that the "new democracies" certainly ought to be invited to join the democratic club of "Western European states" possessing a long, and hopefully strongly anchored rule of law traditions. The door must definitely not be slammed in the face of countries wishing to join a democratic club. (135)

Both Drzemczewski's account and interviews I conducted with people who had worked at the Council during this period depicted a moment of upheaval and potential. This tension came to a head with Council of Europe deputy secretary general Peter Leuprecht's highly public resignation over the inclusion of Russia and Croatia in 1997. According to Drzemczewski, Leuprecht's logic was this:

> Yes, states should be welcome to the Council of Europe, but only if they "have clean hands" and are really willing and able to abide by the principles upon which the organisation is based. Leuprecht thought that these states fell woefully short of the mark as concerns the three Council of Europe basic pillars. . . . Leuprecht reflected, ". . . values were being watered down. That's why I left. I don't believe you can be a dissident and stay in government." (136)

Expansion posed a choice: to draw stark lines (as Leuprecht did) or to create a system that was simultaneously hopeful in its ability to welcome and integrate new members but realistic in its plan to monitor them. The resulting system had to ensure that states, principally the new democracies, were willing and able

> to abide by Council of Europe standards— . . .—they became members of the Organisation on the understanding that they remedy shortcomings in their legal orders as part of the membership package. This would be overseen, in particular, by the Committee of Ministers' confidential, non-discriminatory, consensus-based monitoring. This was process that relied on persuasion, peer pressure and diplomatic negotiation. (136–137)

This approach shaped subsequent power relations and dynamics that are palpable in the Council to this day. It formed the basis for an approach to European integration through the maintenance of difference along the axis of cosmopolitanism and nationalism that is Europe's modern and Cold War inheritance (Judt 2011, 57). It grouped states along different trajectories of progress toward democracy. In one group were like-minded states that continued to refine already well-established systems of democratic principles and practices. For these states, staff, lawyers, and judges saw human rights violations as exceptional problems rather than deep structural contradictions or democratic failure. The role of the Council was to help refine human rights around the edges. In the second track were "the new democracies" that would be called on to demonstrate that they "were 'willing and able' to abide by Council of Europe standards" (Drzemczewski 2017). For these states, the Council acted as pedagogue. It would teach states how to overcome structural deficiencies through a combination of persuasion and pressure. By bringing the "new democracies" into the fold in a graduated system of monitoring and encouragement, Council expansion institutionalized aspirations to supersede Cold War divisions and facilitate integration. The new democracies become part of the system. But they did so in a way that reproduced Cold War distinctions as an internal boundary that kept long-standing power differentials operational and productive (e.g., see Myslinska 2024).

This arrangement shifted pre-accession strategies of hard power and sanctions to those of encouragement, consensus, and negotiation. It made transforming the absolutist position of having "clean hands" into a negotiated compromise that became a unique form of post–Cold War soft power. But it also left Euro-integrationist institutions haunted by the possibility of failure and complicity. For example, Leuprecht's objection to Croatian accession in 1997 was in response to the scale of state violence and crimes against humanity committed during the wars of Yugoslav succession. In addition, processes of transition in former state-socialist countries were often negotiated by many of the same political elites that had ruled during the communist era. For someone of Leuprecht's generation, who came of age in opposition to these regimes, one can see how this was at best complicity. And at worst it was a thin papering over new states' nondemocratic pasts.

In the end, the pro-expansion camp won the day. The once unshakeable external boundary that grounded Council values became a mechanism for authorizing and structuring expansion itself. Membership in the Council of

Europe was a pathway for states to full integration into a post–Cold War European community (Reichel et al. 2020). To become a member, one had to sign onto a series of Conventions, including the ECHR. These served as both a marker of and aspiration toward a state's commitments to democracy, rule of law, and human rights. Participation provided access to diplomatic, political, and legal institutions. It was also a kind of moral stamp of approval that a country met the conditions for European democratic belonging.

In signing on to Council membership and its binding Conventions, new member states were compelled toward oversight and monitoring, not necessarily on their terms. The original founding members had concrete visions of what mature and functioning democratic orders looked like. But what it means to be "democratic" is neither absolute nor ahistorical (Paley 2008). It matters in this context that the ECHR system, as a legacy of the UN Declaration of Human Rights, emerged as a minimalist instrument for political and civil rights rather than economic and social rights (Messer 1993). When people spoke of democratic guarantees, they largely meant in the areas of civil and political rights: property rights; freedom of expression, conscience, and religion; and civil and criminal procedural guarantees. These were the kinds of rights that many of the drafters saw at stake in the emerging Cold War divide. In addition, the lessons of fascism and state violence left their mark in a series of so-called non-derogable rights that protected the sanctity and life of persons: prohibitions on torture and degrading treatment, on slavery and forced labor, and protections of the right to life. Absent in this balance of rule of law, human rights and democracy were explicit references to economic and social rights, which many communist states in the mid to late twentieth century also enshrined. Since expansion, the Convention system has been remarkably flexible in accommodating areas that might be classed as economic and social rights, particularly in the area of labor and collective action (Fudge 2011). But it remains a civil and political instrument first and foremost. And it was always these achievements that marked this transitological arc of progress against which new states were measured.

Who and What Is the European Convention For?

As I demonstrated in the previous section, expansion made clear two different underlying visions of Council membership and the role of the Convention system. The first was that the grounds of the system rest on an already shared commitment to human rights and the rule of law that united Europe's democratic community of nation states. The second was premised on the pedagogical function of the Council, a role that drew an external line between democratic and undemocratic contexts and created internal hierarchies among members. How the system would manage difference within the framework of integration was a thus a litmus test for how it would manage expansion more broadly. It was necessary for all members to be bound to one another and the Convention. And they necessarily did so while accepting the fact of hierarchies within that community. Alexander, a high-level staff member at the Council who had experience in the Court, in the human rights directorate, and with the Committee of Ministers, put the persuasive task that held this system together more directly: the key to the Council approach was to convince states that it was "better to be in the system than out of it."

This comment points to the tenuousness of a system that ultimately rests in moral and political persuasion and relationships. It relies on country representatives to not only stay in the system but abide by its rules. Yet not all member states had the same relationship to those rules or norms institutionally, legally, and sometimes politically. Compromise and negotiation were thus necessary. But compromise needed to stay within bounds. It should not throw the sanctity of those norms totally into question. After all, if the goal is to keep countries "in," at what point does everyone become responsible for sanctioning violence committed by member states? How much difference is too much? How much persuasion and compromise are necessary to make difference workable? And when do new patterns of human rights violations threaten the underlying legitimacy of the system as a whole?

These questions were not only theoretical. As new states brought new challenges, the realities of compromise also became more concrete. Alexander explained this through a powerful example in our conversation on the history of expansion. I asked how he had approached the balance between upholding system values and compromising in order to persuade state representatives to work within the system. He answered by posing a counter-question: "Is it braver" to call out human rights violations or to compromise and work within the system. He described an instance several years prior to our conversation, when he had been on a fact-finding mission to a Council of Europe country to investigate prison conditions. He did not tell me the country out of confidentiality. But he did not need to indicate that it was a more recent accession state. The association of prison condition cases and post-1990 membership is so naturalized as to go without saying. The delegation he was with visited the cells where detainees were held in isolation. The conditions were so terrible they could hardly be believed. The fact-finding team encountered a particular prisoner in isolation, suffering terribly. They agreed with the country representatives that if the prisoner could be moved out of isolation into better conditions, the Council task force would not publicize the violation. "What should we have done?" he mused. Should the Council lawyers have drawn attention to the conditions and made it an issue? Would the prisoner still then be in that cell if they had? Or was it better to have compromised to ensure some better conditions for that person?

His painful dilemma echoed other conversations I had with Council and Court staff, particularly around the time of Russia's invasion of Ukraine in 2022. Indeed, many reflected back on similar conversations they had had in 2014, with Russia's invasion of Crimea. Was compromise the right path then? These conversations were particularly hard when facing large-scale state violence of one member state against another. But they were not new. The tension Alexander pointed to in his anecdote was also resonant with the original debate among Council staff at the time of expansion. Prior to 1990, the European Commission saw a fair share of difficult human rights issues. But for a system largely built around a shared sense of trust in national institutions, rightly or wrongly, the role of the Court was to oversee "like-minded" states.

Perhaps an institution premised on binding legal authority and soft diplomacy is always haunted by complicity with violence among members in its ranks. But this became much more evident when a small cadre of Eurocrats in Strasbourg encountered "shocking" conditions, clustered in new types of rights violations. In turn, *different* kinds of rights issues became a way that people made sense of the rapidly changing definition of European community, still deeply marked by Cold War distrust. Like Alexander, people struggled with these contradictions and tensions and posed serious questions about the compromises they made along the way. In response, a central tension in the system itself could be expressed as a specific relationship between kinds of states with different kinds of rights problems.

Expansion, Backlog and Difference in Administrative Practice

How then to deal with difference? After all, making distinctions can be destabilizing in an institution premised on equality before the law. Is it an institution tasked with generating singular instances of brilliant legal reason and the development of human rights principles? Is it the last, best hope for thousands of individuals in need of human rights protections that are legally repetitive but vital from a human perspective? Of course, the answer is very much both, but as it turns out, reconciling these two different goals meant the institution itself would have to change. In rethinking what the Court was for, it was necessary to make changes at the organizational level. In the process, reforms reproduced forms of difference (geographic, legal, and bureaucratic) even as the Court became a site for producing new forms of post–Cold War European unity. Managing this tension led to the ECtHR registry creating new systems for processing and adjudicating differently categorized and tracked cases.

Reorganization was a key pressure valve for some of the contradictions and pressure points of Council expansion. Yet few framed the need to develop different ECHR systems explicitly in terms of geopolitical or ideological hierarchies. Instead, differences were naturalized in relationship to administrative and staffing demands that expansion posed. Development of different mechanisms for filtering and tracking was both a mundane and geopolitical act. Tracking this requires explaining how cases travel the system and relate back to national domestic legal systems. Not every application is reviewed in the same way. Registry staff make distinctions about the appropriate pathway for review based on several factors, including the legal issues cases raise, their level of legal complexity, and where they sit within Court systems for prioritizing or expediting cases.

For example, following a series of reforms in the mid-2010s, the Court was authorized to implement new judicial formations, including single- or three-judge panels to address rising caseloads and the impact they had on overwhelmed staff and judges. These smaller formations allowed judges to review cases that do not raise overly complex legal issues and fit existing patterns of human rights violations in a given context. Alongside these processes, the Court registry streamlined other systems of processing and categorizing types of cases. Well-established case law (WECL) emerged as a response to cases that are so prevalent, similar, and clearly in violation of the ECHR that they can be decided in an expedited manner. To ensure efficiency and timeliness, court staff developed innovations in the technological interface for sorting and generating quicker judgments (such as pre-generated form letters).

The ECHR system's response after expansion was to accommodate difference, in the name of unity, by institutionalizing flexibility for how cases were sorted and processed. The move to single-judge formations and mechanisms for processing repetitive cases and well-established case law helped shape a multitrack system within the Court. But this was not only a practical matter of who and how cases would be processed. It also had implications for the broader meaning of cases and case law in shaping community obligations and interpretations of Convention rights. The Court system is organized around the premise of subsidiarity, or deference to sovereign state power and national specificity of member states. At the same time, when the Court finds a violation of the ECHR and issues a judgment, that judgment is not only binding on the state that breached Convention principles. That judgment is binding in concrete ways on the violating state. But it also sets standards that all member states must incorporate within their own domestic systems. Within a multitrack system, not all cases become shared baselines for general principles. Some remain at the level of particular country conditions that are not readily generalizable—especially to more "mature" democratic contexts.

Who adjudicates the case, how many judges are involved, and what kind of legal issue is raised determine how powerfully binding a case may be on every member state and whether that case becomes a baseline for new universally applicable European standards. While one could technically cite any of the Court's case law, the most powerful precedents are those set by the Grand Chamber. This body is the highest legal authority in the Court. Not only is it composed of seventeen judges, but its rulings cannot be appealed or overturned. The cases the Grand Chamber hears are those of the most legally complex nature. They have the power to shift the scope and interpretation of the Convention in ways that will have potentially significant impact on the legal systems of the member states. It is for this reason that many scholars talk about the ECtHR's "constitutionalizing function" (Stone Sweet 2009; Wildhaber 2011).

The Grand Chamber does not hear every case that comes through the system; it is an exception to the right of individual petition. But when the Grand Chamber does rule, a case against a particular country can reverberate across the entire Council system, pushing states to make reforms to legal systems. An excellent example is the near-revolutionary impact that ECtHR case law has had on criminal procedure and defendant rights in recent years. Article 6 of the Convention guarantees fair-trial protections, including equality of arms and right to counsel as part of a cluster of rights of the accused. In 2008, the Grand Chamber ruled for the applicant in the case of *Salduz v. Turkey*, finding that the defendant had a right to custodial legal assistance. The case codified the so-called Salduz Doctrine, a case that rippled through the Council membership, leading to criminal procedure reforms and an expansion of rights of the accused in multiple countries (Giannoulopoulos 2016).

Key subsequent cases have weakened the general applicability of *Salduz*, in part because powerful states pushed back on the limits to sovereignty it imposed in cases of national security.[5] But the case is illustrative of how the influence of case law works. A particular instance in one country becomes precedent and even leads to semi-standardized rights guarantees when the Grand Chamber issues a strong ruling with specific doctrinal or interpretive tests that are widely applicable. This leads to legal reform throughout the Council to bring legal systems into compliance with these newly clarified rights.

It is quite remarkable that a violation judgment against a small state or a state not considered a "mature" democracy sets legal precedent for a longstanding or original member state. But it is perhaps the exception that proves the rule. To reach generalizability requires a kind of legal novelty or complexity rarely associated with cases and places associated with structural deficits in transitioning contexts. This is not to say that Grand Chamber and precedentially significant cases don't come from across Council Member states. It is to say, however, that new judicial formations, ways of bundling cases, or categories like well-established case law designate certain kinds of problems as repetitive and less legally relevant to the system as a whole.

In this sense, who and what the Court is for and the kind of power it has to compel changes in domestic systems depend on the kind of case involved and the country from which it originates. Universality does not inhere in every case, for every country equally. As I noted in the introduction, some projections of European categories come to take on universal and often binding force in the world. It is this process that Trouillot (2002) refers to as North Atlantic universals. And it is also this process by which parochial histories of Western human rights, themselves always vernacular and situational (Merry 2006a), become global norms. In tracking how certain kinds of cases become legally consequential at different orders or scales, we can see precisely how vernacular forms of human rights become universals. They take on abstract qualities when they are channeled through different institutional pathways.

As legally "interesting" and novel cases move through the Grand Chamber, they are projected out as universally, legally binding, and relevant for Council members. As case law of a certain order, they become globally salient. As other cases, designated legally repetitive, are tracked through lower institutional

orders, they too take on the character of particularity. Well-established or repetitive cases of prison conditions, for example, come to stand in as instances
of concrete national deficits or structural failures. The system has both the
power to generate important lessons and standards across the member states.
But it also has the power to erase the legal significance of some kinds of case
law by filtering it through judicial mechanisms not likely to be picked up or
used as precedent outside that country context. This is not necessarily a problem from a strict human rights perspective. But it is one way that the system
has been fundamentally reshaped by the questions of who and what the Court
is for in the wake of expansion.

Embodiments of Difference: Experiences of Case Law Significance

What makes something *legally significant* does not necessarily make it important from a human rights perspective. And sometimes, people naturalize
the different trajectories of cases through cultural characterizations that link
human rights problems to certain places or even hierarchies of legal and political development. In the previous section I addressed how what and who
the ECHR system and the Court are for depends on whether you look at
well-established case law or, Grand Chamber judgments. Variations in both
kinds of cases and how they are adjudicated creates flexibility within the
system. This was particularly salient in the post-expansion period. But these
tensions are not only technical. They also are something that shapes registry
lawyers', judges', and advocates' experience of the work they do and why it
is important.

Whether registry staff or judges find the work "interesting" from a legal
perspective or impactful from a human rights one often depends on the kinds
of cases they deal with. This alone is not surprising. What is interesting is how
the association between kinds of cases and *kinds of places* continues to shape
people's experience of the Court through geopolitical hierarchies of East and
West or mature and immature democracies. This often happens at an everyday level that passes below notice or comment in daily interactions. But when
I asked people to reflect on what the ECHR system is for, I encountered consistent patterns in the way that they linked types of legal questions regarding the
qualities of files and other material aspects of applications to their assumptions
about places. We can see this in contrasting positions that emerged in interviews I conducted about the importance of the Court. These examples reflect

how the legacies of the categories that structured expansion were expressed through the language of culture and context. And in turn, the idea of cultural difference became naturalized as different approaches to legal interpretation and administrative processing.

For example, one question I frequently asked judges was how much social context they needed to decide cases. Judges must decide on cases from countries with which they have little familiarity from a legal and even cultural or historical perspective. In some cases, judges relied on each other, registry staff, and their own research (if they had time) to fill in the context. Sometimes this knowledge came from experience. Sometimes judges relied on past cases to understand country contexts. One strategy came from the encounter with repetitive cases from a given country. For example, when I spoke with a judge from a Northern European country, she noted that when she reads her twentieth case on Ukrainian prison conditions, she doesn't need that much information. She was very clear to say she doesn't go into a case looking to find a violation; she examines all the facts before her. But in these cases, she explained, the country context is less important because the cases are so similar and legally straightforward.

In this case, we can see how the category of well-established case law (WECL) moves from an administrative process that clusters cases together to an epistemological stance that shapes judicial interpretation. More importantly, the judge then translated this combination of administrative and interpretative categories into an ethical perspective on the role of the Court more generally. Here and as described in other interviews, judges and registry staff aligned legal complexity, repetition, and the essential question of who the Court was for and what role it was meant to play. The judge referred to "a big debate in the academic literature" and noted that it reflects conversations in the Court as well. One path was to "embrace a constitutionalizing role" and emphasize cases that were legally significant in a singular sense. You might get fascinating cases from Finland, Ireland, and Germany, she noted. But then you wouldn't address the countries where "the big problems were happening." Balancing this tension was key to the judicial function.

This interaction echoes other conversations that I had about internal distinctions among European regions. People mapped what were legally complex or "fascinating" and what were urgent but relatively straightforward cases of "big problems" onto a post-expansion geography. Exemplary are two conversations I had about the role of the Court. The first was with registry lawyers and the second was with a strategic litigator with long-standing experience working on cases of forced disappearances, torture, and prison conditions in parts of Eastern Europe and the Caucasus. In both conversations, my interlocutors drew distinctions between cases that were interesting and cases that were important in a pressing human rights sense. And in both conversations, this divide between what was interesting and what was pressing was expressed in geographies of the pre- and post-expansion map of Europe.

In the first conversation, two senior registry lawyers, Sarah and Jane, drew distinctions between cases that were "fascinating" and those that were higher stakes but less legally interesting. Both women were from Western European countries that had been original founding members of the ECHR system. This meant that when processing cases from their countries, their job was to "apply the rules as written." "I am from a very ruly legal culture," one of them noted. Because they "rarely had to deal with many difficult, repetitive cases" or really "egregious violations," the work was more interesting. But it was also, in their words, "lower stakes." For the most part, forced disappearances, torture, prison conditions, and right to life didn't occur back home. In addition, they noted that when cases did come to them from their home countries, they were already well dissected by the domestic courts, so they have a chance to work through some of the more interesting legal issues that the national judiciary might raise—for example, on gender equity. Sarah reflected on feeling lucky to work with these more challenging cases, noting that they get to focus on such big issues because "the Court is divided" by country.

For Sarah and Jane, what was *legally* important was not necessarily what was high stakes from a human rights perspective. This view was shared by Jasmine, a longtime human rights lawyer based in London. She had extensive experience with cases of systematic state violence, police brutality, and forced disappearance across Russia and the Caucasus. In arguing passionately for the importance of the work she was doing, she told me: "The intention of the drafters of the Convention in the wake of the Second World War was to stop authoritarians and to facilitate peace. It was not actually about equal pension rights in Belgium. . . . what is more important: equal pension rights in Belgium or somebody being imprisoned because of their opposition to the government?"

Jasmine juxtaposed pension rights in Belgium and defense of political prisoners to argue for the relevance and importance of a Convention system. It was more important to counter authoritarian violence than to hash out rights in a functioning Western democracy. In doing so, she turns the logic of expansion on its head. For some Council staff from the "old" democracies, expansion posed a problem of watering down the system. For Jasmine, expansion to new countries and pressing issues they faced were the true realization of the goals of the ECHR system as envisioned by its founders. It is a reversal of expansion as "a problem." Instead Jasmine reframes the focus on cases of economic and social rights in older member states as less urgent from a human rights perspective.

The significance of these perspectives is not that one kind of case is inherently more important than another. Pensioner rights, gender equality, freeing political prisoners, and holding states accountable for forced disappearance are all critical accomplishments for the Court. What is significant is that the question of what and who the ECHR system is for maps onto types of cases, which in turn map onto the political geography of expansion. In this way, people interpret internal differentiation among countries as a legitimate and important part of the Council and Court's mission. The fact that the Court does different work in different places is not a problem from the perspective of rule of law per se. But people manage this difference by imagining different tracks and articulating different kinds of significance for the work they do. In the process different *kinds of legal questions* are linked to different places, such that the original tension posed by expansion of how bringing the "outside" into the system takes a new form: that of distinctions with case law and administrative procedure. This happens at the level of people's commitments and experiences of work at the everyday level. As a result, the problem of difference moves from a reflexive issue at the level of ideological or political contradiction. It becomes a more mundane issues of the professional goals and duties required to manage cases in appropriate ways through the application of rules and procedures. In other words, hierarchies of difference become naturalized through experiential encounters with different kinds of cases and the mechanisms by which the Court manages them.

Not all political or legal systems are the same or even similarly prepared to deal with some kinds of rights violations. The fact of difference is not necessarily a problem in and of itself. It becomes more difficult to manage from a rule-of-law and equality perspective if people attribute or assume meanings about those differences. Court expansion took place within a deeply ideological context of unequal geopolitical power relations, culturalist, and even at times nationalist assumptions about who does or does not have the "mentality" or "cultural capacity" to be truly democratic (Borocz 2006). Dealing with the legacies of this culture concept and civilizational hierarchies on which it rests became a material and administrative reality at the center of European integration.

More than anything else, Council expansion led to both innovations in and tensions over the role of the Court and the meaning of human rights. This sensitive dilemma was well summed up by a former registry lawyer, Nikola, who had been witness to the tensions of expansion when he first began at the Court. He worked in the registry section for one of the new Eastern European member states. Now working on rule of law and democracy in an office elsewhere in the Council, he characterized the tension between equality and difference in the system incisively:

> The problem arises when you don't have that sort of faith in the national judicial system which you are reviewing or whose decisions you are reviewing. Obviously, what happened from the 1990s onwards was the Court was suddenly faced with situations which it hadn't really been faced with before, where it wasn't wholly convinced of the effectiveness of the proceedings that had been conducted at national level. And so, it found itself having to be much more invasive, intrusive in the extent of its review and in some cases operating as a court of first instance, which it simply wasn't designed to do and isn't equipped to do. . . . Because if you're dealing with courts which are at entirely different stages of development and entirely different states of confidence as far the population are concerned, then you cannot treat their decisions in exactly the same way. It's a very sensitive and difficult problem.

The idea of trust in different national institutions was a theme that came up in several interviews, particularly when I spoke to judges about how they managed caseloads across very different contexts and legal orders. Often, judges signaled a high level of faith in their registry lawyer assistants and deference to other judges' experiences and knowledge—particularly about their home country. In this way, generating trust (or distrust) in particular national institutions was also a product of intersubjective professional relationships at the Court itself. But the geographies of institutional trust discussed above were nonetheless present at the judicial level as well.

These hierarchies of knowledge could cut both ways as people across the system relied on each other as cultural brokers in interpreting the law in particular contexts. For example, a former judge who was raised and practiced law in a socialist state explained these differences through his own perspective coming from an Eastern European context. He noted, concerning his dissenting opinion in a ruling on one high-profile case: "That is really for an anthropologist because I think I understood the case better than some of the judges who were not from the eastern part of Europe. The [applicant] was trying to cheat. It was so obvious." While judges often served as interpreters for each other when it came to domestic legal systems, understanding not just law and even social context but "culture" required a kind of cynical self-positioning.

Judges and lawyers from formerly state-socialist countries participated in this co-construction of distrust and opacity. And like the former judge cited above, they drew on their knowledge and expertise in navigating the subtle cues and clues about trustworthiness in contexts with which they were more familiar. Another now former judge from a formerly state-socialist country commented on this in a conversation we had about a dissent he wrote. I was particularly interested in the case because it seemed to involve a dispute on facts, which is rare in the Strasbourg context, The Court is explicitly not engaged in such assessments (to use the technical term, it is not a court of fourth instance). He explained that sometimes review of cases involved making judgment calls about what was or was not a reliable source of information, noting, "We had a Ukrainian case recently. The issue was the applicant complained about not having a lawyer during his first interview [during which] he confessed to a murder charge." He went on to explain that the domestic court countered the applicant's claim that he did not have a lawyer, dismissing it in one line, without providing substantiating evidence. The judge explained, "It was also a bit of an example of the way our background does influence us, coming from a more structured judicial environment where you would have more trust in the judiciary and you would not question a judge on their finding [and] would say, 'Yes, if the domestic court looked into the matter and said there was a lawyer, there must have been a lawyer.' Coming from where I come from, I would be a bit more demanding in having review of these complaints on what basis did the domestic court say there was a lawyer or not." It was this distrust of state institutions that informed his more critical perspective, coming from his own experience that impacted a different relationship to facts in the case.

In these examples, the presumption of trust in institutions shapes experiences of a very different Court and a very different relationship to doctrine and subsidiarity. Neither interpretation is necessarily right or wrong. Rather, people justify their interpretations in relationship to cultural and experiential frameworks. These are bound to different kinds of evidential materials and shaped by socially located presumptions about what kind of world we live in. Across these examples, the material encounters with the Court—from particular files to kinds of evidence and the faith one has in state representatives, judicial systems, and even applicants themselves—are grounded in beliefs about political capacity, institutional trust, and national culture.

Cold War Pedagogies in Post–Cold War Europe

The ECHR system is shaped by differences across institutional and political histories; linguistic, social, and religious practice; economic organization; and legal culture. This heterogeneity becomes more complicated when layered into long-standing European civilizational hierarchies and ideologies of regional difference. While such categories preexist the Court and Council, they are also perpetuated through them at the level of everyday practice and experience. The idea here is not merely to point to power imbalances and hierarchies within a complex, multinational institution. It is to ask how people manage, track, and respond to these forms of differentiation in the context of commitments to shared rule-of-law frameworks and democratic norms. This tension between equality before the law (and through the law) and the different weight afforded to some cases or some voices over others shaped how people enacted rule of law in practice. Attending to this experiential level demonstrates how rule of law works as a kind of sociality, composed of normative commitments, aspirations, and interpersonal relationships.

This is particularly clear, for example, in the area of diplomatic negotiations. Within the Court, legal and administrative pathways allow for the management of tension around implicit hierarchies manageable through shared legal commitments and terms. Diplomacy is a more political sphere by design. It requires a different approach to understanding how people managed the tensions difference, and power dynamics of post-expansion approaches to Council diplomacy.

For example, a legal affairs attaché from a Western European country explained to me (in an interview in February 2022) that what made the Committee of Ministers and the Committee of Ministers' Human Rights (CMDH) meetings successful was that operating behind closed doors and in relative obscurity created conditions for successful persuasion and consensus. They "try to do everything by unanimity here," which shapes the negotiation and dynamics of meetings. Unlike the majority system in Brussels, the Council is a consensus-based context in which "we try to keep everyone involved as long as possible. We do have voting, but we try to avoid it. . . . It's a collective thing." In part this is because, while the Court judgments are legally binding, the rest of the process is not legally binding; it's politically binding, but we "need states to be on board themselves."

A reader might hear echoes here of the quote early in this chapter in which Drzemczewski described something similar as key to post-expansion strategies for the Council system: "persuasion, peer pressure and diplomatic negotiation" (2017, 136–137). Several interviewees credited those practices of confidentiality and soft diplomacy as some of the most unique and important features of the ECHR system.

From this perspective, *not* drawing a line in the sand and not creating hard and fast distinctions—clean hands or not clean hands—was a feature, not a bug of the system. To return to my conversation with Alexander, who explained: "What is the power of the ECHR system? It is to convince states that it's in their interest to have a system where member states comply." This required convincing states that "what they are doing is not correct or could threaten the system. Rather, it is in their interest to have a dialogue." Thus, on one hand, the system of negotiated power was a way to create a legal and diplomatic consensus that allowed rule of law to function, even at the moments in which it was being violated. As long as countries were willing to "stay in the system" and saw this as a question of their own self-interest, the Committee of Ministers could manage violations of human rights internal to a European community.

At the same time, the power relations outlined in Drzemczewski's article continued to shape subtle distinctions around who was monitoring whom. The consensus-based system of negotiating rule of law took place on the grounds of deeper institutional divisions that shaped everyday interactions in subtle ways. These differential power dynamics were expressed as a question of who felt authorized to speak (and judge) whom in supervision of ECtHR judgments.

This was expressed clearly in an interview with a legal attaché from a Western Balkan country. We were talking about his participation in the CMDH meetings. I had talked to a few diplomatic staff who noted that northern and western European state representatives tended to take lead on coordinating diplomatic pressure and negotiations in executing judgments. I asked if his country representatives also felt a responsibility to speak to cases that affected European citizens more broadly. He said they did, but this took time. It was not in the "national character of his country" to speak out right away and criticize. But the experience of a significant structural (pilot) judgment being successfully implemented really changed their relationship to the larger process. His delegation didn't feel it could criticize or get involved until it had addressed its own issues and cases. This gave it a sense of confidence and credibility to take on other issues. In this telling, the sense of who is authorized to speak is not only a question of "national character" although it is interesting that my interlocutor framed it this way. It is also a subtle index of who is authorized to speak grounded in confidence about one's status as a fully realized democratic country.

Negotiations over execution of judgments take place in a context in which geopolitical difference is the spoken and unspoken premise of many interactions across the ECHR. It wasn't only interviewees from newer accession states who observed these imbalances in diplomatic negotiations. In an interview, a western European ambassador reflected on this directly. In talking about dynamics among different state representatives, she noted with humor and grace that when her regional group of countries got together, they could be "very righteous." She was aware that some countries felt picked on and that the specter of double standards was a constant debate "underlying the surface more or less all the time." For this reason, she noted that those countries with fewer problems (e.g., human rights violations to be executed) have to be very self-critical. "We need to be constantly welcoming critique against ourselves, have the courage to raise it in order to be credible discussants with those who have many problems." She gave the example of domestic violence in her country. Having a critical awareness of the scope of this issue at home allowed for a way to "open a conversation." She noted at times her colleagues would begin a conversation on human rights by saying, "We have this big problem." It was a way of trying to counter the image of unfairness and double standards. "We are able to say, 'Please monitor us. We will do our best, we are far from perfect, but we are trying.'"

In response, I asked her if others might perceive this kind of response to "double standards" as cynical or disingenuous. The issue of domestic violence that she raised was unquestionably an important human rights issue. Yet it was not one that threatened her country's status as a fundamentally democratic country or a "mature" democracy of the West. Indeed, if anything, the demand to be monitored and pushed on just such an issue could be read as evidence of the well-functioning aspect of the rest of society—a place where true gender equality was possible and desirable and also a place where the deeper structural mechanisms of democracy and rule of law were so well established they need not even be discussed. My interlocutor agreed that the issue of domestic violence might not be the same in kind or structural significance. But about that, she said, "Well, then we might take another tack . . . that we have succeeded in a number of ways in human rights, and so should you." She explained that in such a case, an element of competition might kick into play. Since her country's metrics and indicators are good, that might awaken a competitive drive in other country representatives to improve. And of course, she noted, they would offer help in such a case.

Central to the ambassador's comment is not just how people mobilize repertoires of comparative cultural difference or maturity. It is her vision of a competitive field in which people are motivated by the desire to be good students or by internal competition and self-interest. Underlying democratic maturity was not only a commitment to rights and rule of law. It necessitated the cultivation of a rational, self-interested personhood. Within these distinctions, monitoring, pedagogy, and incentives operated to both reproduce difference and project a future of unity (you can become like us). Some countries served as models of best practice that marked the gap between fully mature democracies and those who were motivated to catch up. This reinscription of difference becomes an argument for the continued relevance of the Court and Convention system, even and indeed precisely at moments in which the fragility of the system becomes most evident. In other words, by inscribing difference within the system through the cultivation of correct democratic dispositions, actors within the ECHR system both project unity through shared commitments to abstract terms and rights. And they generate subtle distinctions, forms of power and hierarchies that continue to shore up the Council's relevance as a guardian of core values.

Conclusion

In many ways, expansion greatly increased the ECHR's impact and significance, if the rapid growth in applications and judgments issued is any indication. The ECHR became more relevant to more people than ever before. With a growing caseload, lawyers, judges, and staff developed innovative approaches to legal interpretation, diplomatic negotiation, and the execution of judgments. These included new administrative procedures and pathways, as well as classifications for grouping a new class of structural human rights violations. Yet expansion also produced institutional anxieties about how to manage difference within the system. Post–Cold War expansion required that people within the Council of Europe system rework diplomatic and professional practices. They did so through new legal, administrative procedures and interpersonal relationships, as once external others became key partners in European integration.

In this context, my interlocutors often described managing the tensions and pressures of accession by reframing who and what the ECHR system was for. An expanded Council required flexibility that allowed for integration in the context of legal, cultural difference and long-standing ideological and geopolitical hierarchies. People within the ECHR system created and reworked once external distinctions into internal pathways and relationships of power, pedagogy, and persuasion. Geopolitical distinctions became much more intimately mapped through the administrative systems of the Court. This shaped the projected meaning of cases and case law, and the interpersonal dynamics including who felt entitled to speak (or not) in the authoritative voice of democratic Europe. Because many of these shifts followed from technical and administrative shifts in everyday legal and administrative practice, they flew beneath the radar of overt ideological tensions and distinctions. And they shaped the ways in which the meaning and expression of legal and democratic capacity took on material and affective shape, as instances of "messy files," boring and repetitive case law, or legally interesting or shocking contexts. Within this common but heterogenous community of law, some countries would guide others toward the realization of democracy, human rights, and rule of law through gentle pedagogy and carrot-and-stick diplomacy. The educative function that served as an overt aspect of the justification of Council expansion took on its own life in ongoing interpersonal interactions as well as the formal mechanisms of differentiation discussed throughout this chapter.

THREE

Performing the Rule of Law

Communicative Modalities and Legal Publics

ACCORDING TO THE OXFORD *English Dictionary*, the rule of law is "the restriction of the arbitrary exercise of power by subordinating it to well-defined and established laws." As a normative principle, it implies "the regularity and predictability of law; access to forms of redress, and the subordination of individual and political interest to legal principles." But what all this means in practice is harder to define. Depending on the emphasis or definition, the rule of law requires different, even contradictory actions and institutional relationships. Rachel Kleinfeld (2006) has argued that there are at least five competing definitions of the rule of law. These are based on distinct normative goals that are often conflated in scholarly accounts but cannot be reducible to each other: states abiding by law, equality before the law, law and order, efficient and impartial justice, and upholding human rights (35).

In 2011 the Council of Europe's Commission for Democracy through Law, better known as the Venice Commission, issued a comprehensive report on the meaning of the Rule of Law. An internationally respected body of constitutional experts, the Commission displayed remarkable self-reflexivity and humility. It concluded that it was not possible to come up with a strict definition at all. Rather, the 2011 report

> reached the conclusion that the Rule of Law was indefinable. . . . Rather than searching for a theoretical definition, [it] concentrated on identifying the core elements of the Rule of Law [and identifying] common features: Legality; Legal certainty; Prevention of abuse/misuse of powers; Access to justice.[1]

In lieu of a strict definition, the Venice Commission produced a checklist. This could be used, according to an interviewee familiar with the process, to narrow down what rule of law was not rather than what it was. The meaning of rule of law was thus contextually dependent, at least to some extent. And one of the contexts that mattered for defining and maintaining it was the Council community in Strasbourg. The Council itself was part of what the report calls "an enabling environment." "The Rule of Law can only flourish in an environment where people feel collectively responsible for the implementation of the concept."

The idea that people must feel collectively responsible for the rule of law signals that beyond a set of norms, it is a form of sociality and professional, ethical responsibility. A means, rather than an end itself, it is inseparable from people's commitment to enact and uphold it iteratively and across relationships. As an "enabling environment," a rule-of-law framework helps to cultivate dispositions, authorize ways of interacting, and represent those interactions to others. As with abstract political categories like citizenship, the rule of law is inseparable from how it is discursively performed, embodied, and authorized (Paz 2018). It operates interactionally and intertextually at different orders of reception and uptake. Yet across these contexts, what it looks like and how it might be discursively figured can differ widely. And yet, because it is a process, not a definition, the ways in which it is expressed and communicated will inevitably be messy, contradictory, and at times irreconcilable.

How then, do people come to feel collectively responsible for a concept? And how do actors within institutions like the ECtHR reconcile competing and sometimes contradictory norms among their founding principles? In this chapter, I argue that the rule of law is inseparable from the ways people communicate it and the publics and audiences those performances call into being. In this sense, rule of law is an interactional achievement rather than a set of a priori definitions. Enacting the rule of law, performing democracy, or effectively articulating rights claims across different publics are inextricable from the material forms of media and registers of speech that structure those interactions (Cody 2023; Paz 2018; Bishara 2013). Here, I examine three discrete modalities through which people express the rule of law: efficiency, consistency, and transparency. These communicative modalities organize and govern the normative relationships among people and texts, the flow of information, and hierarchies of power across the institution. Contradictions in approaches to the rule of law need not be inherently problematic. Rather, the flexibility of moving across communicative modalities allows people operating with different professional needs and normative assumptions to coordinate across the ECHR system. At the same time, these tensions can generate confusion and frustration when normative principles come into conflict in everyday interactions.

Communicative Modalities, Legal Publics, and Institutional Legitimacy

In this chapter, I track how people within the ECHR system translate different understandings of the rule of law into different communicative practices, which in turn hail linked, but non-identical legal publics. Scholars often overlook the role of nonstandard linguistic forms in constituting shared notions of European belonging, either through mass-mediated publics or shared communicative frameworks (Gal 2006). I follow Susan Gal's call to "conceptualize publics as reliant on inter-discursive links across occasions of talk, and often across languages. The circulation of face-to-face and mass mediated messages creates viewers and listeners who, by virtue of their own listening and their reflexive awareness of others listening to them, come to see themselves as members of a public" (2006, 166). Whether and how people adopt, take up, and perpetuate these communicative forms create both a sense of connection and perpetuates political and institutional authority (Gal and Woolard 2001). Approaching rule of law in this way allows us to track the juridical construction of Europe as an ideological and social proceses. These are shaped by the legal publics that international courts call into being, through the circulation of legal norms or case law principles.

In attending to rule of law and human rights as communicative frameworks, I draw from interviews with registry lawyers, judges, diplomatic staff, NGO and human rights advocates, and Council media specialists. All these interlocutors drew on widely circulating theories from scholarly literature, legal doctrine, and Council of Europe policy to define the rule of law. It operated as a guiding framework through which they tried to both uphold and navigate among authorized ways of talking about and analyzing the world from a human rights perspective. Rule of law was inseparable from the interactions in which it was performed and expressed (Buyse et al. 2021; Rajah 2012). And it also could not be separated from people's reflexive awareness that their actions were being watched and assessed by other stakeholders as more or less transparent, efficient, and fair (Tsampi 2021).

As law-and-society scholar Jothie Rajah has argued, rule of law is a performance embedded in regimes of publicity (Rajah 2015, 2023; see also Cheesman 2018) It is through inhabiting certain forms or genres of speech that institutional actors, such as judges and lawyers, conform to and shape expectations for what legal authority looks and sounds like. Linguistic anthropologists have referred to this process of linking speech, personae, and institutional authority as enregisterment (Agha 2005; Urciuoli 2009). Enregisterment is particularly important to the production of institutional authority and legitimacy when these bundles of normative principles, forms of personhood, embodied comportment, and types of speech extend out through interactions beyond the four walls of the institution itself. People persuade themselves and others that institutions have legal legitimacy by repeatedly and iteratively performing styles of communication and interpretation for a wide variety of publics.

I call this intersection of interaction, persuasion, and norms a communicative modality. Rule of law works as a communicative modality in two ways. First, it entails putting normative goals and commitments into practice. As a legal institution, these practices are most frequently grounded in ways of handling texts like judgments or the Convention itself, face-to-face interactions like judicial or diplomatic negotiations, or information like schedules and agendas. The second understanding includes the ways in which text and talk about the rule of law are projected and taken up by a wide range of audiences (Gal and Woolard 2001). People enact rule of law through professional codes of conduct, hierarchies of judicial authority, and citational practices when drafting judgments. But this nexus of ideas, practices, and ethical and professional commitments is not only an internal institutional matter. It also pulls in audiences within and outside those institutional frameworks. It is with specific audiences in mind that people representing the ECHR system continuously work to achieve and safeguard institutional legitimacy. They do so by linking kinds of professional practices and ethical commitments to the legitimacy of the system as a whole. For example, in interviews and multiple public settings, I have heard judges invoke what they can and cannot say about the ECtHR as an important part of preserving judicial authority and the legitimacy of the system. In so doing, they perform links between personhood and institutional authority. They also comment reflexively on these links to socialize ways of thinking about what rule of law looks and sounds like. In talking about and enacting judicial restraint publicly, judges embody certain principles through speech (or non-speech) and comportment. In turn they perform and project the rule of law via specific genres of legal publicity.

Managerial Efficiency: Registry Practice as Rule of Law Publicity

As I noted in chapter 2, the Court has been under enormous pressure to process an ever-increasing number of cases since expansion. To remind the reader, this massive explosion was an effect of Council expansion in the 1990s. Public awareness of the Court, the growth of domestic and international networks of NGOs, and strategic litigators incorporating Strasbourg into their advocacy and social change efforts also contributed to this increase. And, as I wrote in earlier chapters, it was a function of the official recognition of the individual right to petition codified in Protocol 11 in 1998.

The question of efficiency became more than just a managerial problem. For many, the backlog crisis threatened to undermine the legitimacy of the whole system. Across the Council of Europe, people were increasingly aware that people were watching how the Court handled the massive caseload. The crisis was not only one of practical staffing and budget. Many people I spoke with framed it in terms of the Court's obligations to applicants, its image, and indeed its ability to uphold the rule of law. Applicants, watchdog groups, and state officials explicitly assessed the Court's effectiveness in these terms. Backlog, time to judgment, and other matters of efficient bureaucratic function became a common way to talk about the legitimacy of the ECHR system. After all, if the European Court of Human Rights could not abide by its own Convention principles—such as a reasonable length of time to trial—what did that say for its capacity to adjudicate those matters in its member states?

In response, the Council introduced a series of high-level reforms through binding protocols, beginning with Protocol 14, which went into effect in 2010. These have had impacts for how cases were processed. Protocol 14 introduced single- and three-judge judicial formations and changes to admissibility criteria and filing deadlines, among other measures. While the concern about backlog has eased since the mid-2010s, it forced registry staff to confront the fact that internal procedural matters were also a question of the Court's reputation. Reputation was central to maintenance of its legitimacy, particularly in the context of critiques in domestic systems in which the Court had come under fire. Procedures were a form of communication internal to professional practice at the Court and for a range of other audiences as well. Judgments, press releases, and other texts communicated certain messages about the Court and case law in a direct and literal sense. But how the system handled these bundles of texts also became a channel for equally powerful and influential communications about the system and its legitimacy.

These links between rule of law, legitimacy, and efficiency were clear in a 2021 conversation with a senior registry official, who I will call Frances. Frances had helped oversee implementation of some of these new managerial practices. At the time of our interview, Frances had worked her way up through the Court system to an important role in the registry. She knew its institutional, professional, and legal contexts from the inside out. Her senior registry position demanded that she navigate a range of roles that included assisting in workplace management of a large bureaucratic organization and helping to align those managerial processes as part of a public-facing effort to improve the Court's image. In her comments to me, Frances linked communication within the institution and the need to reach external audiences, like state representatives and domestic legal institutions. She spoke of the Court's role as a public institution in generating a clear and persuasive body of case law and judicial reasoning that was central to its wider legitimacy. Managerial efficiency was key to holding all these different expectations together. Frances referred to this process as "rationalizing" the Court and registry system.

Efficiency was not only a guiding principle for how people ought to communicate with each other and the broader public through judgments. It was also a means for enacting and performing the legitimacy of the Court. Professional practices, management styles, and institutional organization also act semiotically. Institutions taken as a whole act as communicative forms and messages. This includes not merely what official texts formally say but what they signal through shared assumptions about their material qualities, forms, and genres (Cavanaugh and Shankar 2017; Jamison 2016). Arrangements of texts in relationship to texts as well as texts in relationship to people can stand in for whole professional communities. Similarly, crafting and circulating texts of a certain type and variety (thick reams of paper for Grand Chamber decisions or organizational charts that both guide and communicate "efficiency" within the registry) is an important part of legal publicity. Organizational charts help to guide and shape actual registry practice and order relationships among management and staff. In turn, these changes produced shifts in the temporality, rhythm, and flow of work at the registry. Registry staff then represent these shifts outward through charts, statistics that demonstrate the reduction of backlog, and other talk about the institution. In turn, the whole registry comes to stand in as the embodiment of rule-of-law efficiency. The whole functional organization of the institution acts itself a sign—a way of communicating a second-order significance beyond the practical effect that managerial practices were intended to produce.

This was evident in the managerial charts and reorganized registry structure that Frances shared with me when we spoke. The charts represented a flow of texts and decisionmaking that also mapped onto relationships among lawyers and judges. The goal of efficiency and clarity was achieved through textual and communicative forms and standards (shorter judgments, more direct language, standardized citational practice). In turn, the need to generate these new kinds of texts created the need for new professional orientations and practices that shape the material organization of the Court itself.

One set of tools available to Frances was administrative and managerial categories for the filtering and processing of cases in efficient and timely ways. For example, in recent years, the registry has worked with a system of prioritizing cases through which staff filter applications and determine how (and how quickly) each is to be processed. Examples include cases that concern life and death or "life at risk." These can sometimes be addressed immediately through "interim measures." In these cases, applicants (through their lawyers) can request an immediate halt to an action, such as deportation, until their case is examined. The speed of processing a case stands in for the efficiency of the system in responding to urgent life-or-death matters.

The Court can also move priority cases more quickly through the system of processing and judgment. Frances explained that if a case has immediate implications for a pressing issue in domestic policy—say, the handling of mandatory vaccinations during the pandemic—it might also be expedited. These new impact criteria link the efficiency of Court workflow to the significance of a case for domestic lawmaking or policy. Frances gave me two examples of recent cases. In the first, the Court sped up review of a case on the compliance of a Czech mandatory vaccination policy under COVID.[2] This case was pressing due to its immediate implications for public health policy in a global health crisis. The second case concerned Iceland. This was an Article 6 case concerning fair trial rights, which would not normally be a priority issue for two reasons. First, as a common kind of case, legally speaking, it would likely not be legally complex enough to go beyond a seven-judge Chamber judgment. Second, it was not a matter of life-or-death urgency.

Frances explained why it was given priority. While it was a "normal chamber case," the entire judiciary of the country was waiting for the ECtHR decision. "If it was processed according to our existing policy, it would still be waiting." Here, Frances configured a member state, Iceland, as an important audience and party to managerial process. As Frances explained to me, this new system of prioritizing impact helped it to be "a Court that matters." It gave the registry a "new way of looking into things in order to be more relevant."

This idea of being a Court that matters speaks to the way that management practice is oriented toward broader audiences. In turn, these managerial concerns extended to styles and genres of judgments. Being a court that matters was not only about the speed of processing. It also included how the language of judgments might be taken up and circulated. Frances linked judgment writing styles to the Court's broader image. She explained a new focus on producing standardized and shorter Court judgments in terms of justice, noting, "It is more important that we give replies to most applicants, rather than spend one year drafting a judgment that is a master of legal analysis." It is important to not keep "64,000 applicants waiting"; at the end of the day, the Court's role was to "say if states complied with the Convention or not. We are not here to create literature and show how well we master law. We are here to deliver justice rather than high intellectual projects." I took this reference to "high intellectual projects" to mean long, more legally complex judgments. While such judgments are often of scholarly interest, they don't generally have a wider audience. Frances, by contrast, linked the Court's relevance to simpler, more direct language. She framed the clarity of expression not only as a pathway to legitimacy; efficient modes of communication were iconic with the rule of law itself.

Human rights scholars have at times pitted the managerial, neoliberal logics of international human rights against more substantive justice claims (Zigon 2013; Moyn 2018). Yet officials invest ethical meaning in effective bureaucratic workflow and the genres of texts that enable it (Hull 2012; Mathur 2016; Bernstein 2017; Ballestero 2015). Efficiency and simplicity can also have persuasive effect. And it can serve to signal that the rule of law, as defined through accessibility and timeliness of legal decisions, is in effect. For example, Frances explained a recent emphasis in the registry on training drafting lawyers in new citational practices and styles. While there used to be "a mélange" of case law principles and citations that were more haphazard, the Court was introducing a more standardized approach that "synthesizes case law" and focuses on what is most relevant. This includes not only citational practices but a standardizing link between conventional phrasing and general principles coming out of specific case law. From her perspective, this prevented drafting lawyers from falling into the previous problem of "mistaking underlying words for the overarching principle" when reading and applying past case law. The standardization also helps those in charge of quality checking to keep case law consistent. I discuss this principle more below.

Frances described how this focus on certain ways of communicating could also shape professional comportment in ways that socialized a certain relationship to rule of law. Standardization allows lawyers to "resist trying to please everyone." But judges have to "deliver judgments that are solid" and guarantee the right of individual applications; "our role . . . is [not] to try to convince or justify or please." I understood her to be making a point that it was the role of judges to rule through application of principles and law and not to persuade or please within the text itself. And yet, efficiency itself was a communicative modality that was in some sense meant to persuade or convince others that the Court was working as it should. The goal was not to please but to reason—and to reason effectively and in a timely manner.

It was through the reformulation of texts and styles of writing, citation, and argumentation that the registry turned the goal of efficiency into a field of practice. This had implications for actual organization of registry work at the daily level as well as the professional and ethical experience of lawyers within the Court. Changes to ways in which people communicated were also about changes in their interpersonal and subjective experiences, as they related to professional norms and conduct. Frances described to me her belief that more efficient relationships and managerial systems would shift professional practice and people's relationships to their work. She described the new workflows in the charts she showed me as part of an effort to bring more junior lawyers closer to cases and give them a greater sense of ownership and closer working relationships with senior lawyers and judges. Such "proximity creates good relations," Frances noted, while still operating within an essentially hierarchical system. Communicative practices then become the basis for (and are reproduced through) new work arrangements, temporalities and rhythms of work, relationships among staff, and between the Court and applicants. And in turn these shifting relationships—from everyday interactions at work to managerial flow charts and guides for citational practices—came together as the basis for the registry to project, perform, and communicate efficiency within the Court and to outside audiences. This took place through the actual form and prose of judgments that circulate widely beyond the Court's four walls.

One cannot be sure that registry lawyers felt closer to cases in the way that Frances described. But it was clear in other interviews that new managerial styles impacted lawyers' and judges' relationship to cases in professional and affective ways. For example, in 2018 I interviewed a judge who often worked with the kind of repetitive cases that had prompted new managerial systems to address backlog. We sat in her bright, airy office in Strasbourg. The sun streamed in, lighting the papers spread out on the table between us. The surroundings could not have been more removed from the topic of discussion: detention conditions in Russian prisons. We were looking through a thick, stapled document of page after page of charts. On one side was a column with case numbers running down the page. Across the top, headings detailed key categories: size of prison cell; distance from eating area to toilet; presence of lice, bedbugs, and cockroaches. Between the serial numbers of the cases and the general categories of violations, the chart contained the briefest of accounts: the individuals who suffer these "inhumane and degrading" conditions, in the language of Article 3 of the Convention.

Such prison detention conditions are part of well-established case law (WECL). These cases are so prevalent, so similar, and so clearly in violation of the Convention that they can be decided in an expedited manner. While applicants bringing individual cases, Court lawyers group them into aggregated types and categories. Judges then decide violations by comparing an individual application with these aggregate pictures. Successful applicants receive individual restitution in the form of monetary compensation. As discussed in chapter 4 and 5, if the details of enough cases bundled together reveal patterns of systemic violations, advocates and lawyers may then be able to translate these into demands for structural and institutional reform.

The judge had pulled out the chart to help illustrate how she managed the massive caseload at the ECtHR. She described a pragmatic and distanced approach to the cases. Yet, hearing her talk about detention conditions, I wondered how she coped with the emotionally loaded aspects of the cases. She responded:

> JUDGE: Sometimes you can have a case in the Grand Chamber and Chamber with lengthy discussions and you find that the details are really horrific, the facts are awful. . . . I do WECL communications. . . . There you have these . . . tables. . . . I can show you an example, and you can see just how it's structured. (*She pulls out the papers.*) So we have the complaints, and it looks like this: So here are people complaining about Article 3—that's torture. So there are conditions of detention. So you would have these kinds of tables.
>
> JESSICA: Wow. It's the most distilled language that you could have.
>
> JUDGE: This is the most distilled language you can have. . . . And you sit here and read this. . . . And there is page after page. . . . These are the ones we can't

deal with because it's after [the time limit for an admissible application]. This is the square meters that they are contained in.

JESSICA: It's so basic.

JUDGE: Exactly, it's so basic. And this will take me a day to go through this. These are shocking, shocking things to read.

JESSICA: Because you imagine there is a human being behind each one of these?

JUDGE: Of course. But this is what we have to do when we have fifty to sixty thousand applications on the docket. And I have no problem with that. When you talk about the horrors people are suffering . . . I can't sit here and cry. These are serious and life-changing situations. Of course it grabs you. But I think my job as a judge is to frame it in the judicial context. And for that, I don't need to use feelings. It's not necessary.

In this encounter, the judge grounds judicial reason in her ability to maintain emotional distance and professionalism. It is precisely efficiency that allows her to do her job. The charts offer a representational infrastructure through which she can maintain judicial comportment and enact rule of law. The stark black and white spreadsheet is a material representation of the scale of the problem. It is expressed through the collective weight of serialized cases. The boiled-down, sparse language invites an emotionally distanced reaction.[3] "I can't sit here and cry" is a theory of the proper judicial disposition, an affective stance that allows reason to prevail over emotion. This may not seem, for some, like justice. But it is a way to enact and represent (in charts and judgments) rule of law, from one perspective.

Efficiency and the Problem of Justice

New administrative arrangements led to new ways of communicating through and about applications. These in turn supported the argument that the European Court of Human Rights was becoming increasingly efficient following a period of backlog crisis. People represented this efficiency to themselves and others through organizational flow charts, training manuals, statistics about case-time processing on the Court website, and other mass-mediated channels. People also used these charts of cases, numbers processed, reductions in backlog, and changes to writing styles of judgments to shape internal professional practice, ideally bringing it in line with particular visions of the rule of law. In this way, densely woven interactions and interpretative practices were materialized in shorthand texts and images that could be mobilized as persuasive evidence of Court legitimacy for different audiences and publics.

Yet every form of communication is subject to reinterpretation and re-contextualization. Not everyone saw these bureaucratic changes as positive expressions of legal and judicial transparency or effectiveness. For example, in the name of reducing backlog and making processing more efficient, the Court also introduced other more controversial mechanisms, including changing the admissibility criteria for applications from six to four months. This made it harder to file admissible applications and meant fewer cases ever reached judges. From this perspective, efficiency reduced access and stood at odds with the very rule-of-law goals that Frances and others were trying to achieve.

For example, one new genre that was meant to communicate efficiency was the form letter that simply indicated a case was inadmissible. The inadmissibility letter is an object much hated by Court observers and dreaded by applicants. Basak Çalı, a highly regarded legal scholar who has analyzed the Court's communicative forms and its commitments to transparency and rule of law, refers to this new form as simply "the letter." In a poignant and critical blog post, she uses this shorthand to convey how brief, alienating, and legally and ethically inadequate this mode of communication could be.[4] Another blogger on the popular Strasbourg Observers site noted shortly after the practice began that "while it is true that, in absolute number, the Court has created more efficiency thanks to the filtering capacity of the single judges, . . . this cannot justify the lack of reasoning in individual decisions. It is a dangerous evolution that a judge can take decisions unmotivated, creating an aura of arbitrariness, which affects the legitimacy of the Court as a whole."[5]

The Court eventually responded to these critiques, and judges now have to give some reasons for inadmissibility. But the inadmissibility letter is an example of how internal communications, intended to produce efficiency, are taken up as part of outward-facing interactions with other stakeholders in the ECHR system (Helfer 2008). The letter had a life beyond communicating the status of a case to an applicant or serving as a mechanism for streamlined case processing. The texts the Court produces are also picked up among other publics. This includes scholars, bloggers, and human rights advocates. In turn, people within the Court system are aware of these critiques and respond directly or indirectly. In a 2016 conversation with William, a senior registry lawyer who had witnessed the full history of reforms firsthand, he argued that that the single-judge system and inadmissibility letters simply couldn't be helped. Eighty to eighty-five percent of cases were simply not admissible and could "never see the light of day." William recognized that sometimes people are upset, that they feel the least a human rights court could do is give them reasons for their rejection. But to produce reasons for each inadmissible case would run counter to the purpose of speeding up the Court's processes and "would effectively bring the Court under." These cases are managed by "skilled lawyers" who filter those cases from the admissible complaints, which are then subject to "adversarial procedures."

For William, openness and consistency were important. But these principles were sometimes at odds with other commitments to uphold the rule of law. Efficiency necessitated developing internal forms of communication, which might stand at odds with the idea that the Court should be more transparent. This came up in a conversation with Sarah, an administrative assistant who worked at the registry. We discussed the issue of how much information the Court could or should feel compelled to share. I commented that some people were upset at how short and formulaic these inadmissibility letters are. Sarah was sympathetic, but longer letters would be too timely. "We know internally what we have done, You have to draw a line somewhere."

The process of drawing a line is an apt metaphor. Indeed, it is precisely such practices of drawing and redrawing distinctions, transparency, and opacity that have produced a palpable sense of inside and outside the Court, with unintended effects. These contradictions highlight different understandings of what rule of law and human rights mean—or ought to mean in practice. I will address the question of access in the section "Access and Transparency as Rule-of-Law Principles" below. But for now, this tension marks the importance of attending to how different conceptions of the rule of law give rise not only to a range of expectations but also to a variety of concrete practices and professional roles.

Consistency as a Communicative Modality

In approaching the rule of law as a managerial problem, registry lawyers align legal norms with professional commitments through organizational infrastructures and forms of communication. These goals are central to one version of the rule of law in which access to justice is timely and requires keeping cases moving through the system. But efficiency is not the only principle at work at the Court. Producing case law that is high quality and consistent is also a key way people perform and enact institutional legitimacy.

Judges and lawyers achieve such consistency when they interpret and decide new cases in light of past case law principles and established legal doctrines. This is important for several reasons. From a legal perspective, consistency is linked to the legitimate exercise of judicial and Court authority. Citational practices signal that judicial decisions are not arbitrary; they are derived from past institutional and judicial authority (Goodman et al. 2014). This supports a notion of rule of law based on the principle that authoritative norms ought to govern future action. Consistency allows for the predictability of rules that sanction social behavior within a given jurisdictional space.

Achieving case law consistency is a complicated practical and legal matter within the ECtHR. The Court is technically not a precedential system. Rather it must balance its role as an interpreter of the ECHR as a treaty with doctrine, derived from case law. This balance authorizes judges to interpret the Convention in evolving and creative ways (Mowbray 2005). Judges toggle between Convention principles and concrete legal situations that require ongoing interpretation. The triangulation of Convention principles, domestic law and practice, and a body of case law is what keeps the institution legitimate and relevant. The weight or emphasis may shift; this is what makes the Convention a "living instrument" subject to changes in line with evolving values and political, social, or technological contexts (see *Tyrer v. UK*). But achieving and projecting some form of consistency is the necessary condition for the fair and equal application of a shared framework to which all member states are bound.

Like efficiency, consistency is an effect of distributed labor. People create links between present and past cases in different ways. They may group cases as "similar" based on interpretation of context, prior judicial reason at the domestic level, or resonance between fact patterns. They may draw links between cases by triangulating aspects of a case file in relationship to past case law or shared doctrinal principles. Regardless, achieving consistency is a massive undertaking with its own unique form of interpretative and administrative labor. After all, the Court oversees forty-six discrete legal orders. What's more, it has produced almost twenty-five thousand judgments. Even with advances in digitization and text searchability, the practical work of tracking and keeping case law consistent is daunting. The registry has responded to this challenge in a few ways. First, it has a unique office of the jurisconsult. This is a group of lawyers whose main task is to review and ensure consistency of case law and the application of principles in Court judgments. This group is also responsible for production of case law reports and guides, all of

which are available on the ECtHR's website. The jurisconsult analyzes and cat-
alogues case law principles and key cases on a regular basis. It organizes case
law guides around specific Convention rights. It also identifies emerging areas
of law unforeseen by the founders: privacy in the age of internet and advances
in women's reproductive health, to name two examples.

Within this massive collection of texts, not all judgments have the same
impact on case law. Some have different weight or authority, depending on how
many judges were involved in deciding them. The legal weight of a judgment
is tied to the judicial body that issued it: from single- or three-judge formations, Chamber decisions, or Grand Chamber rulings. That Grand Chamber
judgments are weightier in precedential relevance is often reflected in their
actual weight and heft. Unlike the more efficient judgments that Frances spoke
of, with their shorter, direct arguments and writing styles, Grand Chamber
judgments can be as long as eighty to one hundred pages. It is a small example
of how the legal categories and practices that define rule-of-law relationships
in the Court are reflected in the materiality of documents themselves (Philips
2016; Jamison 2016).

Across these bodies of texts, it is the jurisconsult's job to oversee consistency. This happens through coordinated practice and communication
among jurisconsult lawyers and judges, review of case citations within judgments, and the production and oversight of case law "quality" through regular
checks of citations. The challenges in managing this sprawling relationship
among texts were evident in two conversations two years apart (2016 and 2018)
with a senior member within the jurisconsult. William had vast experience
with the work of the jurisconsult as the "eyes and ears of the Court." As in
my discussion with Frances, the notion of the jurisconsult as "the eyes and
ears" signals William's awareness that his work necessitated anticipating and
communicating with different audiences. "Coherence, quality and vigilance,"
William told me, were central to upholding case law and the legitimacy of the
Court. But coherence and consistency were not just practical issues. They were
ways of understanding the fundamental relationships that gave the Court
meaning and representing them to others.

William had an unshakably calm demeanor, soft voice, and a reputation
for encyclopedic knowledge of case law. He was held in high regard within
the Court. I could see why, from his thoughtful responses and generosity in
responding to my layperson's naivete. For William, consistency was a theory
of human rights expressed through mundane forms of everyday practices of

coordinated communication. He explained to me how the jurisconsult system works through regular meetings with registry lawyers and consultation with judges. This is necessary because of the Court's organization into five administrative units called sections that work relatively independently. Each is made up of a section president and seven judges. It is from these discrete administrative units that Chambers are formed.[6] These divisions operate relatively autonomously. He explained that it is possible that a section can decide on a case and not know that another section issued a relevant judgment a few months before. This is where the jurisconsult stepped in to play a key coordinating role.

Every week, the head of the jurisconsult gets five bundles of draft judgments (from the five sections). Lawyers review the drafts to determine if they raise conflicts and respect past Grand Chamber decisions and if the reasoning is based on the most recent precedents. Without careful coordination of communication, he told me, "The right hand doesn't always know what the left is doing." The concern is that if a chamber is "oblivious to a case," it might diverge too widely from another chamber's reasoning. To avoid this, lawyers review the quality and consistency of judgments through "quality checks." The goal for the Court is that it must be able to "respect its own reasoning."

Consistency is not a feature that inheres in static texts like judgments. It is an effect of relationships across the registry as people triangulate their interpretation of texts, and signal that work through citational practices in future judgments. These practices exemplify the kinds of distributed agency central to producing legal authority (Latour 2009). In addition, as an everyday form of practice, consistency, like efficiency, shapes people's relationship to time and the rhythm of workflow. For example, William described to me the frenetic energy of writing and finalizing judgments, as people coordinate across the institution. He explained that when a judgment is being drafted, a "flurry of amendments (so-called pigeonhole amendments)" fly back and forth. Another member of the jurisconsult team, Sonja, also noted the intense pace of communication that is at times necessary for the Court to ensure quality. These short bursts of intense activity alternate with the slow, plodding work of case law as it links past, present, and future in a unified arc. In this sense, consistency invites its own mini-temporalities, like eddies in a swiftly moving stream. Speed contrasts with the slow, plodding, and materially grounded experience of case law. This produces incremental change grounded in recursive legal reason and dense citational practice.

Case law consistency produces different material weight and heft for differently consequential documents: thick files for cases and lengthy judgments for important Grand Chamber decisions, dense with case background and citations to past case law. They might include lengthy addenda, such as concurring opinions or dissents, in which judges weigh in on the importance of a case. Such thickness—the quality of careful, slow deliberation and documentation—was also the condition for reversals of case law. A break with past case law is something that usually happens at the Grand Chamber and can result in a decision that may shift the direction of Court reasoning. This decision is not taken lightly. For example, I asked Sonja about the procedures for breaking with principles of consistency. How could that be justified, given the importance of respecting past reason? She explained, with enthusiasm, that the registry was developing new techniques for just this kind of question. A Grand Chamber judgment is "this thick," she said, holding her thumb and pointer finger two inches apart and gesturing to a blue folder on her desk that indeed looked thick and particularly daunting. She noted that the response is to read the judgment and deliver on the same day a one or two page document called a "page flash," a "synthetic document" that identifies what is new and important in the case. It is, in her words, a way to say, for example, "Hey guys, don't worry. This case only really brings us two new things." Putting case law consistency first means, in her words, that changes happen not as "a quantum leap" but an "incremental change in the case law."

These examples demonstrate how consistency as a communicative modality gives rise to organizational practice, epistemological commitments (synthesis over information), and practical ways of approaching, reading, and communicating about texts. Consistency creates the effect of predictability and foreseeability at the heart of rule of law. But it also gives rise to hierarchies of authority within the Court. Continuity inheres in "smaller" and "lower" spaces within the Court, while challenges to continuity are supported by larger and higher judicial formations. "If you are going to reverse the case law, you need to do it authoritatively, and it should go to the Grand Chamber," William told me. This sense of Court and registry as defined by such hierarchical relationships gives the appearance of a coherent institutional space, adding a sense of weight and authority through comparative frameworks (higher or lower, bigger and smaller) that map onto the gravity of what it means to reverse case law. Thus, smaller judicial formations—a single judge or group of three—decide cases that fall within well-established case law principles or fact patterns. Chamber decisions of seven judges may deal with more legally complex or unique issues. But it is the Grand Chamber, composed of seventeen judges drawn from across five sections, that has the authority to depart in meaningful way from case law. When an important judgment is "this thick," as Sonja noted, it signals heft and gravitas. It also stands in as a record in and of itself for the paths and channels a judgment travels in order to take on the qualities of an authoritative legal document (see Greenberg 2024).

Consistency, Efficiency, and the Question of Justice

To be consistent requires practices that are not always efficient. But both approaches to rule of law must be incorporated into everyday practice at the Court. Yet these principles also stand in relationship to another definition of the rule of law: the delivery of justice. Consistency and efficiency are not about justice per se. They are about justice in the sense that the rule of law requires infrastructures that ensure the fair and even application of legal principles. When I asked William how case law consistency related to justice, I was met with a gentle rebuke. He told me that it was "hazardous to introduce the notion of justice" into the work they do at the Court and the system of processing cases. He noted that justice is not the right concept for describing how the Court treats cases. Indeed, it may be "the last thing on my mind." Justice as an abstract concept could not substitute for justice as a particular relationship between consistency and coherency of case law. These goals are foremost in the service of the image of the Court: its "integrity, authority, and legitimacy," he explained. Justice was a matter for domestic court systems; the Court's role was to support the conditions where that could happen, through general guidelines and rules.

Consistency, rather than justice, was the underlying commitment that kept the Court, in his words, the "most important judicial institution on the planet." Consistency creates the conditions for institutional legitimacy but also for "fairness" in the application of the law. However, within the context of rule of law, justice and fairness are not the same. A court, William explained, must be accountable to the parties, including the governments and the applicants. It should deliver judgments based in principle with a clear logic and be able to defend its decisionmaking, and "internally," it needs to be democratic. The judges need to uphold principles and reasoning that are consistent and sound.

William offered a powerful example of the ways in which different stake-holders in the system approached justice and rule of law while orienting around the same texts. We were discussing the different roles that people play in producing case law through "dialogue" (the process of non-Court actors communicating with the Court via documents, texts, reports, or analysis). He noted that perspectives, such as amicus briefs, from experts, scholars, or NGOs can provide helpful context and information. Many such amicus submissions are written by NGOs to assist the court. Yet, he added, NGOs tend to be "more adventurous" and more sympathetic to the victim. These serve not only as outside pressure. They are, in his words, ways of "encouraging judges to dream about a better world." Of course, William was careful to remind me that judges have the ultimate say in deliberation. But consistency emerges as a different relationship to time and space than dreaming. To dream is to look ahead to a possible alternative future, one linked to creative imagining inspired by case law but not wholly bound to it. It was thus not a surprise that William drew a distinction between law and justice as they mapped on to different roles within the institution and different modes of address intended for various publics. In contrasting the "dreams" of judges to the grounded work of jurisconsult staff, we can sense the way that competing roles and relationships to human rights work through contrasting relationships across different institutional spaces and temporal arcs.

Access and Transparency as Rule-of-Law Principles

In the last section I looked at how lawyers and judges in the registry uphold rule of law principles of consistency. And I examined how lawyers, like those in the jurisconsult division materialize those principles by creating linkages between past and present cases through citation. They also concretize and represent these chains and connections through texts, such as case law guides. And they enact consistency through professional and organizational tasks, such as quality checks, regular meetings or "pigeon-hole amendments." These forms of interaction and communication create the effect of coherence or consistency. When ruptures do happen, they are the exceptions that prove the rule, reinforcing the hierarchies and authority within the Court. Only some people can break with precedent and dream. Others are, in William's self-designation, "just civil servants."

What happens, though, when rule-of-law norms to achieve institutional authority clash with norms about transparency and access to the institution itself? Efficiency, timeliness, and consistency can create practices that feel opaque or confusing, arbitrary or unjust. Other stakeholders, such as human rights advocates or applicants, have different expectations for how a human rights and rule-of-law institution ought to communicate and function.

In this section, I show how NGO and civil society representatives, including human rights lawyers, make demands on the ECHR system in the name of transparency. While people within the registry try to make the Court accessible, their genres of communication, their internal logics, not to mention the sheer volume of texts involved, often create a sense that the institution is opaque and difficult to navigate. This stands in direct contrast to definitions of rule of law based in access to and transparency of legal and political decisionmaking.

One need look no further than the ECtHR building itself to appreciate that transparency is central to how the ECHR system communicates and projects rule of law principles. With post–Cold War Council expansion, builders broke ground on a new Court building in 1991. Designed by a team of architects, gathered as the Rogers Partnership, the building was part of a growing architectural movement to concretize a new European era of unity and open democracy. Like other buildings designed at the time, the use of ample natural light and glass was intended to signal the ECHR system's transparency (Sperling 2011). In this view, the workings of institutions should be open to public scrutiny to prevent the exercise of arbitrary power or undemocratic decisionmaking.

Court and institutional actors also perform transparency in several ways that shape the material and infrastructural flow of information. These include an online database, known as HuDOC that provides access to the case law of the Court. The Court website has translations of cases in relevant country languages; updated case guides; links to talks, conferences, and other public events; and full videos of Grand Chamber hearings. At the same time, some kinds of information are simply off limits, also, in the name of rule-of-law principles. Judicial deliberations are strictly confidential to protect judges from outside influence or political pressure. This helps to project the all-important sense of consensus and one shared voice that many in the system also attribute to judicial authority and legitimacy (Cohen 2014).

The demands of accountability and transparency can bump up against demands of confidentiality in judicial deliberation. Confidentiality protects individuals from the pressure to serve state interests, thereby ensuring that politics and personal interest are kept out of judicial reason. Deliberation also promotes consensus-based decisionmaking, removing the responsibility for decisions from any one individual (Cohen 2014). As Çalı and Cunningham argue, the structure of the ECtHR is characterized by prioritizing "judicial independence at the expense of accountability with a 'mixed picture' for transparency" (2018). These practices produce "spaces to think": confidential carve-outs for people within European governance institutions that pit deliberation against transparency (see Hillebrandt and Novak 2016).

Within the Council of Europe, diplomatic, judicial, and civil society understandings of rule of law often clash around access to information and decisionmaking. This is clearest in the process of supervising the execution of judgments. As I have discussed elsewhere in this book, when the Court issues a binding judgment of a violation against a member state, it is the first step in a long process to seeing that judgment implemented in practice. In the past several years, the Department for the Execution of Judgments (DEJ) and the Committee of Ministers have been much more attuned to the role that civil society actors might play in the execution process. This was in part a pragmatic choice. The DEJ is overworked and understaffed. Execution often requires up-to-date in-country information about the status of cases, human rights policy, and legal contexts. Regular communications with state representatives and civil society members provide important updates that allow Strasbourg to keep pace with the necessary information required for execution.

In addition, these expanded opportunities for civil society input support transparency and democratic participation as core principles of the Council more broadly. They are also responses to concerted, long-term organizing on the part of civil society representatives for more formal channels for accountability. And yet, as anthropologists have noted, there is a difference between access to information and deliberation and how people experience that access as transparent, accessible, or meaningful (Muir and Gupta 2018). In his ethnography of campesinos in Paraguay who try to hold state actors accountable for land claims, Kregg Hetherington demonstrates how legal documents obscure information as often as they render it transparent. This is because "the practices of representation that go into creating transparency are saturated at every turn with precisely that aspect of social life that they are meant to get rid of: politics" (2011, 7). In other words, documents do not have a one-to-one relationship to information. They are sites where "abstracted representations meet actual, messy contexts, inciting confusion and competing interpretations (8)." While transparency is a central norm for democratic land reform in Paraguay in Hetherington's analysis, it is equally central to notions of rule of law more broadly. Yet there is almost always slippage between access to information and the translation of that information into actionable forms of engagement.

Descriptive information is simply not the same as embodied or meaningful knowledge that allows people to act effectively in the world (Edwards 2024). Access and transparency can only ever be realized in concrete interactions and *ways of communicating*. Calls for more transparency in Strasbourg are thus also metapragmatic comments on implicit power relations and communicative modalities that shape how arguments and information circulate across the ECHR system. Transparency often comes down to whether people experience themselves as participating *effectively* in processes of argumentation, persuasion, and influence. It is an interactional stance and an affective experience of being listened to that resonates with Matej's explanation of what it means to "knock on Strasbourg's door" (see Introduction).

For example, I frequently heard advocates complain about how difficult it was to access practical knowledge about the ECHR system in NGO workshops and trainings. One consistent complaint among civil society representatives was never knowing which cases would be discussed in the twice-yearly Committee of Ministers Human Rights meetings (CMDH). It was during these meetings that the Committee of Ministers would review and debate execution measures, potentially using diplomatic negotiations to move the process forward. Knowing which cases were on the agenda and which ones would be the subject of debate was critical to getting the right information to the right people at the right time.

Yet, I encountered more than one occasion when advocates suggested that making that information available would hugely improve relationships between civil society and the ECHR system offices—only for Council staff to point out precisely where on the website that information was available or explain how to access it through existing systems. For example, in one training I attended specifically designed to facilitate communication about executions between civil society, the Committee of Ministers, and the Department for Execution of Judgments, the issue of access was, once again, on the table. The training, convened in Strasbourg, included about twenty-five participants with a handful of observers, including me. The event focused on how civil society groups could use formal channels to make submissions to the Committee of Ministers, providing additional detail and framing on cases to assist in execution of the judgment. The organizers saw these official communicative channels as important ways to shape the implementation process and make it more effective as a tool of broader social change. Formal communications were part of making the execution process "more transparent." Indeed, as one of the workshop organizers told the group, a recent survey they had conducted demonstrated that many international organizations felt that there was "no transparency" in the system. One could see this idea at work both as a concern among civil society representatives and frustration from people working with the Council, as they struggled to make information available and usable.

A representative from the Council, Lucas, had extensive experience in executions. He urged those present to get involved. He repeatedly tried to demystify what went on behind the scenes, in the name of access and transparency. One sticking point people continued to clarify was how cases get on the list for discussion at Committee of Ministers' Human Rights (CMDH) meetings. The meetings are closed-door and devoted to supervision of cases and steps the Committee of Ministers can take to move that process along. They are a kind of accountability seeking through discussion and diplomatic negotiation, as I discuss more below. The agenda includes a list of cases that is made publicly available prior to the meetings. On the list are the cases to be discussed, usually those that have been designated as "enhanced" supervision, which means they might be diplomatically or legally tricky and require more time and attention. Indeed, how to get one's case on the enhanced list was a question NGO and human rights lawyers advocating around a particular judgment would often ask.

It was thus not a surprise that this very question came up early on during Lucas's presentation. One of the participants referred to a 2003 Turkish case, still awaiting execution, and expressed frustration about the lack of a timeline for this process. Lucas agreed, informing the participant that the case would be examined that coming September. "I get this question [about the timeline for execution] all the time," he noted and suggested that the participant could check the agenda for meeting discussions online. The fact that a case is pending, he explained doesn't mean that "nothing happens." This was a "misunderstanding" among the general public, linked in part to the slow pace of execution. But, he added, the execution process had become much more "participatory." Since 2006, there was a "U-turn" in the execution process and a shift from a "top-down to a bottom-up approach . . . to involve more actors."

This frustration and miscommunication were not an indication of bad faith or lack of trying. They are evidence that accessibility and transparency are rarely about information in its inert form—for example, website calendars that list the dates of upcoming CMDH meetings, recommendations for when to submit supplementary materials to be considered by the Department of Executions, or back documents outlining what was argued and decided at past meetings or public hearings. Rather, when NGO representatives were calling on registry, executions, and Committee of Ministers staff for more information, what they were seeking was a sense of the institutional and political contexts in which their interventions might have an impact on the direction and outcome of conversations.

Lucas was speaking in the language of transparency because it was an important sticking point for many in the room. Being able to find information was key. But more important was the ability to navigate a system in which power and influence could happen at different points, sometimes publicly and sometimes behind closed doors. The participants in the room pushed back against Lucas's account of accessibility and transparency. They all seemed to agree that it was a goal, but the question was whether there was enough of it. One participant spoke of the recent Copenhagen Declaration, which was a controversial document at the time, proposing reforms to the ECHR system. The declaration referred to the need for increased NGO involvement, the participant noted, but she explained that this was difficult to achieve when they weren't informed about meetings, agendas, and other actions by national authorities. Others agreed, pointing to insufficient information coming from national governments. When one of the trainers noted that it was precisely these kinds of gaps that required NGOs to use new, formal mechanisms for communication with the Committee of Ministers, another participant pushed back again. She suggested that one reason NGOs weren't using these channels was a "lack of transparency" about which cases would be discussed at the Committee of Ministers meeting. This left human rights advocates and NGOs scrambling to prepare submissions for cases that might not be discussed when planned. It required a huge amount of work to update the submissions as cases and contexts changed.

Lucas responded with some frustration, as the critiques of lack of transparency mounted. He pointed out once again that the information was on the website. But beyond this, he noted that some of the participants were missing the point. "Let me give you some advice," he noted. "Don't concentrate on cases to be debated. Debate is not a catalyst for changes. . . . It's more important that a case is on the agenda." By this, he seemed to mean that the NGO representatives were overly focused on the technical aspect of getting a case discussed rather than on the long-term process of execution, of which a CMDH meeting was only one part. And yet, when it came to navigating transparency, many of the workshop participants were trying to figure out where and when decisionmaking took place and how they might actually have influence.

People's encounters with large, bureaucratic institutions or complex state processes often take the form of narratives of suspicion and distrust (Paz 2018; Das 2019). Underlying these is often an ideology about language and knowledge that we can call the "Wizard of Oz" theory of power. The behind-the-curtain theory imputes a kind of centralized agency and clarity between intention and action, which is rarely true of any complex social organization, particularly bureaucracies (Mathur 2016; Hull 2012). Indeed, time and again, despite their access to information, I encountered human rights advocates who felt frustrated that they couldn't get the *real* information they needed or that deliberation processes were still shrouded in mystery and secrecy. Advocates and lawyers struggled to figure out what was "behind" the information they did have access to. The sense of the secrecy of the Court or the lack of clear communication between the Court and execution came up in many interviews with people across the Convention system.

The problem of opacity and frustration is linked not only to closed door processes, such as confidential deliberations among judges, or a caginess around internal workplace dynamics within the Court and Council institutions. It is also the fact that knowledge is given form and substance through different linguistic registers and social practices. It is indicative of the mismatch between the fact that information might be available and the experience that makes information useful and intelligible. Participants in workshops placed an emphasis on communication as a series of commitments and relationships they might develop with people "inside" the institution. Representatives from the institution placed an emphasis on more technical aspects of access—where to find and download documents or how to check calendars and agendas. Being effective and persuasive was about figuring out how to be heard, and how to be heard was bundled in people's experiences with access to information. These different approaches reflected not content but the pragmatics of information—the contextual aspects and details of documents and decisions that would make it possible to interpret and use that information in shared ways.

What became clear to me in this and other similar interactions was that transparency and access meant different things to people, depending on whether they were or were not "in the room where it happened" (with a nod to Lin-Manuel Miranda). For NGO participants, transparency meant not only knowing when meetings might take place and what was on the agenda but actually the social conditions and contexts through which they might have an impact. As a rule-of-law principle, Lucas could confidently say that the Department for the Execution of Judgments and the Committee of Ministers were making information available and giving civil-society groups a welcome chance to weigh in. But as a communicative modality, civil society representatives saw transparency not as a neutral availability of information on a website. Transparency was embedded in social relationships. Lucas's presentation about technical channels of communication, timelines, and even how to format and write effective communications to the Committee of Ministers was met with questions about the power dynamics and conditions of actually being heard.

Transparency from Diplomacy and Media Perspectives: Maintaining Reputation and Trust

The NGO representatives I write about above struggled both with how to hold states accountable and how to know if they had an impact on actual decision-making. From their perspective, transparency as a communicative modality meant meaningful access to information and actual input into negotiations among diplomats and state representatives. This was where and how execution really took place, at least in Strasbourg. Indeed, over the course of my research, the question of why Committee of Ministers meetings couldn't be open to NGO observers came up in several contexts and continues to be a heated issue from all sides. What publics were hailed and how inclusive would they be were thus among the terms of debate for what true participation might look like. It was thus that the very terms of producing the rule of law were grounds for production of frustration and critique.

These issues of power and exclusion become even more fraught when considering how transparency intersects with diplomatic trust on one hand and the need for a public-facing media strategy on the other. The ECHR system works as a system of soft power and persuasion. Many lawyers, judges, and diplomatic representatives I spoke to credit its effectiveness in regulating state power and human rights violations to confidential forms of negotiation. This applies to deliberations among judges and to the diplomatic deliberations about how judgments are to be implemented. In theory, the veil of confidentiality protects individuals from the pressure to serve state interests, thereby ensuring that politics and personal interest are kept out of judicial reason. Individuals also are protected through consensus-based decisionmaking, removing the responsibility for decisions from any one individual.

What you make public and how will always produce boundaries, particularly in the context of democratic deliberations and discussions (Greenberg 2014). There is always the practical matter of meetings behind closed doors, like confidential deliberations. But within democratic publics, not everyone is equally able to speak with authority, participate, embody and perform the conversational rules of the game (Fraser 1990). The ideas of equality in arms as a rule-of-law principle or transparency of governance and decisionmaking are a response to the inequalities built into communicative channels and interactions.

While in theory, accountability and transparency are often linked, in practice some of my interlocutors saw them as at odds. For example, as I noted in chapter 2, diplomats directly linked confidentiality and trust in closed-door meetings to effective negotiations and the ability to persuade states to comply with Court judgments. Several people told me with frustration that few in Europe understand the importance of the system, its impact on people's lives, and the very human stories at its heart. Yet others (and even sometimes the same people) told me that being off the radar was part of the whole system's success. This paradox of publicity and secrecy, then, was not only an effect of failures to communicate outwardly. It was an ambivalence at the heart of the system that stemmed from the juggling of publics and how best to serve the cause of human rights in the context of the rule of law. This was particularly important for those involved in the diplomatic end of things. From this perspective, the rule of law is a fragile achievement that needs to be nurtured and protected. One member of the diplomatic core that I interviewed, a lawyer who had worked for several years in Strasbourg and had inside knowledge of Committee of Ministers negotiations, noted, "We try to everything by unanimity here. It shapes the negotiation and the dynamics of meetings." She compared this to Brussels (the European Union), which is a majority system. By contrast, Strasbourg is based on consensus. "We try to keep everyone involved as long as possible. We do have voting but we try to avoid it." She added, "It's a collective thing." She explained that this is in part because, although the Court judgments are legally binding, the rest of the process is politically rather than strictly legally binding. "We need states to be on board themselves." In the same moment that she acknowledged the fragility of the system—the kernel of consensus at the heart of binding rule of law—she acknowledged her surprise when she "steps back and realize[s] how well its works." She added that it is easy to forget that "cases do get implemented, things do change. . . . We have this system here which is so unique and works and so few people know about it. It's bizarre."

Likewise, the media teams at the Council must juggle preserving trust in the system, protecting diplomatic negotiations, and communicating to broader publics about the relevance and successes in the system. This creates a complicated squeeze between the requirements of diplomacy and trust at the Council and responding to journalists and news cycles that are, in the words of one interviewee who handles media strategy, "conflict driven." He explained the different strategies for creating events out of what is an ongoing and often difficult-to-understand process in executions. For example, whenever there is an interim measure at the Committee of Ministers, they issue a press release. But they need to translate why this is newsworthy to journalists, who may not get the process or significance. At the same time, he acknowledged the Committee of Ministers and member states are very sensitive to being in the news. From the Council of Europe media office's perspective, it is important for diplomatic relations to standardize press releases, so no countries feel singled out or treated unfairly. Once again, echoing the "delicate balancing act" that defines so much of the ECHR system, he noted they are "trying to attract journalistic attention." On one hand, media "thrive on conflict, and on the other, we have to keep the member states on board because they pay the bills and they don't want to be in the media, especially if they are criticized." Indeed, the dangers can be real, and when local news agencies get it wrong, misinformation "can spread like wildfire." Yet, as an institution that serves 700 million Europeans, it is nonetheless important, he noted, to tell people's stories and to highlight the importance of the system.

Like the balance between publicity and confidentiality at the Court, the conditions for performing and enacting the rule of law requires managing the distinction between public and confidential knowledge. Confidentiality stood in for trust, but it was also an expression of diplomatic power—the ability to negotiate and create consensus. And this consensus (rather than the processes that produced it) could in turn be made public to project certain messages about the system and its functioning. This was a careful balancing act in that all that diplomats have is soft power and persuasion. It was thus all the more important to them to manage negotiations carefully.

Conclusion

The rule of law has become a global imperative since the end of the Cold War (Carothers 2006). It shapes diplomacy, geopolitical relations, and global democratization and humanitarian interventions. Yet even as rule of law has become the name of the game, its practical ambiguity often presents as many challenges as it resolves (Cheesman 2018). I have hoped to show in this chapter how the rule of law operates nonnormatively, as different communicative modalities that emerge from and shape everyday actions across the ECHR system. The hope is that in asking what communicative work rule-of-law frameworks enable and foreclose, we can move beyond metrics of success and failure. At stake is understanding how ambiguous terms work in and across scales of action—sometimes creating flexibility on which the legitimacy of legal systems is enacted and performed and at others shaping the terrain for challenges and contestation.

FOUR

Enumerating Justice and the "Treadmill of Paradox"

Human Rights and the Language of Numbers

There's a kind of paradox involved in all of this. The more efficient the court will become, the more cases it will get. The more cases it will get, the more problems it will run into. . . . You might call it the treadmill of paradox. . . . [It] will mean the court will always be concerned about its procedures and whether they're appropriate for dealing with huge numbers of cases.

—Former Deputy Registrar of the ECtHR, 2016

THE 1998 SHIFT TO PROTOCOL 11 was a sea change in the ECHR system. In addition to establishing the permanent Court in Strasbourg, it codified the right to individual petition for hundreds of millions of people on European territory. This right to individual petition is unique among regional human rights courts (Hampson et al. 2018). Unlike other apex courts that hear only a selection of cases that speak to broader legal issues, the ECtHR is obligated to hear all cases that meet admissibility criteria. This means the building blocks of one of the most expansive human rights regimes in the world are serial, individual cases. This commitment to individual petition is now one of the Court's defining features. At the same time, rising case numbers necessitated new ways to classify cases for faster and easier processing. This resulted in a paradox: at the very moment right to individual petition was formalized, the ECHR system introduced managerial and legal ways to aggregate individual claims into groups. This raised important questions about what and who the

Court was for. Is it a system where every person counts as an individual? Or are cases, at the end of the day, about communicating the need for structural reform to state actors? And if the answer is both, how do people—strategic litigators, human rights advocates, lawyers, judges, and diplomats—juggle these different roles?

The right to individual petition also raised the question: If you must hear all individual cases, how do you differentiate their significance and meaning? In this chapter I analyze the uses of numbers and the different kinds of narratives and analyses they support. I argue that shifting among different ways of counting and accounting allowed registry lawyers and Council staff to navigate and balance the individual versus structural potential of human rights. Scholars have argued that the quantification of human rights has led to atomization and disaggregation of underlying structural issues (Merry 2016). While this is certainly true for some aspects of the ECHR system, it is not the whole story. Not all quantification is the same. It can take on political import when people frame identify, and persuade others to recognize and group numbers through different categories and patterns. This politics of aggregation is best analyzed in terms of the arguments it supports. Within human rights and international governance, numbers and accounting are central to how people tack between legal and policy analysis, individual rights protections, and structural human rights problems.

Numbers are neither definitive nor absolute representations of the world (Newfield et al. 2022). They are epistemological moves in a field of play. Any form of accounting is also a form of knowledge production that shapes how people define and act on problems (Poovey 1998). People can use numbers to make complex and disparate representations of the world commensurate in service of political, legal, and economic arguments (Espeland and Stevens 1998). Speaking in and with different ways of accounting provides a plasticity to how people ground their actions in the name of law (Ballestero 2015; Espeland and Vannebo 2007). Numbers are ways to talk about efficiency and to project legitimacy, as I showed in the last chapter. They are a mechanism for diagnosing and analyzing the ECHR system to hold it to account, as I discuss below. People use numbers, taken as individual cases, to tell stories about rights. They generate perspectives grounded in a singular, compelling narrative example. And they use numbers and ideas about grouping and aggregating to tell structural stories about rights as well. In so doing, people across the ECHR system move between talking about cases as legal artifacts and cases as vehicles for policy or political change. The move back and forth among numbers—made to stand in for qualities and quantities—can also support competing visions of the proper relationship between institutions, sovereign states and international legal bodies.

Talking Numbers in the Court Registry

There are lots of different ways to talk in and through numbers at the European Court of Human Rights: how many cases have been filed, how many violations found, how many applications pending, how many years to judgment. Even the everyday patois of the Court rests in numbered shorthand: references to articles (2, 3, 4, 5, 6, etc.); single-, triple-, seven-, or seventeen-judge formations; the endless circulation of charts and tables ranking country statistics on violations found, articles breached, and judgments executed. As I argued in chapter 3, numbers are central to debates about the system's success or shortcomings and the way people make political and ethical claims about its importance. People invoke numbers as a form of critique by pointing to backlogs of cases or increases in inadmissible applications or unexecuted judgments. Numbers as one key form of accounting live in everyday conversations across Council offices, the Court website, training-workshop presentations, and analysis of the Convention system in mainstream and social media. They are both a shared and contested resource for making sense of the ECHR system across multiple formats, interactions, and audiences.

It was thus not a surprise that when I walked into the office of a senior registry official, James, in 2018 for a follow-up interview, he greeted me with numbers. I settled into my chair and inquired how he was doing. He responded with a litany of figures. Leaning over the coffee table between us, James launched into a discussion of the recent Burmych case. This was a controversial decision in which the Court struck out over 12,000 cases, removing them from the docket and sending them to executions to be counted under a single leading judgment. He explained that if we took the Burmych cases, and put them aside, then we take all the repetitive cases (which, he noted, are really about execution and so wouldn't count against Court numbers), and then the detention cases (which, he pointed out, are getting better), and all the interstate conflict cases, (which [the Court] won't ever be able to solve on their own) . . . then that really only left the Court with 15,000 cases to decide. As he spoke, he moved his hands above the table, as if sorting and organizing this mass of thousands of cases. He divided them—through qualifying asides and hand gestures—into invisible piles, noting, "It's still a lot [of cases]." But with characteristically good humor, he added, "It is not so bad, or as bad as it seems."

James wasn't making light of the seriousness of these numbers. He was trying to help me make sense of the scale of cases and the urgency of the Court's response. Like metrics of good governance and human rights indicators (Anders 2008; Merry 2016; Cowan 2013), he used numbers to express the smooth institutional functioning that underpins a particular understanding of the rule of law. Sorting in this way expressed a world view with practical consequences. He was narrating an account of running a massive institution, managing a huge staff, and being responsive (without bending) to external pressures and critique. James was also using numbers to group and classify cases as *types* of problems to be solved. Some were a matter of law. Others were a matter of diplomatic negotiations. Some cases could be reduced to one underlying issue and should be counted as such. And yet, nothing here was purely quantitative. Quantities, groups of cases, and numeric representations took on qualities that aligned with the proper role of the Court (Nelson 2015). Determining how many cases the Court was managing had everything to do with the categories through which they were grouped and ultimately adjudicated. In sweeping a group to the right—let's take these cases as if they were the same— James performed an epistemological operation that argued for a particular understanding of what the institution was for and what its role ought to be. Adjudicating every clone case as if it stemmed from the same policy shortcoming moved it from a legal problem to a policy problem, from the mandate of the Court to that of executions. It was a moment in which numbers were central to creating a distinction between law and politics and to transferring cases across the divide. It was also a way to explain to me what the Court was designed to do and to be persuasive that it was achieving those goals.

Whatever critics thought of these solutions, people had experimented with multiple new strategies for accounting in the mid-2010s. As I described at length in chapters 2 and 3, the Council of Europe and the Court's jurisdiction grew significantly with the 1990s Council of Europe expansion. Many of these cases were repetitive in character. They stemmed from shared, underlying causes that generated tens and sometimes hundreds of violations of the Convention. New procedures helped the Court to deal with these cases in one fell swoop. By 2018, reforms of the early 2000s had helped reduce the caseload. Changes in admissibility criteria meant fewer cases were eligible for judgment.

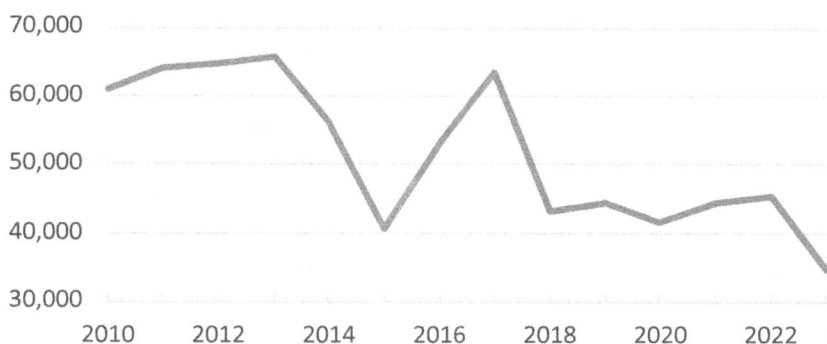

FIGURE 4.1.   Backlog and decline of applications allocated to a judicial formation 2010–2022. Although the numbers remain high, the graph illustrates the impact of new administrative procedures on reducing backlog during this period. Source: Council of Europe, *Annual Report of the European Court of Human Rights, 2020–2023*, https://www.echr.coe.int/annual-reports.

This resulted in fewer applications making their way through the system. By creating smaller judicial formations, processing more cases quickly, and using stricter admissibility criteria, the Court could support a narrative of greater efficiency. For those admissible cases that were repetitive in nature, new methods of accounting allowed the Court to aggregate and rule on groups of cases, speeding the process along.

One formal method for this approach was the pilot judgment procedure.[1] Pilot judgments were an innovative response to processing large numbers of similar cases stemming from a shared structural human rights problem. Rather than issue an extensive ruling on each case individually, judges could consider the issues raised by a "leading case" that stood in for the rest. If a violation was found, each applicant could receive just satisfaction—usually monetary compensation. The more complicated and nuanced task of figuring out the case law—how the cases related to the Convention and precedent— could be worked out in one exemplary case. This avoided the time-consuming task of adjudicating many instances of the same issue. It allowed the Court to package tens, hundreds, and even thousands of violations together, which could then be cleared from the docket in one fell swoop.

These new categories and techniques for managing cases gave rise to a new object of legal intervention: the structural human rights problem. As the Court began to bundle cases together for adjudication, it also impacted how the

Department for the Execution of Judgments handled oversight and implementation of judgments. For example, if one hundred cases all stem from the same problematic law in a country, those cases will be grouped together. Each individual can receive monetary compensation for the violation. But for the cases to be fully resolved, the member state will need to address the structural issue that generates the cases in the first place. This may include legislative change at the domestic level. It is one way the court takes the additive logic (1+1+1) of cases and bundles "types" of cases together to create more efficiency. This allows the system to translate additive elements into arguments for structural and political change. This diagnosis of cases as stemming from a shared underlying structural issue shifted the legal burden of analysis to a diplomatic and policy question of identifying that problem and addressing it within domestic systems.

From Judgments to Execution: Building Structural Analysis of Rights Back In

From James's perspective, being able to group multiple cases under a leading case was a method of accounting that helped the image and legitimacy of the Court. It is in this sense that James's aside that some cases were really about execution and not judgments was an important clue to deeper debates at the time. People used different methods of accounting to toggle between the different legal and diplomatic functions of the ECHR system. In reframing the problem as a matter of administrative approaches to execution rather than a string of legal questions and cases, the Court could move more quickly and effectively. At the same time, some long-standing Council staff expressed concern that the problem hadn't been resolved so much as shifted to another part of the ECHR system. As a result, the length of time to executing the judgments had grown. It was one thing to deliver violations. But tracking these through to meaningful change on the ground was also essential to the process. After all, if member states could solve the systemic problems that generated cases in the first place, then the Court's caseload would be reduced. And from a legitimacy standpoint, this would mean that human rights reforms were happening at the domestic level, within the context of sovereign states, in keeping with principles of subsidiarity.

While states are bound to execute judgments, the scope in how far they do so is a matter of negotiation and diplomatic and civil society pressure. Most states agree to pay out just satisfaction to individual applicants. But given enough cases about like violations, the lawyers in the Department for the Execution of Judgments (DEJ), supporting the Committee of Ministers, can make plausible arguments that more than individual measures need to be taken. The DEJ derives this diagnosis from reading judgments, analyzing shared patterns in similar cases, and putting this information in the context of additional data coming through formal channels. This can include information from the applicant's lawyers, civil society groups, and official reports from Council offices, such as the Commissioner for Human Rights. In other words, they build a picture out of aggregate data to move from the legal warrant of a case to potential policy recommendations. The fact of multiple legal cases can authorize diplomats and execution lawyers to transit from individual measures to general ones. It is for this reason that implementation is such a critical site for the actually meaningful practice of human rights on the ground in a given domestic context.

The process of executing a judgment almost always requires additional information to understand a violation's social context, domestic legal norms, or the ongoing harms to applicants or other affected groups. Judgments can include that information. This depends on the kinds of texts and narratives that drafting lawyers choose to include. But just as often, the information might be lacking, outdated, or insufficient for addressing contemporary conditions.

When I asked Theresa, a senior registry lawyer at the DEJ, to clarify what kinds of information she needed to implement judgments, she told me, "In order to be executable, a judgment needs a certain amount of information." But at the same time, they could "only ask for implementation of violations" from judgments. They "can't make it up." In this sense, the judgment is the ultimate mandate and source of information for the execution process. The DEJ lawyers rely on it to do their work. But lawyers in the DEJ can also shape the scope of implementation by working with the text. To do this, they must wait for information through additional channels of communication. For example, Theresa described strategies for gaining additional context for a judgment through authorized legal channels. She explained, "They can . . . say to the Court, 'There is a particular situation in a country we need more information or background on. . . . We could use a judgment that clarifies this particular issue.'" Thus, context could come either from direct communication with lawyers at the Court or in the form of new judgments on similar issues. This creates new chained, intertextual links in which similar cases could be read against each other via processes of analogy.

Speaking through and about judgments is what creates institutional channels through which supplemental context and information flows. For example, if a strategic litigator or a human rights advocate wants to frame a case as part of a larger structural issue, one strategy is to keep bringing cases with similar fact patterns from the same country context. This gives the Court material to build out a legally authorized picture of broader structural conditions. The *fact* of similar cases in aggregate can be translated into a warrant for legal interpretation that adds to the weight of each individual judgment. In turn this added weightiness allows a judgment to stand in for more than itself. It can then be used as the grounds for diagnosing structural human rights problems.

Another lawyer for the DEJ, Thomas, described this interpretative labor to me in some detail. He told me that "the Court is quite cautious" in pronouncing "when it sees or when it knows that there are structural problems in a particular country." This means it is reluctant to "go deeper into" issues raised by cases and the context in which violations emerge. Thomas explained that this is "why in order to understand the dimensions of the problem, which is tackled by a specific judgment, one sometimes has to go beyond the document."

Thomas relied on a deep understanding of the context of a case to, in his words, "read between the lines." It was not enough for facts, figures, or descriptive accounts to appear in a judgment. Contextualization including reading such details against knowledge of an in-country situation, diagnosing underlying causes, and potential responses that a state ought to take. Such a process is labor intensive. "Reading between the lines" was necessary to supersede the often narrow or, in his words, "casuistic" reasoning (and prose) of a judgment. To go deeper (between the lines) required going broader. He might achieve this effect by bringing multiple cases into relationship with one another. In this way he could derive (or ground) shared context through likeness among cases to create a deeper understanding of country conditions. This is how he got from law to policy or general measures.

Classing and aggregating judgments as the same creates a new interpretative context. The *fact* of multiple judgments grouped as the same can be the basis to reframe individual legal harm, requiring monetary compensation, to collective structural political or legal failing, justifying general measures. Such connections acted as warrants for transforming legal into political action. To return to the pilot judgment example, if there are one hundred cases all stemming from the same problematic law in country, lawyers at the Court will group them together. Every individual receives just satisfaction for a violation that similarly affects everyone in the group. But for the cases to be fully resolved, the member state will need to address the structural issue that generates the cases in the first place—for example, introduction of a new administrative procedure for property restitution. This is one way the Court takes the individual token cases and bundles types of cases together. Pilot procedures make the processing of cases more efficient. But they also support arguments for structural and political change that will prevent future violations from happening.

Susan Philips (2016) discusses how particular crimes comes to be scaled as more serious through their mapping onto different hierarchies across the Tongan judicial system. Similarly, the scale of a violation in Strasbourg is figured via the statistical aggregation of cases: more like cases stand in for scope of the problem. Aggregate likeness scales to seriousness of the underlying issues, which authorizes oversight and general measures. Thomas told me, "In many cases . . . we actually wait for more judgments to come. It's a rather common method we adopt. We [are] in touch with the Court or the registry of the Court. We always ask them, 'Do you have more judgments of this kind coming?'" He added:

> If we see that there are more judgments coming on many cases, we wait; we don't close cases. [When] we group all the judgments together . . . we have a clearer picture. And we can also go before the Committee of Ministers and say, "Here we have ten or twenty judgments of the same issue; there is something structural'—even if the court does not really identify the issue as structural.

This grouping, he added, allows "a more holistic approach, and it facilitates our own examination."

One can see in his comments how bundling multiple judgments together as the same allows people to shift from a legal to a policy interpretation. This allows lawyers to anticipate the future moment when new intertextual relations will transform the meaning and thus the warrant of existing judgments. Lawyers cannot stretch beyond what judgments name as the violation to be addressed. But they can link those violations to other kinds of contexts by reading between the lines for qualitative contextual information and by using additive logics of statistical grouping. This process relies on channels that move judgments from one point to the other while holding them in suspension until they can be reframed with new and more context.

Importantly, this is not just an in-office set of interpretative practices. These processes involve shared strategies as people learn to work within the ECHR system. This reflexivity is also key to the pedagogical work of the ECHR system and its official institutional representatives. Indeed, I first encountered Thomas at an NGO training where he was explaining his strategies for "reading between the lines" to human rights advocates. I later asked for an interview because he was so instructive about how to read judgments in a way that both retained their authoritative *legal* grounding but allowed people to stretch their social mandate through (re)contextualization. The practices within the DEJ are also sharable interpretive strategies through which NGO advocates and human rights activists learn how to work with the bundling of cases as well. In all of these instances, people use different methods of accounting for and counting cases to support arguments for certain institutional responses, as a matter of legal authority or policy response.

Defining the Scope of the Problem: Numbers from a Civil Society Perspective

Lawyers working in the DEJ ground structural and contextual analysis by clustering or aggregating case numbers, in addition to using the supplemental information that comes in new judgments. But human rights advocates also shape persuasive narrative and analysis through case numbers, and especially open or unexecuted judgments. It was this competing attempt to tell stories via numbers that made the Court's accounting for pilot cases an object of criticism in the late 2010s. Because cases were grouped under a leading judgment, they counted as one instance of a judgment to be executed, rather than many hundreds or thousands. Some in the civil society community found this frustrating. It seemed like an unfair representation of backlog and the work yet to be done at the stage of executing judgments. How unexecuted cases are calculated was not only a technical matter. It impacted the weight, persuasiveness, and influence of human rights advocates' ability to pressure violating states to take meaningful action.

What people do with numbers and methods of accounting depends on what they think those numbers are for. Are they intended to facilitate processing of cases to keep the court efficient? Are numbers a way to diagnose and represent the underlying human rights situation in member states? Is the audience for such accounting internal—other registry lawyers and judges—or external—member states representatives, media outlets, civil society groups? In theory, this need not be either/or. But in practice different approaches to accounting allow for very different ways of narrating the significance of cases. This has consequences for the kinds of advocacy that might follow. For example, if a member state has a large number of unresolved cases, under a leading judgment, civil society advocates can argue that the case is in need of enhanced supervision. This is a designation that means that a group of cases will be discussed at the quarterly Committee of Ministers' Human Rights meetings and might receive extra diplomatic attention. Sometimes an enhanced case involves only one judgment that is particularly politically sensitive or complicated to execute (see chapter 6 for an example). And sometimes it is a series of cases in which the underlying structural cause of a violation is dauntingly large in scope.

It matters then if the Court or Department for the Execution of Judgments counts only leading cases, turning the number of cases to still be addressed from several thousand into one. Arguments for counting *all* the cases in a pilot group (as opposed to just the leading case under which they are grouped) impact the persuasive effect of advocacy efforts to pressure national governments to comply with Committee of Ministers' directives. While it looks better from the Court registry perspective to have fifteen thousand cases grouped under one leading case, it also looks better for member states who have the violation. This impacts advocates' ability to argue for increased diplomatic pressure by the Committee of Ministers. As implementation or execution becomes more important to the efficacy of the ECHR system as a whole, these numbers come to matter more and more.

This tension and the different role that accounting and numbers play was made clear in a two-part essay that was published in the respected legal blog, EJIL Talk in 2019. The author, George Stafford, was at the time director of the European Implementation Network, a respected NGO that monitors execution of ECtHR judgments. The two-part series focused on a shift in how the Council calculated statistics on implementation of judgments. In the articles, Stafford argued that numbers and accounting matter from an advocacy standpoint. The posts took issue with how the DEJ had ported over the accounting strategies for pilot judgments into the execution process. This calculation followed the same logic of the pilot judgments that James cited in my opening vignette. It grouped unexecuted cases under one leading judgment and counted only that against member states' obligations to meet their obligations in executions.

The posts made the point that these accounting methods were counter-productive to human rights advocacy. Counting many open cases as only *one* case undermined the potential of the execution process to support long-term structural change and ECHR compliance. For James, numbers or statistics supported legitimacy for the Court and Convention system through metrics of efficiency and time to judgment. For Stafford, the question was how numbers and statistics worked diagnostically to identify underlying structural causes for human rights violations. In turn, numbers talk enabled different kinds of conversations and communication with respondent states. Statistics could be mobilized for pressure and to support social change on the ground. This made possible different and potentially new kinds of action and advocacy. It also pointed to a central aspect of numbers and accounting: more than a representation of the world, they are about knowledge production (Poovey 1998). This includes defining the scope of a problem in ways that open up forms of action and intervention into that problem.

Stafford argued that the way the Council calculates the execution of judgments (and thus closes cases and moves them off the books) is misleading because it hides the scope of an underlying human rights problem in a given country context. This means of calculation supported a narrative of success and effectiveness that alleviated pressure points on states thus removing a diplomatic and advocacy lever for generating compliance. Comparing the ways of counting executed cases to "grade inflation," Stafford cited several social media and official annual reports as a "general 'good news story'" and a "pervasive narrative about the system for the implementation of judgments . . . that . . . is getting more and more effective." The blog acknowledged the pressure on the ECHR system from previous methods of accounting for large numbers of pending cases. Yet the move to a new system for calculating figures, he noted, "created an opportunity for states to quickly close thousands and thousands of cases, many of which could be closed simply by paying the compensation due." At stake was not whether the new approach was good or bad or true or false in relationship to cases but "the narrative that resulted from it—the good news story—concerning the overall effectiveness of the ECHR implementation system." This narrative, the author argued, was problematic because it mispresented what it means to be effective as an institution, which was as a means of effecting structural change and compliance with the ECHR on the ground.

Talking about methods of accounting was also a way to talk about what counted as meaningful participation and transparency within the ECHR system. The blog posts argued that current statistical practices closed channels of communication and knowledge that were central for advocates and others "outside" the institution to engage with the Convention system in meaningful ways. As I argued in chapter 3, whether and how civil society groups had access to the "inner" workings of the ECHR system was a constant issue in interactions between Council staff and advocates. This wasn't just about being in the room where decisions were made. It was also a matter of being able to participate meaningfully and effectively in those conversations. These groups include human rights NGOs, funders, and "guardians of the ECHR system" who need to be "able to accurately audit the effectiveness of the system." Numbers and accounting mattered tremendously in this regard. They were simultaneously forms of communication, knowledge, and the grounds for action. Thus according to Stafford's analysis "a clear, well-understood evidence base is necessary in order to gauge the scale of the non-implementation problem. Only if we are able to see the true nature of the problem will we be able to respond appropriately to it in the next era of the Convention system." In the second post, the author goes on to compare the situation to a hole in the roof of house. Without an accurate assessment of the size of the hole and the materials needed to fix it, it is impossible to mend. Here the metaphor operates to argue that statistics and judgments not executed ought to work diagnostically. They are not only a source of political pressure and moral authority but a means of knowledge production necessary to understanding and responding to human rights as systemic "holes" in our democratic systems. If, as the posts argue, "the scale of the problem is being underestimated" then corresponding responses will be insufficient. From this perspective, democratizing that knowledge is key to the healthy functioning of an institution defined not just as offices in Strasbourg but a larger community that it serves. Knowledge practices via different approaches to numbers invited different publics and communities of participation.

If James was concerned with protecting the legitimacy of the institution as both a professional and ethical goal, Stafford also pegged the language of numbers—and the work it should do—to ethical practice. He closes the blog by noting:

> If the system is to function effectively, judgments from the Strasbourg Court need to result not just in justice for the individual, but in the legal or practical reforms necessary to ensure that the same violation does not happen again in the society as a whole. . . . If leading judgments are not being closed, that

means the underlying human rights issues are not being dealt with. Each un-implemented leading judgment represents an ethical problem for Europe (be-cause of the ongoing violation of human rights); and a practical problem for the Court (because they can lead to repeat applications, which increase the backlog and threaten its ongoing viability).

Interviews with and reflections by registry lawyers, DEJ staff, and civil society representatives reveal that how the Court and DEJ account for cases have legal and political significance for different audiences—member states, applicants, Council staff, media outlets, and scholars. And persuading these audiences that accounting for cases ought to work in a certain way was central to arguments and advocacy within the framework of the ECHR system. Grouping leading and trailing cases was a way to both understand the scope of a problem and engage in the advocacy and persuasive means available within the diplomatic and Council systems created to address it. This was inextricably linked to their diagnostic, or epistemological function. But it also represented an ethical problem for a system that self-designates as "the conscience of Europe." From this perspective, numbers make sense only in relationship to the narrative frameworks in which they are embedded. It is a common "semiotic ideology," or "underlying assumption about what signs are, what functions signs serve, and what consequences they might produce" that numbers offer transparent views onto the state of things in the world (Keane 2018). But as the cases here demonstrate, it is difficult to separate what numbers represent from what people invoking them claim they mean. Numbers work as persuasive strategies, then, when people put them in relationship to interpretive frameworks and ethical claims. It is this fact that animates the tensions between the two ways of classifying or accounting for leading and trailing cases. At stake is the ability to use numbers to "know" different things about how many cases are yet to be executed. But beyond that, it is also the possibility to ground diplomatic or civil society pressure on states—in other words the processes that underlie the functioning of the ECHR as a negotiated form of power and persuasion.

From Numbers to Knowledge

People often make claims to knowledge of the world through the language of numbers. They also argue for particular kinds of correspondence between quantities (such as human rights cases) and qualities for which they stand in

(Nelson 2015). For example, when registry staff and lawyers speak with confidence about the human rights situation on the ground in a particular member state, they often support this knowledge with visual and narrative representations of numbers and types of cases. The Court undertakes little fact-finding of its own. Its role is explicitly *not* to fact-find (in legal terminology, it is not a court of fourth instance). It can access the substance, qualities, and meanings of harm or violence only through the traces of procedural recordkeeping and documents. And it is thus the case that registry lawyers, judges, and Court staff must rely on cases in aggregate (large quantities of like cases) to figure out something qualitatively specific about people's experiences of human rights violations on the ground. Part of the contradictory mandate of the ECtHR is to assess and know on-the-ground experiences of violence, harm, and suffering. Yet as an international body, it has limited access to the local contexts, fact patterns, and experiences of those suffering harm.

Beyond helping people to understand the situation in each context, these numbers also support the idea that judges might know enough about on-the-ground conditions to enact the supervisory role necessary to the functioning of the Court system. I touched on one such example in chapter 3. There I wrote of my 2018 conversation with a judge at the Court about her work on well-established case law (WECL). To remind the reader, she shared with me a computer-generated chart that listed hundreds of cases of prison detention, many from the same penal colonies. On one side was a column with case numbers. Across the top, headings detailed key categories: size of prison cell; distance from eating area to toilet; presence of lice, bedbugs, and roaches. Between the serial numbers of the cases and the general categories of violations, the chart contained the briefest of accounts: the individuals who suffered these "inhumane and degrading" conditions, in the language of Article 3 of the Convention.

Such prison detention conditions are part of WECL. These cases are so prevalent, so similar, and so clearly in violation of the European Convention of Human Rights (ECHR) that they can be decided in an expedited manner. This process includes applicants bringing individual cases and Court lawyers comparing and bundling these cases into distilled and aggregated types of harm. Judges then decide violations by comparing and contrasting an individual application with these aggregated pictures. In this way, an aggregate picture of multiple like cases makes any one individual case more easily justiciable. One case and one instance takes on legal significance in a relationship of comparison and contrast to statistically organized representations of a given country context.

The work of aggregating cases allows registry staff and judges to "know" the scale or scope of a problem, moving from the additive logic of 1+1+1 to a more general assessment of a human rights situation in each domestic legal context. The work of aggregation and the comparisons it affords require a well-functioning bureaucratic infrastructure. It was thus that during the same summer, I found myself discussing IT systems, form letters, and filing systems with Astrid, a staff member at the Court. Discussing WECL detention cases, she explained that the first step is to input the information: location and dates of detention, the square meters of cell, the specific defects in the cell (rodents, insects, nonfunctioning toilets). This was the technical work that generated the spreadsheet I had seen in the judge's office. On rare occasions, one of these complaints might raise an issue not within well-established case law. A registry lawyer could refer such a case forward to be reviewed by a larger group of judges. But for the most part, she explained to me, "We have a machinery going."

The Court has moved to a system of templates and grouping like cases to manage a massive workflow. Yet for all the standardization, there is a high level of contextually specific knowledge that allows such templates to function. Astrid—who was central in developing these template systems for repetitive cases—described processes of removing everything extraneous and irrelevant in data from applications. This allowed quick, standardized responses to so-called clone cases. I was skeptical and asked whether all these cases could really be that similar. Yes, she nodded her head and explained to me that by now they have tens of cases from the same penal colonies. Someone in one of these colonies would get a judgment of a violation, receive compensation, and "go and tell his friend." The conditions in each colony at a given time are so well documented that when a case comes in, registry staff can enter the name of a penal colony and the dates and generate a judgment with only the specific grievances outlined in the case.

I was struck by Astrid's account because it entailed stripping down human suffering to its most technical and impersonal components. This process was paradoxically enabled by the contextual knowledge of specific penal colonies. They used documents, evidence, and cases of individual suffering to build up into a picture of a specific time and place. Registry staff could enter the dates and the prison location and "know" those penal colonies well enough to assess the validity and significance of any individual application. This required drawing from a detailed and specific body of knowledge. Astrid had no doubt that prisoners also talked—passing on specific knowledge and understanding of the ECtHR to their fellow inmates. This brings the distant Court into close and immediate proximity to prisoners' everyday lives. Thus she represented (real or imagined) sociality within the prison as a technology of access and knowledge-making through which prisoners translated harm into cash (if not justice). In turn, registry lawyers translated serial cases into a more complex and intimate knowledge of specific times and places in which harm unfolded.

The idea that prisoners in penal colonies (in this case in Russia) monetized the Court (cash in exchange for documented suffering) was something I encountered in other interviews with registry lawyers. While no one contested the appalling conditions of the prisons, people also recognized the limits of a single case to provide more than immediate monetary compensation. The translation between individual suffering and structural harm was not only a technical exercise. It also involved registry lawyers taking a stance on the moral, geopolitical and legal meaning of individual cases versus cases in the aggregate. Hundreds of Russian prison detention cases could be made to serve as evidence of the need for structural reform. In this way lawyers could translate countable units, individual violations, into a collective mass of human suffering. Quantity became a quality: structural political deficiencies in human rights compliance. At the same time, the mass of numbers took on meaning through background and foreground that shaped the meaning of an individual case. A violation of prison detention conditions for an individual applicant was given credence or made weighty by virtue of its similarity within a matrix of like cases. A lawyer could then translate this relationship of token and type from the symbolic economy of suffering into a monetary logic.

It is often the case that moving across ways of (ac)counting have moral as well as pragmatic effects. In her work on legal redress for Japanese colonial and wartime violence against Chinese forced laborers, anthropologist Yukiko Koga (2013) analyzes the "convergence of monetary and moral economies" (495) and translations among three forms of accounting for debt: giving voice to victims of violence, monetary compensation and legal responsibility. Similarly, in attributing cynical motives to prisoners to use the Court system like a cash machine, the lawyers I spoke to were assessing the moral standing of applicants, even as they acknowledged the tremendous suffering these victims faced. At the same time, they were also assessing their own moral standing as agents of a bureaucratic institution that could provide monetary compensation but not necessarily justice. It was not clear whether Astrid really knew that prisoners were talking. But her projected scene of intimacy, derived from her interpretation of serially submitted similar cases from the same space, created a sense of connection. It was an ethos of care in which distant places became proximate through specific kinds of knowledge: we know these prisoners, just as prisoners come to know us at the Court. This produced a feeling that such sites and places were known and seen, even in the moment they were being standardized. In the process, intimacy and understanding from the Court perspective and receipt of monetary compensation for prisoners replaced meaningful institutional change, at least from a short-term, individual perspective.

This familiarity paradoxically came from hundreds and hundreds of interchangeable, repetitive cases. Vera, another lawyer who also worked on prison cases, told me that she had quickly learned to recognize what kinds of language or complaints were really going to reach the level of a violation of human rights standards. She noted that if an applicant complains that "my bed is to narrow, my sheet is too thin," that is not sufficient to trigger the beginning of a case. If prisoners have "to sleep in turns, that's bad; if the toilet is too close to the table, that's pretty bad." Anything that hints at overcrowding "is a red flag," she said. She drew both on a set of genre conventions that prisoners used (and had learned to use) and specific knowledge of particular penal colonies. She told me that by this point, when they get a case from a particular prison, they know "in this particular jail the conditions are appalling."

Čarna Brković (2016) has argued that at a local scale, humanitarian subjects retain and even rely on complex social relations and networks. They are thus far from being bare life. Similarly, for the lawyers I spoke with, people in penal colonies are not (only) figures of bare life. They are also part of a contextual matrix of relations that make their situation knowable, actionable, and above all specific. This was clear when the registry staff I spoke with imagined the scene of prisoner interactions or spoke with intimate familiarity with specific penal colony conditions in particular places and times. Prisoners are represented in the most basic and socially stripped-down ways in the chart. However, getting to that chart was a socially embedded process. This is a different kind of "knowing" people than that described by Brković within a tightly knit Bosnian community. But when lawyers spoke in the idiom of knowing someone in a local context, it produced a deeper and more nuanced understanding of the scale of suffering. They then translated this knowledge into the kind of standardized and "distant" representation that allowed the judge to get through 50,000–60,000 cases and to maintain professional and emotional distance.

Intimacy and distance are thus effects of a massive bureaucratic apparatus in which people transit across quantities and qualities to ground relations of proximity and distanced perspective. At times, the number of cases distances workers at the Court from applicants, and at times, it brings them into intimate proximity. Such knowledge does not generally shift the work lawyers do or shape specific interactions between actual prisoners and lawyers. But it does enable different kinds of stances and action vis-à-vis human rights cases. Occasionally lawyers also bridged those stances. For example, Angelina, a lawyer who had been at the Court about five years and who worked on WECL cases, told me that the interaction with applicants is minimal. While it is not very "sympathique" for the applicants, in WECL cases, they no longer reply if the applicants write to follow up. Prisoners, she told me, have a lot of time and may write continuously. Answering them is not possible given their time constraints. However, she recounted one time in which she was "very proud" of herself. It involved a case in which the applicant had been so severely beaten by the police that he was rendered an invalid. After lodging the complaint, the applicant disappeared. The Court staff lost all contact. This had saddened her, because the case was so serious. It was also well-founded and close to completion. Angelina told me she had been able to dig through the huge file (she held out her hands to illustrate how thick it was) and find one old document with an old phone number. She called the number, and the applicant was there! It made her happy because, as she noted, it was the case of "a really innocent man."

As she recounted this incident to me, Angelina switched framings from a moment of immediacy and contact with an individual—mediated by the thick file in which she drew out information specific enough to reach out and connect with him. In countless other cases, inmates or applicants may reach out to her to no avail. The weightiness, the experience of distance come into clear perspective only against the one moment of narrating a fleeting encounter of closeness and connection.

Scholars have argued that scalemaking is a semiotically mediated process through which people organize knowledge through comparison across categories of space, size, and hierarchy (Gal and Irvine 2019; Carr and Lempert 2016) Such translations allow people to move across different epistemological and moral frameworks. These perspectives together point to how scaling works by helping people frame the meaning of particular events or actions through metaphors and terms that bundle moral, affective, political, economic, or technical meaning. One death becomes a legal injury; a quantity of deaths becomes a matter of geopolitical significance that calls for state level or interstate action; a larger quantity of deaths becomes legally actionable as a quality of moral harm (genocide) (Nelson 2015). Similarly, one can represent knowledge of the same contexts (say, Russian prison conditions) through metaphors or narratives of intimacy and closeness or of distance. One can "know" a Russian prison through idioms of familiarity that produce a sense of closeness. For example, one might imagine a scene of specific conversations, action, and planning (prisoners who meet to talk about success at the ECtHR). Likewise, one can create distance from that same knowledge through representations that emphasize the generic aspects of some Russian detention facilities: producing spreadsheets that reduce knowledge to the most basic and most general expression of specific contexts. This creates an effect of distancing. A judge may then take up the material or semiotic expression of that distancing (a spreadsheet) and use it to frame an affective experience of distance ("I can't and won't cry"). Key to this process is the movement between anchoring metaphors of quality (an incommensurable quality of suffering for one individual human being) or quantity (a multipage chart of all the instances of individual suffering reduced to commensurable and comparable instances of human harm).

Numbers as Narrative-Producing Perspective

By foregrounding individual cases against the background of similar cases, Court actors can claim to understand complex social settings and human rights harms. They ground evidence of their knowledge through bundling minimalist elements—even if this entails a projection or fantasy of the true local story. In so doing, they respond to the epistemological problem built into the heart of the human rights convention system, as well as the sovereignty problem, which hinges on the Court's ability to grasp the meaning of individual human rights violations better than domestic courts. In situating the one against the many and the many in terms of the one, Court actors manage the contradictions of the human rights system—not by solving them but through a dynamic movement among the positions and points.

Numbers then are ways to talk about perspective. Perspective in this case is also a way to ground the scope and scale of knowledge: what people can know about the world they are supposed to interpret through international human rights obligations. One can't interpret numbers without other kinds of reading practices. In the examples above, people work with aggregate numbers to stretch from individual cases to an analysis of structural problems. But not everyone I spoke to was totally convinced that the right to individual petition nor the aggregating logic of the ECHR system was the most just or effective way of handling cases. I spoke to one registry lawyer who was adamant that the Court ought to pick and choose exemplary cases. This would bring it into line with the practice of most other apex and constitutional systems. While Nada's perspective was less common among my interlocutors, her example reveals the importance of numbers as a way to ground narratives. A carefully selected individual case, she argued, could be just as, if not more important than the thousands of repetitive cases swamping the Court.

Nada was a passionate and eloquent interlocutor. Her ideas on the Court were somewhat controversial, but it was clear she had thought long and hard about how to make the Convention system work. We spoke about what an individual case means and what role it ought to play. For Nada, an individual case is important only as far as illuminates or serves as evidence of a general problem through the concrete specificity of a specific fact pattern. She explained to me that the right to individual petition gave the Court too narrow a perspective on individual cases. She contrasted this to the Department for the Execution of Judgments' "problem-based approach." She explained cases are grouped in execution depending on the problem that they raise. This created a very different logic and approach. In part, she noted that the problem with the Court was that it is still wedded to the "right of individual application."

Nada raised important points in our conversation: How can you really understand a particular context through an individual case? What is "perspective"? How do you know what you think you know is accurate or true? This epistemological problem requires finding creative ways to build structure and knowledge back into a human rights system composed of minimalist blocks. Nada's frustration with the individual approach was evident in her comments to me, as well as in the charts covering the walls of her office. She took me through them—charts that outlined the historical role and logic of the Convention system, Protocol 11, and the relationship among different parts of the institution, including flows of relationships among cases, judgments, and execution.

Nada's narrative pivoted as she walked me through her charts. In so doing, she embodied the dynamism among the individual case and the larger context that the convention institutions made possible. She used the charts to explain to me how the individualizing logic created specific problems. She argued that the Court should return to its pre–Protocol 11 days when a commission filtered cases and took on only a few of its choosing. Nada noted that with the elimination of this system and the massive influx of eastern European cases in the 1990s, the Court was now "paying the consequences."

When Nada noted the Court was paying the consequences, she meant it figuratively and literally. Individual petition was slowing down the work of structural change. But it also created a system where rights were translated into a monetary logic. The right to individual petition fueled the focus on monetary compensation for violations. Thus the additive and quantitative logic of the Court became the additive and quantitative logic of cash. The Court has "to be brought back to reality" and needs to understand how things work on the ground, she told me. It has the "reflex that everything can be solved by money," but, she explained, if that's the response, then you increase the Court's caseload, because many people come to Court with repetitive cases looking for monetary compensation at the individual level. This, she said, "is conducive to no one solving the problem." The Court treats each case separately and thus it is hard to deal with the underlying structural issue. People bring cases for money, reinforcing the relationship between a quantity of cases (one) and a quantity of cash. This equivalence displaced other acts of scaling from quantity (one violation) into qualities (structural violence). Here Nada flagged an epistemological problem. The focus on the individual case in and cash payment out stymies the work of a deeper analysis of state violence. As individual cases are monetized, the system is locked into a logic that can never scale from one to many. This makes it hard, in her words, "to figure out what the underlying problem really is."

Nada believed there was a role to play for the individual case but only if a singular case is translated not into monetary compensation but into political will and advantage. In other words, for the one to scale to the many—from a quantity of one to a quality of political change—it needs to be made commensurable not with cash but with narrative significance. I asked Nada, with all the problems of backlog and the failure to change things structurally, what was the role for the Court? She told me that the Court "remains important political leverage. People come here as a measure of last resort. . . . They want the problem to be fixed." The Court, she went on to say, has the "privilege to address general problems through individual cases." The stories and specifics of personal suffering, the "human aspect" is "what gives you leverage." Nada pointed to the constitutional system in the United States—a system that does not grant the right to individual petition but picks and chooses cases that advance case law in significant ways. One case can stand in for the principles and values enshrined in a founding document (the Constitution) such that its meaning is enhanced or translated into the qualities of constitutional law. This translation from an individual case to legal and constitutional principle makes an individual case more than the sum of its parts. It is the opposite of a logic where justice as compensation rests in the commensurability of suffering and money. Pointing to the constitutional approach, Nada emphasized the role of narrative. She referred to the iconic imagery and narrative of *Brown v. Board of Education*: a young African American girl being escorted by police into school during the era of segregation. That narrative and imagery had power because it was a shared story of "a little Black girl having to walk into school." She added, "Everyone knew there was a little girl. . . . Without the individual story, it wouldn't be legitimate to ask for changes."

My conversation with Nada demonstrated the complex acts of translation and possible pathways of analyzing and framing individual cases to reach different ends: an individual case could be commensurable with cash in a logic of monetization. Or it could be made to anchor a politically authoritative call for structural change if one case was interpreted through narrative and tropes that framed an individual story. Or cases could be bundled—as they are in the execution process or pilot judgments to generate evidence of a need for structural change. Either way, the function of the Convention system and the ability of legal actors operating within and through it relied on orientations toward their work that demanded they make sense of numbers, quantities, and qualities.

However, between individual or aggregate logics, what made Nada's talk of numbers remarkable was the effect she generated in moving dynamically and constantly among the coordinates defined by qualities and quantities. For Nada, knowledge and perspective took the form of "seeing" a problem. Here sight or vision was also a kind of motion or relationship to one's body—reading documents becomes vision—or seeing the contour of real-world problems. An individualizing logic made such vision impossible. Treating cases individually meant that "the Court doesn't see" the larger issues at hand. She used the example of a famous optical illusion—the old woman or the young woman—in which entirely different pictures are generated out of the same image, depending on perspective (see figure 4.2). In this case, the difference in interpretation has serious consequences. "Everyone is looking at the same thing and seeing something different. The Court sees the individual circumstances, but not the problem behind it," she told me.

Perspective was a recurring theme in our discussion. She spoke of her perspective moving among institutions at the Council of Europe, her perspective as someone not from France, with training in both her home country and the French legal system, and the importance of her own complex family history,

FIGURE 4.2. "My Wife and Mother-in-Law," by W. E. Hill (1915). This is the optical illusion to which Nada referred in our conversation. Source: Library of Congress Prints and Photographs Division, Washington, DC, http://hdl.loc.gov/loc.pnp/ds.00175.

which positioned her in multiply minoritized ways in a long history of European state violence against ethnic and religious minorities. Nada's comments were shot through with metaphors of perspective, part-whole relationships, and the impossibility of knowing. No one, she told me, is seeing the system or the problems "as a whole." Yet seeing and knowing—perspective—required different interpretive frameworks to scale from numbers to qualities. Nada reached for the following example to make this clear: She had recently taken her son and father to Italy, and they were standing in a cathedral in Rome. There were two statues on the wall, facing each other. From the perspective on the ground, they seemed equal in size to her. Then the guide explained they were each fifteen meters tall. That, she said, is what the Convention is (and here she took the Convention booklet and held it up for me to see). Standing with this in their hands, applicants feel equal in size to states, and can face them. It makes them feel equal with the state. The Court, she told me, gives her hope. "People still come here, people who suffer, trying to change things in their daily life." The idea that the Convention system could give enough perspective to tackle persistent forms of state violence was something she kept reaching for. Doing so entailed fixing a relationship between cases—individual cases at the Court—and perspective—an understanding of the structural issues on the ground.

In Nada's analysis, we can see how it is not just the existence of different ways of approaching numbers across the system that is most significant. It is the play between them. The act of comparison and contrast among and between different theories of numbers gives the ECHR system its dynamism and helps manage constitutive tensions and institutional impossibilities. The comparison and contrast between *kinds of numeric accounting* is absolutely central to how people project and experience the authority of an international legal institution. Numbers in this sense serve as a perspectival medium—they allow for what legal anthropologist Charles Goodwin (1994) has called "professional vision." As he noted in his analysis of the legal use of video evidence in the Rodney King trial, "the ability to see a meaningful event is not a transparent, psychological process but instead a socially situated activity accomplished through the deployment of a range of historically constituted discursive practices. . . . All vision is perspectival and lodged within endogenous communities of practice" (606). Perspective, then, is an effect of mechanisms for counting and accounting for cases and the representational narratives they make possible.

Pivoting among quantities and qualities, the one and the many, and the individual case and the bundling of cases into pictures of structural violence created a perpetual, dynamic motion with comparative purchase. Nada's comparisons that took on the metaphors of space, hierarchy, and ultimately perspective. Her pivots were a response to an epistemological problem grounded in the commitment to knowing and understanding human rights harms and state violence from a distance, one case at a time.

Conclusion

What effectiveness or justice mean and for whom depends on the narratives in which cases are embedded and the kinds of actions that those narratives make possible. Differences in accounting are not a problem per se. And one can look at cases from different perspectives to identify or highlight their narrative and legal significance. In this sense, heterogeneous forms of accounting are important in creating a flexible and workable human rights system. Different methods of calculation support and legitimate contrasting ways to define the scope of a problem and determine the scale and methods of intervention. This flexibility can be frustrating. But it is also one of the resources that draw and bind people to an international human rights system in the pursuit of judicialized approaches to social change. Beyond just the quantification of rights as an effect of power, accounting has implications for people's experience of rights as a way of being in and acting on the world.

As Anne Meike Fechter (2023) has argued in her analysis of vernacular humanitarianism in Cambodia, the idea of making "every person count" allows her interlocutors to scale seemingly singular, small acts of care into an ethos that far exceeds the meaning of any one act. By this logic, individual petition expands rather than diminishes the reach of care, because it supports a quality (of conscience, as in the conscience of Europe) that exceeds the rationalizing and economistic logics of law. From this perspective an individual (as a singular quantity) can support a narrative rendered commensurable with justice (as a quality). And yet, as Nada argues, the conditions of possibility for this are that the ECHR system does *not* hear every case. Individual significance is an effect of institutional constraint. It is a different, although related version of the "treadmill of paradox" that an interlocutor pointed to in the epigraph to this chapter. Individual petition is both the condition of possibility for every person to count and yet threatens to overwhelm the system such that nobody does. This tension lies at the heart of whether the ECHR system ought to function as a true constitutional order that would hear cases based on legal significance versus individual right to petition.

I have argued in this chapter that number talk allows diverse actors within and across the Court to communicate. It is a shared framework for evidence to argue for what has been done and what is left to do. When talking in numbers, judges, registry lawyers, and advocates always also must stretch from numbers to patterns and from patterns to qualities or types of action. Counting cases will never add up to a singular number because the act of producing discrete, countable units is fundamentally an act of evaluation and intervention (Mol 2003). These different kinds of "professional visions" are also ethical commitments to the ECHR system. They shape people's ideas about what it is for, and whom it serves. At the same time, number talk circumscribes how expansive that conversation will ever be. In situating the one against the many and the many in terms of the one, Court actors manage the contradictions of the human rights system—not by solving them but by moving dynamically among positions and points.

FIVE

Litigating Human Rights in Time
Strategic Litigation and Temporal Advocacy

SHORTLY AFTER I BEGAN interviews and fieldwork on the ECHR system in 2016, I began to hear about crises in the system. Whether it was the "crisis of implementation," the "crisis of noncompliance with judgments," or the "backlog crisis," people narrated an ECHR system that had moved from a golden age to one of decline. Some cited external threats, backlash in domestic political agendas, or rising conflicts within and between member states. Others turned inward to critique the administrative and workflow systems of the Court. These evaluative positions often took the form of comments on the speed or intensity of the work in the ECHR system and the Court especially. Those who felt the Court had pulled back too much from a pro-human rights agenda talked of the Court slipping backwards to more conservative early days. Others saw the Court's sluggishness in processing cases as a threat to justice. Still others equated particular judicial decisions as moving case law too fast. In each instance, the metaphor of speed was a way to comment on the rule of law, subsidiarity, and the Court's jurisdiction.

Narratives of crisis, rupture, and reversal are examples of time talk in the ECHR system. As Georgina Ramsay has noted in her analysis of tropes of displacement and people on the move, the talk of crisis is often used to "signal a distinct temporality of urgency and exceptionality that works to overlook the need for more longitudinal and in-depth attention to particular circumstances and events" (2020, 386). Crisis talk, then, is a way to make sense of long-standing, often structural issues. Yet the framing of urgency or rupture

FIGURE 5.1.   Council of Europe sign with graffito asking "When" in response to the placard's claims to be "Guardian of Human Rights, Democracy and the Rule of Law." Source: Photo by author.

can paradoxically make it hard to keep those structural issues at the fore. Crisis often signals people's experiences of disorder in how the world *ought* to work. It is thus more a prescriptive theory of the relationship between time and agency than a descriptive picture of the state of the world (Muir 2021; Roitman 2013).

Planning or talking about the time legal processes *ought* to take was also a way to authorize the role the Court should play and whom it should serve. For example, a lawyer who had moved from the registry to another part of the Council expressed the problem in terms of the speed and tempo of case law. He noted:

> It is a question of tempo . . . a question of speed. I think the Court at some point develop[ed] certain areas too quickly. . . . People of the older generation . . . see this speed [as] damaging the court. [In response] it is important to recede a

little bit, to entrench, to protect some core set of values and principles, and not to rush into developing new unexplored areas.

That my interlocutor took a stance through the language of tempo makes sense. People's relationship to the European Convention system is shot through with different experiences of time—heterogeneous rhythms, horizons, and intensities.[1] These may shift over the course of a day, a case, or a lifetime. Registry lawyers talked about the flurry of communications in conjunction with a Grand Chamber judgment (see chapter 3). And they characterized the job as slow and routinized, checking the clock against stacks of files on their desk. Lawyers working on the execution of judgments faced intense, short-term cycles of preparation for Committee of Ministers' Human Rights meetings. These ran parallel to the painstaking tracking of cases over long periods. Judges, too, spoke of the massive workload in terms of temporally mediated experience. A seasoned judge reflecting on his early years in Strasbourg noted:

> It's interesting, because when you land here . . . the working methods are totally different. Practically, you don't know what's hit you. . . . . The first thing I remember is arriving here, and two days after I had taken my office, a number of drafts land on my desk, and I [had to] decide all these cases. . . . To be honest, it took me more than four years to understand finally . . . not to understand, but to accept how the Court works.

Yet in the same interview, he also spoke in different temporal terms—as many judges did when they described their ethical commitments to human rights and justice. Invoking cosmic imaginaries to describe the inevitable progress of the Court, he noted Galileo's quietly muttered riposte to his inquisitors about the movement of the earth around the sun. "And yet it moves," the judge told me. "Like Galileo . . . said, 'Yes, I recant. But . . . in spite of that, it moves.' . . . So in spite of everything, it [the Court] works." Like the cosmic time through which the earth inscribes an orbit around the sun, so too do the daily rhythms of the Court allow it to move toward some arc of justice.

Others who participate in the ECHR system also narrate their experiences in temporal terms. Although I was unable to interview applicants directly, I spoke with human rights lawyers who represented their clients' experience of harm and violence as both eventful moments and a slow grind of waiting years for resolution of their cases. One litigator told me, "The worst case I was involved in was [X], which is a rape case. [The applicant] was raped shortly before her fourteenth birthday, and she got judgment when she was twenty-three. . . . It takes a pretty extraordinary person to go through that kind of process." From this perspective, the slow grind of cases through the system is antithetical to justice rather than its building block. In turn, those advocates and strategic litigators who brought cases had to tack back and forth between the individual experiences of an applicant, the painstaking steps of exhausting domestic remedies over years, and an imagined future for the case's life as enduring precedent.

Managing a case's tolls on clients required litigators to work across the differential temporalities of cases. One interlocutor, a longtime London-based litigator, Sarah, recounted speaking to an applicant on the eve of her appearance before Strasbourg. Sarah described the client's sense of defeat: "There were a few things about the hearing that were upsetting. One is that the night before, I sat down with [the applicant] and said, 'This is what we're going to say on your behalf.' . . . And she just put her hands up and said, 'I don't care what you say. Doesn't matter'—she'd just been so disempowered by the process." That Sarah's case was high stakes and would continue to be a significant win from a gender-justice perspective didn't matter to the applicant, at least in that moment. The case has had a significant afterlife and endures through precedent and subsequent organizing in reproductive rights. But what is powerfully enduring from a legal standpoint is painfully so for applicants themselves. Lawyers were not alone in expressing frustration with the tolls of the system on applicants. One judge who had extensive human rights litigation experience prior to coming to the Court noted, "Quite often we have cases raising issues of custody rights, and because of the way the whole process works, we come to hear those cases five, six years down the road. Those kids are already adults. I mean, what the hell are we doing here? We're deciding something that's completely gone by the time we decided. That is frustrating." In the next chapter, I examine the stakes of keeping cases open and what that means for a broader sense of justice, weighed against slow, incremental change.

Across my interviews with judges, lawyers, and NGO advocates, people made sense of the slowness of institutional time against the punctuated rhythm of events or shocks to the system: a coup and a subsequent government crackdown in Turkey, Brexit, the war in Ukraine, and Russia's exit from the Council of Europe. Such punctuated experiences of crisis or shock could throw the entire system into new perspective, highlighting both a lifetime of investment in human rights and the system's fragility. One senior registry lawyer I interviewed days after the Brexit vote greeted my question "How are you doing?" with the dark humored reply, "Oh, you mean besides the world going to hell and the undoing of everything we've worked for the last thirty years?" Yet in that conversation and over multiple conversations we had, this sense of crisis did not stop him from patiently talking with me about the nitty-gritty of day-to-day rhythms of the Court in equally powerful ways.

In this chapter I explore temporalities of human rights through an analysis of their material and narrative structure. And I examine the kinds of action that such temporal frameworks facilitate. I argue that talking about time isn't only a way to make sense of law. It is a way to harness and navigate the contradictory and heterogeneous affordances of legal institutions. When people narrate their experience of time, they are also crafting a sense of agency and efficacy in the world. In this sense, learning how to manage contrasting experiences of time, speed, and intensity is central to the art of human rights advocacy (Greenberg 2024, 2021b). This includes formulating and enacting different goals and strategies that make sense within different temporal arcs (Ahmann 2018). When people work with human rights, they learn to engage in temporal arbitrage, through which they juggle competing and at times contradictory goals and professional commitments.

To make this argument, I focus on strategic litigators or cause lawyers, a group who are skilled in working across different temporal orders. Litigators are highly attuned to the multiple temporalities of rights. And they have learned to effectively harness the flows, rhythms, and intensities of the ECHR system. They also participate in framing and reframing the meaning of litigation through shifting narratives of time—what a case means, how long it ought to take, and against what timelines it ought to be judged as effective. Such competing experiences of time have sparked new advocacy strategies, ethical commitments, and litigator subjectivities. These professional identities are often tied up in the contradictions of the job (Sarat and Scheingold 2001; Marshall and Hale 2014). This includes the immediate needs of individual applicants and the goal to build out an enduring legacy through jurisprudence.

Material for this chapter is drawn from interviews with several strategic litigators who came from the same professional networks and organizations in the mid-1990s to early 2000s. Many of them have shaped contemporary strategic litigation in the ECtHR. They provided the earliest and most widely circulating models of strategic litigation and have trained a generation of lawyers across the Council member states. Using long-term advocacy strategies, litigators have learned to use time itself as a human rights resource. They do so not only by bringing cases but by using litigation to engage different institutional channels and forms of publicity. They also use cases as a diagnostic tool for analyzing the conditions for long-term change (Greenberg 2024).

As I show, this knowledge was hard won. At times their goals bring litigators into conflict with the clients and constituents to whom they are beholden. But in seeking to shape not only cases but their reception and meaning within ECHR institutional channels, they have helped produce what one senior lawyer in the Council's DEJ called the system's "institutional patience." This means using the institutional channels for moving and working a case slowly through the system. This has the benefit of keeping a case open and alive until a coalition of diplomats, lawyers, and civil society advocates can create conditions for more robust implementation of a judgment to support structural and social change (Greenberg 2024). Litigators inhabit the slowness and exhaustion of building a case as well as the excitement of winning. Through it all, strategic litigators self-reflexively play and experiment with the duration, rhythm, intensity, and speed of litigation-driven change, while also self-consciously reflecting on its pitfalls and limits—a process I call temporal advocacy.

Strategic Litigation and Cause Lawyering at the ECHR

Strategic litigators, or cause lawyers, bring cases to advance legal principles by building precedent.[2] They might attempt to establish new doctrinal norms—for example, what kinds of evidence judges ought to use when interpreting the specific facts of a case (see chapter 6). Or the strategy might include expanding rights to new protected groups. For example, several litigators have brought Article 8 cases to the ECHR. These are cases that fall under the right to private life through which people might try to expand the notion of the family to include same-sex partnerships (see chapter 1). Other strategic cases might push the scope of the Court's jurisdiction, creating new linkages among Court protections and people outside geographic European territory—for example, on the high seas (*Hirsi Jamaa and Others v. Italy*) or in countries with a large European military or peacekeeping presence (*Al Skeini and Others v. The United Kingdom*). Litigators can also bring serial cases on a similar issue—for example, to make patterns of state violence visible (Kurban 2016).

Most people I spoke with dated ECHR strategic litigation efforts to the late 1990s and early 2000s. The combination of institutional changes and an explosion of post-1989 civil society development and donor funding created a climate for experimentation and organizing (Hann and Dunn 1996; Guilhot 2005). In addition, the post–Cold War realignment of state power and the rise of an international democratization industry created global conditions for cause lawyering across state borders and at the international level (Sarat and Scheingold 2001). These shifts were central to what Garth and Dezalay (2012) have called the construction of transnational justice, a period in which there was a proliferation of new international legal fora and transnational legal professionals.

Early strategic litigation in Strasbourg relied on models coming out of North America. But it can be traced to a handful of organizations based in the UK with ties to local partners and lawyers (see also chapter 6). These included the Kurdish human rights project, the European Roma Rights Center, and Interrights, a London-based strategic litigation group that brought many landmark cases to the ECtHR in the early 2000s. Although these are by no means the only groups of people bringing cases, these networks were a hub for experimentation. Many of these lawyers would go on to other organizations, such as Amnesty International and the Open Society Justice Initiative, European Human Rights Advocacy Center, and the Aire Center.

This period of ECHR strategic litigation is best described by those who were involved from the beginning. In 2018 I conducted an interview with a UK-based lawyer, Darian, who had been involved in human rights since 1990. He first got involved while working in his home country just after the fall of state socialism. His narrative is exemplary because it embodies the chaotic energy, hopefulness, and contingency of human rights approaches in Eastern Europe just after 1989. His career trajectory conveys how early litigators experimented with strategic approaches to legal temporalities. Initially a flurry of activity, litigation then gave rise to slower, long-term strategies of bringing cases from the beginning through domestic systems all the way to Strasbourg. As the years went on, strategic litigators sense of the time necessary for their advocacy also lengthened. Rather than focusing on one case, going through the system, and ending with the punctuated event of a legal victory, litigators began to consider an even longer temporal arc for judging the efficacy of their work. This is evident in a collective shift in litigation zeitgeist in the mid 2010s. Focus shifted from winning a case to execution of a judgment and implementation of subsequent policies on the ground.

The links between litigation strategies and temporal advocacy are clear in Darian's account of the stages of his career. He first described in vivid detail how he had become involved in democratization efforts in 1990 as an election observer for his country's first democratic elections. The interview setting—a professional office in a high-rise building in London, with cool air conditioning and noise-dampening carpet—could not have been more different from the scene he described as the very beginning of his human rights career:

> I started as a volunteer in [the] first months of 1990 for an NDI [National Democratic Institute]-funded election observation. . . . I had the car, so my thing was I drove around for voter education. . . . I think everyone contributed; some contributed time. I think they [the NDI] paid for my petrol, but Saturday and Sunday I would drive. The car was a Trabant. And so driving six hours in a Trabant. I'm not sure I can do it now.

Even in retrospective narrative form, descriptions of early human rights efforts were replete with material and sensorial qualities. Darian's description of those early days had a sense of a thick and embodied present that mapped onto the inchoate and uncertain beginnings of human rights. The experience of time and speed was everywhere, attuning advocates to the rhythms of organizing and shaping uniquely time-inflected narratives and sensitivities. For Darian, the experience of the energy of the moment was inseparable from his memory of

> the noise. There is no radio in [a] Trabant. Because when you sit, your knees are over your ears, and so you can't hear the engine. We would drive like breakneck speed, because it was far—there were no motorways. Cram five people in the Trabant. . . . At some point, I remember that they asked me, I have them somewhere at home, to do like little brochures about human rights. . . . I have no recollection what was in there. . . . I think we translated for the first time the European Convention. And actually when Parliament suddenly decided that they want to ratify, they asked that NGO and they used that text that I translated. . . . Actually they had several terrible mistakes because I didn't understand all the case law.

That early democratization efforts were simultaneous with the experience of driving breakneck speed crowded into a Trabant reflects the car's storied presence in late-socialist and early postsocialist lifeworlds—a car beautifully documented by Daphne Berdahl (2001) that was known for its signature noise. The fly-by-the-seat-of-your-pants speed mapped well to some of the other more contingent and haphazard aspects of those early years of human rights. The speed of the car gives way to the suddenness and contingency of the translation of the Convention, which later becomes institutionalized in much slower moving and textually enduring ways.

As Laura Bear (2014) argues, the rhythms of time and work are inseparable from the embodied experience of embedded political economies. Likewise, Darian noted that there was "a lot of money for the first twenty years." It was also, as others commented to me in interviews, a time of creativity and openness. The combined sense of possibility hit large amounts of funding—part of a broader period of rapid democratization efforts. In addition to funding, the sense of newness and intensity mapped well onto an understanding of social change that was grounded in innovative experimentation. Darian told me, "It was this ferment of creating sophisticated new, entirely new legal systems. So there was general atmosphere: let's have constitutional courts, let's have good legislation, let's reform our criminal code or criminal procedure code. Let's invite everyone under the sun to come and teach us."

This "complete opening" gave way to the ideas to "create the law and then we'll create ecosystem of lawyers, judges, travel, translation." Darian recounted a remarkable example of the combination of funding and circumstance that gave birth to the beginning of a human rights infrastructure and knowledge:

> In fact, when I was a student here (in the UK) in the early 90s, I bumped into a philanthropist at a college reception in Oxford, and she said, "Oh, you're the first [person from his country] I've met. What can I do for [your country]?"
> I said, "Well, how much money do you want to spend?"
> "I have 5,000 pounds."
> I said, "Let's buy all the English language human rights books we can find, because they will prohibit it; you can't get them in the public libraries."
> And she said, "Okay. Well, I don't want to give you a check."
> I said, "Let's go together to Blackwell's. We'll put out a list and you can buy the books." . . .
> And that's what she did. Five thousand pounds. Five boxes.

Five boxes and, in his words, the "feeling that anything's possible" shaped his narrative of the emergence of strategic litigation. In those early years, he noted, "We just invented [legal advocacy] as we went along, based on judgments and memorials of previous lawyers, trying a little bit to push the envelope every single time, expanding their understanding of the rights . . ." The sense of urgency and speed led to a flurry of activity and a quick proliferation of cases. In their efforts to work with and develop local legal partners, the organization didn't have a great deal of control over the quality or coherence of the cases they were bringing. They worked with the domestic records and files they already had. But at some point, these contingent and haphazard approaches gave rise to a longer vision of strategy. It was out of this milieu of experimentation that early litigators eventually hit on a model for working a case slowly through a domestic system.

> The best strategy was to construct a case from the beginning. . . . So let's find a case that just happened, then introduce a Strasbourg argument before the prosecutor . . . basically constructing the case from the very beginning, so you more or less have control over the evidence, how it was produced, kept, interpreted, and presented to domestic courts.

What emerged out of these early efforts was not only a model for individual cases but a rhythm and workflow that operated simultaneously on cyclical time (of monthly trainings with local partners in a two- to three-year cycle) and linear time (of progress on cases and ultimately the building of case law). In the process, litigation as a flow of cases became the basis of litigation as a form of community building and knowledge production. Darian explained:

> So there will be like fifteen or twenty crack troops for Strasbourg litigation, from Georgia, Ukraine, Russia, Poland, Bulgaria. They'll come, say, for Saturday, once a month, and they will deal with freedom of expression and fair trial. And then we'll hold surgeries where they'll come with their cases. . . . Usually a couple of cases will crop up, and then we maintain one with that lawyer. . . . It created cohorts of a small number of very good human rights lawyers, and they started working among themselves. . . . That was essentially an informal structure over a ten-year period to flood the Court, ideally with good cases.

According to Darian, this short-term approach of flooding the Court produced a longer-term flow of cases. In this way, advocates used one set of temporal strategies and rhythms to build out the infrastructure and relationships through which they could sustain longer-term visions and approaches. Cycles of cases give rise to the accumulation of knowledge, relationships, and professional networks. These were enabled by and materialized through the case files themselves. This led not only to organizational changes but to new ways of understanding the arc and significance of their work. And as cases accumulated, Darian and others involved in strategic litigation began to see both the limits and different possibilities of the work that such cases could do. Similarly, the strategic litigation case as a singular win with no follow-up began to hit its limits. Darian noted:

> Litigation was so slow. We needed to figure out a few cases that could become the public face of the problem and eventually could generate pressure from Strasbourg for a changing of the law. But to me, if a country doesn't want to change a law, it can drag its feet by saying, "We have no money [or there is insufficient] political consensus." Very quickly states learned that the sanctions for noncompliance are pretty mild. And so at some point, I think after five or six years, we realized unless the litigation is part of a much bigger thing, then you never really know which one [will be] decisive.
>
> JG: Did you become disillusioned with the possibilities then or just change tactics?
>
> D: I don't know. I mean I became tired of case/case/case after ten years. I just couldn't do it any longer. But also partly I realized that you need this ecosystem approach of civil society. . . . I had ignored it, partly because of the excitement of winning case after case, but at some point, I thought it would be more interesting and more impactful to work on the whole thing rather than only on cases.

As Darian's experience attests, the very mechanism that made litigation effective—slowing it down to work it through a domestic system and accumulate materials—became a barrier to conceptualizing change in more lasting and impactful ways. The excitement of winning a case had fueled an intensity of activity. But the sluggishness of the case as the central mechanism for creating strong, careful argumentation and evidence through the domestic system began to wear litigators down. For Darian it was a question of getting "tired of case after case." Exhaustion shifted from a strategy to a phenomenological experience of strategic litigation. In between the contrast of cases as events and cases as process, Darian offered a different understanding of what litigation was really for. It could also be an anchor for creating a more robust "ecosystem" for social change.

Exhaustion as Temporal Strategy and Experience

Exhaustion of domestic remedies is necessary for any strong case litigated in Strasbourg. For one, the condition of admissibility for a case is that it exhausts—or goes through—all available domestic venues before it can be heard in the ECtHR. But exhaustion is not only a formal requirement. It is a means to use a case to accumulate the necessary materials that become evidence of a potential violation. Exhaustion is the slow-moving process of accumulating case file documents, like testimony, witness statements, and judicial proceedings and rulings, as cases move across every available forum within a domestic judicial system. When applicants bring a case to the ECtHR, they must include in the file evidence of exhaustion. This includes records of court proceedings, judgments, and other material that both establishes attempts at exhaustion and provides evidence of the deliberations, procedures, and approaches of the domestic system. It is these that the judges assess—the records of multiple interactions between the applicant (and their lawyers) and legal and state institutions (for example, police if there is an investigative component) or legislative records (if, for example, the right violated pertains to law or policy).

The accretion of these materials in turn generates the thick materiality of the application, which in turn builds out support for ECtHR jurisdiction and authority. The need for exhaustion is grounded in the notion of subsidiarity. The Court must defer to national legal and political systems in the implementation and protection of the ECHR rights. The domestic system has the first obligation to adjudicate the case in a rights-compliant way. The balance between European supervision and subsidiarity is grounded in this slow-moving process. In this sense, exhaustion is the practical application of rule-of-law principles. It is the check in the system to prevent international judicial overreach into domestic legal and political processes.

To exhaust is thus to build the basis of the ECHR system over time, through documents—to create the materials through which lawyers can assess and categorize cases and on the basis of which future ECtHR judges can rule. It is also necessary for building the legal warrant for judicial authority. A case file creates evidence of exhaustion by layering interactions among applicant, domestic courts, and the Convention. In this sense, intertextuality—or the relationships among texts and the meaning these relationships accrue—requires a temporal component (Mertz 2007). Exhaustion is a technical requirement that produces a material record in which Court authority is enacted at a future point.

But as much as exhaustion was a critical step in building out new precedents, it also had its limits. The slow, serial flow of cases was also professionally and experientially exhausting. In light of this experience, some litigators began to rethink their temporal strategies in relationship to the *experience* of time itself. Was the punctuated eventness of winning a case enough of a victory in relationship to the long arc of litigation strategy? What else might be built in the process? As Darian and other litigators I spoke with noted, after years of winning cases but not seeing judgments implemented, human rights advocates began to contend with the limits of a system. They began to move past the judgment as the ultimate outcome of their work. And with this new perspective, they also reassessed what successful human rights advocacy meant, who was involved, and how long it would take to achieve. As their sense of human rights time changed, so too did their use of institutionally mediated temporalities.

Agatha was a longtime and highly experienced strategic litigator who had operated out of several London-based organizations. This long-haul grind sparked a personal and professional reevaluation of what human rights litigators should be doing from a strategic perspective. She described a career trajectory in which she moved from focusing on litigation as a goal in and of itself to litigation as one part of a larger strategy focused on community building and advocacy *after* a judgment of a violation. This shift was not sparked, in her words, by a "Eureka moment." Rather:

> It's about being a bit exhausted by something and then going to have a chat with a few other people . . . and saying, "Okay, what do you think?" And just sharing and learning from others' experience. . . . I think a shift in strategy . . . also really depends on what you are trying to do with the strategic litigation. Is it actually to obtain a precedent that will have ramifications for everyone? Is it to raise awareness but at the same time perhaps [to] try to solve the problem?

Strategic litigation had really taken off in the early 2000s. But many people remarked to me that it had slowed down and seemingly disappeared by the time I began my research in the mid-2010s. One reason was the drying up of donor money. For donors, the excitement and "eventness" of winning cases was no longer a compelling investment. Just as cases were being exhausted, people spoke of donor litigation fatigue. Those who had been engaged in strategic litigation for almost two decades had to reconsider the scope and meaning of litigation against new professional and personal timelines. They began to revisit not only the time frame for winning a case but what it meant to be an effective litigator.

It was in this context that litigators were increasingly concerned that their efforts were being undermined by growing noncompliance by member states. What was the benefit of winning a case if it couldn't be effectively implemented? As their sense of the time frame for litigation changed, their analysis of the actors involved in upholding the rule of law also expanded. Indeed, as Agatha, who I interviewed with another colleague, Arnold, in their shared London office in 2018 noted,

> I think we are facing various existential questions in the human rights system at the moment. And if we're not getting implementation, even in the European Court decisions . . . it's important that for the rule of law and everything else that these decisions are implemented as well. But that's when you do need to invest time and resources over a longer time in most cases.

This shift to a focus on implementation opened an even longer horizon for a case. It stemmed from a shared awareness that winning the case was not enough for the system to be effective. Cases needed to actually translate into on-the-ground change. And the system needed to produce compliance for the rule of law to work.

Implementation Time

Agatha and Arnold's changing attitudes toward the efficacy of strategic litigation were part of a larger shift that I observed among lawyers and advocates working in the ECHR system. The intensified focus on implementation was evident in a public event that I attended in London in 2018 at the storied Chatham House.[3] I took my seat in an entirely packed house among a chatting and buzzing crowd. I recognized several faces from various human rights organizations across London: heads of local NGOs and international NGO legal staff, strategic litigators, human rights academics and practitioners. The panel discussion was on twenty-five years of lessons learned in strategic litigation. It followed the publication of Open Society Justice Initiative's multiyear inquiry into strategic human rights litigation. The organization had recently published a series of reports (e.g., 2016a, 2016b). These included extensive research and reflection outlining the goals, impacts, and on-the-ground significance of the strategic litigation approach. The speakers who gathered that evening were there to reflect on a range of cases: from the critical case of Roma education rights in Eastern Europe to indigenous land claim cases in West Africa and a South Asian case concerning torture in custody. Each speaker sounded a note of caution in their comments: what they had learned over two and a half decades was that winning the case was not enough to enact real change. Litigation was only the beginning. It required a different investment in time and in strategic partnerships than the earlier "event"-focused approach of simply winning a case.

Shifts in strategic litigation approaches meant moving to a different temporal framework for judging effective action. And this reframing was precisely what happened through collective interactions at the Chatham House event. Presenters and participants reworked the meaning of litigation by reframing the temporal frameworks through which it might be understood. One speaker, longtime strategic litigator Jim Goldstone, began his opening remarks by revisiting popular critiques of litigation as simply taking too long to bring results. In response to these imagined critics, he noted that strategic litigation is "best understood as a process, rather than a single binary outcome. . . . It is a means to the end of change, rather than an end in itself." Goldstone and other participants presented litigation as a framework for building relationships that themselves formed an infrastructure in and through time. These relationships, Goldstone noted, were "recursive and reinforcing." And, he added, "whether litigators or individual plaintiffs or social activists should initiate a case is often less important than that they act in ways that are self-consciously and mutually reinforcing." It is "best as part of a broader social change strategy, not a one-off process, but iterative and incremental as a series of cases that build on one another over time."

This emphasis on cases as processes that build relationships out rather than only forward in time was something I encountered in other interviews around the same time. It is exemplary of the idea that people's experiences of time are often expressed as much in spatial metaphors and understanding (Bakhtin 1982; Munn 1992; Carr and Lempert 2016). In my interview with Agatha in London that same summer, she echoed the idea that the work of cases was necessarily "a tool of empowerment" that was intended to "develop relationships." Both Agatha and Arnold contrasted winning a case with the more important and long-term process of building relationships as a tool to systemic change. Agatha explained:

> The goal is that strategic litigation within any of these models is about creating systemic change. I think that is the model whether you are [dealing with] fifty cases on torture in Turkey or whether you're dealing with one case, which is so big and affects so many people and has so many ramifications and you've got a fifteen-year history of working on it. I think the goal is still to create change. Litigation is an advocacy tool [that needs to be thought out]. Otherwise you can lose sight of what the end goal is and just keep going and going and going.

In contrast to just "going and going," a linear notion of cases stretching out into an uncertain future, litigators described cases as a ground for building and stitching together a range of advocacy efforts. This included both relationships and the knowledge that came from using cases diagnostically to analyze the broader socio-legal issues of a community or country context. Not unlike the use of aggregated cases that I discussed in chapters 3 and 6, litigators spoke of the way that cases were a means of generating knowledge, analyzing a murky and complex human rights situation on the ground, and conveying that to an audience. This might include international legal advocacy organizations, like Amnesty or OSI, that would publicize a human rights violation in context. Or it could include stakeholders within policy or diplomatic circles. And it could include an audience of community members and local activists. Whatever the audience, cases became a mechanism for making human rights harms legible through the language of law. And, as one of the participants in the Chatham House event explained, bringing cases was a way to gather not only legal evidence, but diagnose and "see" the patterns behind regime or state violence. It was a way, she noted, to "unpack the problems we have in the system as a whole . . . and how the regime was operating at the time."

This approach offers a very different perspective on what a human rights case is *for*. Beyond amassing material in the service of winning a case, the legal process becomes a mechanism for seeing or diagnosing forms of state violence and power. This is possible only with a shift in temporal perspective as well—seeing cases not as iterative, one unrelated event after another, but as part of an ongoing *and recursive process*. A case is intended not only to win a legal victory but to build knowledge. As a knowledge-generating process, litigation relied on the time it took a case to wend its way through the system. This became a basis on which to build a recursive relationship by bringing new cases, which could be chained and linked to old ones. A linked chain of cases supported community and NGO participation. In this way, a case formed the infrastructure and framework for either community training, international advocacy, or media.

Keeping Cases Alive and Institutional Patience

Over the years, shifts in advocacy practice moved from using cases to build precedent to using cases to support the thickening of community relations and knowledge production. Litigation programs, such as those at big NGOs like OSI and Amnesty International, supported such advocacy efforts. And new

NGOs emerged that focused on the long-term life of a case. Shortly after I began my research in 2016, I noticed an uptick in talk across the ECHR system of the growing importance of implementation. This also gave rise to new relationships and communicative networks across the Department for Execution of Judgments and the Court. More people within the Council became aware of the importance of as well as new attention to messaging around the meaning and significance of cases. This included generating public support for the Court and the ECHR system by highlighting the impact they could have on ordinary people's lives. Exemplary of this was the Strasbourg-based European Implementation Network's innovative approach to focusing on implementation of cases and their publicity campaign Faces of Implementation, which highlighted experiences of advocates and applicants. The group framed implementation as a robust site for advocacy that linked national contexts to those of Strasbourg.[4] It was through new civil society networks and tactical approaches that people increasingly saw cases as anchors for a broader ecology of practice and communication. This worked after a violation was found and while advocates could continue to lobby to keep cases open. The ECHR system was an institutional framework or mechanism to enable this continued life, even over long periods of time. As long as cases stayed open people could shift their focus to implementation. Institutional frameworks and communicative channels provided opportunities for litigators and advocates to create sustained attention about both a specific violation and the root causes underlying it.

The ECHR system offered human rights advocates a series of institutional opportunities to draw sustained attention to cases among the Strasbourg-based diplomatic corps, national governments, and media outlets back home. Advocates could also draw on other offices that might generate media publicity, reports, research, or fact-finding—such as the Commissioner for Human Rights. People created a sense of momentum or forward motion by moving ideas, cases, and representations of rights from one venue or organizing context to another. This sense that cases were moving forward in time and also receiving notice helped people feel invested in the efficacy of legal advocacy as a social change strategy.

From this perspective, a case was no longer about "culminations," in the words of an English labor lawyer, Christopher, who had been involved with litigation efforts in Strasbourg. It was about the slow, contingent work of organizing over time. Christopher reflected on bringing labor cases to the ECtHR: "It was a very slow, incremental process. So basically, it's about working to develop the jurisprudence, to make it work progressively at a time when human rights, of course, are beginning to . . . I hit a bit of a revolution." When combined with sustained diplomatic attention made possible through formal institutional channels, the case takes on a longevity—punctuated by moments of renewed attention that can become the basis of organizing. Several litigators spoke of the importance of their work in precisely this way.

As in other examples throughout this book, human rights advocates and lawyers kept cases and ideas moving until they gained momentum through the Court or Committee of Ministers. Applicants, NGOs, state officials, human rights advocates, diplomats breathed new life into judgments when they continued to publicize or debate a violation or use it as a basis for media and rights campaigns. The slow pace of uptake could be frustrating, but it also became the basis on which to build other campaigns and interventions. As one strategic litigator reflected on a particularly long-standing open case, "There has definitely been disappointment at the process of change and how in some ways limited the impact of that landmark judgment was. On the other hand, I know very well that that judgment is still being used as an advocacy platform for people around the country . . . and so it is simultaneously a source of frustration and of inspiration."

In shifting from simply winning a case to keeping cases alive, litigators could reframe violations for new audiences, and bring new details, contexts and perspectives to diplomatic negotiations. In addition, by linking cases together, litigators could help build a picture of underlying structural causes in a given country context. As I also showed in chapter 4, multiple cases over time created throughlines or continuities using the materials available to lawyers. This is a key way that the individualizing logic of human rights can become more than the sum of its parts and allow advocates to scale individual cases into something that takes on more weight and significance. From a strategic litigation and advocacy perspective, bringing serial cases over time also had a communicative force, particularly in relationship to noncompliant states. As Agatha put it, it sends a message to states: "You may not have implemented that case ten years ago, but we are still here and we are not going away, and we are going to still keep going with this." The idea that litigation could create different routes or pathways was an important one that I encountered multiple times. Interviewees invoked notions of "routes," "channels," and other metaphors for moving cases along across different institutional spaces, for different audiences, and over time. In many ways, the ECHR system itself was an important site of advocacy precisely because it offered an architecture: channels along which people could move cases, while emphasizing some aspects over others as the basis of advocacy

Keeping a case open and unresolved is one example of how litigators could use time as a resource to build out the persuasive effect of their interventions. Repeated cases meant repeated pressure points on states. And it was through these opportunities that advocacy could contribute to actually meaningful enactment of the rule of law. Staying with cases over time was a means for potentially becoming unstuck—creating space for new ideas and even new narrative modalities when advocacy hit a wall of state resistance, media apathy, or the limits of the political and institutional good will in a particular domain. Litigation could create new energy and materials for shifting how people spoke about an issue. People might use Strasbourg to translate an issue from dysfunctional political institutions to potentially (different or at least differently dysfunctional) legal ones. As Christopher, the English labor lawyer, noted, moving between human rights framing and political framing allows you to just "keep an issue alive." When labor issues were being destroyed politically in the UK, law was something they could use opportunistically: "It's a way of testing the waters, a way to try and push the envelope a little bit. But it's a way also of bringing people together, making people aware of what their rights are."

From Revolution to Long-Term Advocacy: Strategic Litigation Advocacy Models over Time

Different temporal horizons for litigation produced new organizing strategies as well as ethical ways of working with applicants. Milo was a former lawyer at the Court registry who had transitioned to a well-respected advocacy NGO. He spoke powerfully to how he balanced the needs of a case, the big picture, and the immediate material needs of applicants and their communities. His organization worked with often highly marginalized and deeply impoverished Roma communities. They were working on strategies to bundle human rights cases with anti-discrimination efforts. They developed a strategy of setting a few goals over a two-year period, during which time skilled field agents with trust and relationships in affected communities would look for cases. He explained to me through a hypothetical example how this process might start: a field agent in Italy "takes the train from

Milan to Rome and then another train to a village and talks to an old woman" who has inadequate housing. At this point, there is a tension, he noted. The field agent and organization may be thinking that her housing problems are at the intersection of poverty, gender, and racial discrimination. But the woman is pointing to her roof and frustrated because her roof is leaking.

He spoke of the balance among these needs as one of managing expectations in and about time. It is a process that starts with explaining to people that their problem has a legal remedy and setting expectations about what the process might do and will do. "You can't make promises," he told me, and "people have to be aware of the time frame." This required advocates and litigators to simultaneously hold onto a future vision of a case along multiple points in a linear path—as it might move through domestic systems—while anticipating future review at Strasbourg. But they also had to work at the rhythm and speed of a client's experience. This was not only a technical but an ethical dilemma—for example, of not "trying to push *intersectionality*." Here the length of time was not only a challenge but a chance for careful, long-term engagement. It started with explaining to clients that they have remedies, what might realistically happen, and how long it will take. But at the same time, cases needed to fit within their strategic goals and time frame on a two- to five-year cycle, as well as fit within donor time frames as well. All these moves require pivots in orientation as well as the ability to communicate clearly what a case might do and what it could mean over time to so many people involved.

Yet, as he noted, even with the frustrations, the law offered advocacy tools to tack back and forth across these disparate needs and time frames. When I asked about the costs and benefits of legal approaches to advocacy, he responded, "If you veer away from the law, you are less effective." In this instance, being effective was not only a question of ensuring change but being around long enough to see and measure it. Having had experience in the Court registry before moving to legal advocacy gave him a unique perspective and a way to measure change. Citing how judges responded to questions of discrimination in a western Balkan country in which he did extensive work, he noted, "I can say I'm very proud to see" these changes. "I know how judges respond now to how they responded five years ago . . . because five years ago I was at the Court, processing cases" from the other side. He commented that judges from the Balkan country have learned what Article 14 is, and he added that prosecutors also have learned there is some "vague institution in Strasbourg" that might shape their work. He could see the change in specific ways—in the language that domestic courts used and in the increased likelihood a judge would make room for defense evidence. They would no longer just stop with the prosecution's evidence and "say I think we have all the evidence we need." This has changed, he noted, with more room for victim testimony.

Part of the effectiveness of strategic litigation was also the fact of continued watchdog presence on the ground. He said that his organization had field staff to attend hearings and be in the room. The judges and lawyers are aware that they are being watched, and that his organization has the reputation and presence to make this a meaningful strategy as a watchdog. "Part of the story is knowing that someone is watching. They know we are paying attention. But the law has to be there" in order for this strategy to work. In this sense, strategic litigation backed by the ECtHR as an institutional framework, binding obligations, and a diplomatic community generates a unique kind of publicity. As opposed to naming and shaming strategies in human rights vis-à-vis media, the case operates as a vehicle to monitor within the parameters of the law itself.

Strategic litigation, then, broadly defined is one condition of possibility for a continued presence and pressure through the idiom of a case. This might obtain even—or paradoxically, especially—when judgments with violations remain open and unimplemented for long periods of time. This is why, as I noted above, increasingly, human rights advocates and litigators bringing cases to Strasbourg lobby for cases to stay open as long as possible. This allows them to advocate for robust and meaningful implementation of judgments beyond the narrow scope of individual measures and monetary restitution. The paradox of keeping cases open while still serving the needs of clients presents yet another temporal dilemma and set of resources for using the framework of legal-institutional authority.

I spoke to Milo about precisely this dilemma concerning *D. H. and Others v. The Czech Republic*, a case his organization was deeply shaped by. Although he was too young to have participated in the research and litigation for *D. H.*, it remains for him and others the benchmark of an expansive and powerful model for anti-discrimination case law—not despite, but in some ways because it remains open and available as a platform for organizing (see chapter 6). I asked him why he thought it remained open after all these years. He noted it's frustrating it hasn't been implemented, but then again, he reminded me, it was an extremely complex case. It was, he noted, "a case of civilizational weight." And he thoughtfully added, "I don't want it executed in two years" because this means the executing government wouldn't be taking it seriously, that "there's been a trade-off." He noted, "Structural problems need structural solutions, and this will take a decade. It's disappointing, but at the same time, I'm not surprised. . . . It will take fifty years to have some improvement."

And yet even with this long time horizon, fifty years for structural change, Milo pointed to the way the case itself has a punctuating temporality and continues to remind governments that "we are watching." The important thing, he noted, is that "the Czech authorities are reminded about it four times a year." Drawing on a tongue-in-cheek reference to Churchill's famous quip, "This whole execution [process] is shit, but it's the best we've got." And he noted, the benefit was that "if you hold the case long enough, at some point the political climate gets just right. It's about waiting it out. There's not much else to."

Conclusion

In this chapter I have examined how talk about time shapes people's experiences of the Court and the ECtHR system. Focusing on strategic litigation, I analyze time not only as a reflection of heterogenous rhythms and temporalities. It is also a resource for innovating new advocacy strategies and approaches to human rights. On one hand, moments of "crisis" or the eventfulness of winning a case punctuate and mark particular relationships between action, agency, and effect within the ECHR system. This gives rise to a holding pattern that serves as a space of both advocacy and organizing. In this sense, it is paradoxical that strategic litigation, which began as a forward-looking attempt to create eventful moments (winning the case) has resulted in its seeming opposite: an infrastructure of waiting (Greenberg 2024), watching, and developing thick connections among people who inhabit different temporalities simultaneously.

SIX

Making Violence Visible

Antidiscrimination and Evidential Advocacy

IN THE EARLY 2000S, strategic litigators and Roma applicants brought the landmark case *D. H. and Others v. The Czech Republic* to Strasbourg. The applicants claimed a violation of their right to education. They also argued that this interference constituted discrimination, which involved a violation of Article 14 in conjunction with Article 2 of Protocol No. 1. Following a Chamber judgment of no violation, the Grand Chamber found a violation in both counts. The case brought to the fore deep anti-Roma racism in the Czech Republic by highlighting disparities in educational outcomes and opportunities. Drawing on statistical analysis, the applicants established that there was a much higher likelihood that Roma students would be assessed as having "mild mental disabilities." They were thus disproportionately and discriminatorily assigned to special primary schools, with a modified curriculum. In its finding, the Court focused on the disproportionate placement of Roma pupils between 1996 and 1999 and found that more than 50 percent of children attending special schools in the town of Ostrava, where the applicants lived, were Roma. A Roma child in Ostrava at that time was twenty-seven times more likely to be placed in a special school than a non-Roma child.

Most Court observers agree that the key innovations in *D. H. and Others* were the precedent-setting use of statistics as evidence for widespread institutional discrimination, the shift in burden of proof toward the respondent state accused of the violation, and the granting of judicial discretion to use inference in assessing empirical evidence. The case was both the result of and engine for new strategic litigation efforts that wed anti-discrimination cases to North American civil rights approaches. The case served as a model for advocacy efforts in Roma rights, gender justice, and disability rights, particularly in Article 14 cases.[1] At the same time, *D. H.* has become iconic for the slow, difficult process of executing general measures in violation findings. The case left many community members feeling abandoned, both in the litigation and execution process (Open Society Justice Initiative 2016b). Indeed, it remains unimplemented long after the original applicants have aged out of the school system.

D. H. is exemplary of the best and most frustrating aspects of the Strasbourg-based system. It often came up in interviews with registry lawyers, judges, human rights advocates, and strategic litigators. One young Roma rights lawyer spoke of it as the "gold standard" for education and anti-discrimination cases. Others referred to it as the *Brown v. Board of Education* of the European Court of Human Rights. One registry lawyer recounted being in a recent meeting (2018 at the time of the interview) with a senior judge at the Court who was shocked to find out that *D. H.* still wasn't fully executed. But this surprise is the exception that proves the rule. Most people who referenced the case were aware it remained open. When I asked a senior registry lawyer at the Court what case stayed with her most, she immediately responded, "*D. H.*" She had worked on the case years ago when she was at the Department for the Execution of Judgments. At the time she had felt that it "was a stretch in terms of case law." Yet she had also gone on multiple missions to the Czech Republic. When she spoke to people there, she felt that they were doing what the "Convention intended us to do."

This registry lawyer remembered struggling with the case because the judgment tried to address "something huge: systematic discrimination." But it gave no road map for implementation. We were trying to "get at discrimination through execution," she explained. As years pass and the case remains open, she sometimes reflects that another year has gone by in which Czech school children are going through this same education system. Yet, it makes her angry when people point to it to say execution doesn't work. They had been able to reduce instances of discrimination in Czechia. Given the scope of the problem, "if it takes twenty years, so be it."

This lawyer's perspective resonated with other interviewees' perspectives on the case (see chapter 5). Sometimes they were resigned or frustrated. At other times they defended the idea that implementing judgments in such complex cases necessarily took time. As I noted in chapter 5, a senior lawyer in the Department for the Execution of Judgments used the case to argue for the value of the ECHR system as one of "institutional patience" (see also Greenberg 2024). Such patience is central to translating individual cases into social and institutional change. And yet, as another execution lawyer familiar with the *D. H.* execution process mused in a 2024 interview, it is "perhaps an example [of a case] in which law is not the answer."

This comment captures the pervasive sense in Strasbourg that law is critical but not sufficient to address the complexity of racism and structural discrimination as a human rights issue. *D. H.* offers a lens to analyze law as a response to long-standing, intractable forms of chronic violence. It also illustrates another paradox of human rights litigation. Lawyers must zero in on narrow aspects of a case through which to define sprawling, socially complex problems. It is this process that translates patterns of injustice into individualized, actionable, and justiciable objects of *legal* intervention. Yet it is precisely this process that can limit the scope of execution after a violation is found. Implementation requires prying legal frameworks back open to expand the scope of social change, while grounding that change in the legal warrant of the judgment itself.

Whether law is or isn't the answer depends on how one defines the question. In this sense, the ECHR system works as a legal problem space (Scott 2004): a shared epistemic framework and communicative infrastructure through which a range of diverse actors generate a shared diagnosis and response to infinitely complex social and political problems. Human rights provided a framework that brought Roma kids and parents, strategic litigators, Czech state officials, judges, and diplomats together. The case points to the discursive labor through which people turn structural violence into a justiciable human rights problem. And the almost twenty-year story of execution points to the work required to retranslate legal problems back into institutionally meaningful responses to that problem.

Evidence, Human Rights, and Racial Discrimination

Establishing evidence for structural discrimination is not straightforward at the ECtHR. It requires what I call evidential advocacy: a process of shifting how local forms of knowledge enter law so that they become legal and not only social facts. Evidence-making always entails a politics of knowledge that shapes whether and how people can meaningfully claim rights (Weizman 2017; Das 2019). The process of creating evidence with an eye toward legal recognition both reflects and structures advocacy and community relationships on the ground (Sapignoli 2017; Rosenblatt 2015). In this sense, judicialization of politics goes hand in hand with the judicialization of activism and advocacy. It entails a reconceptualization of organizing, community knowledge, and claims-making through legal and evidentiary imaginaries.

The complexity of making discrimination *legally* visible and justiciable is one reason why the Court so rarely finds violations of Article 14 of the Convention. The system is set up to recognize human rights violations as events or discrete instances of harm. Racism is an ongoing, enduring structure that is difficult to prove within legal and human rights frameworks (Crenshaw 1989; Bruce-Jones 2016; Fuchs 2024). As a so-called parasitic right, the Court cannot find a violation of Article 14 on its own. Rather, it must be bundled with another violation—a more eventful or discrete harm—whose character is shaped by or channeled through discriminatory practice. Finding these links requires unique evidentiary standards (Mačkić 2018). These can be impossibly high, such as proof beyond a reasonable doubt or evidence of intent (Dembour 2023). And like other aspects of the Court's evidentiary regime, these standards are fluid and at times inconsistent (Speck n.d.).

Beyond formal evidential standards, discrimination cases reveal another, deeper tension between legal facts and the social truth of discrimination cases. As Marie-Benedicte Dembour has recently argued (2023), the stakes of getting the facts right in an ECtHR could mean the difference between a judgment of violation or no violation. But, as she argues, getting the facts right is not a simple empirical exercise. It requires interpretative labor on the part of lawyers and judges to establish and narrate facts in legally authorized ways. Defining a problem in one domain does not necessarily translate into making it actionable in a legal sense. It takes distilling something as pervasive as "the weather," in Christina Sharpe's (2016) powerful formulation for the all-encompassing climate of racism, into a series of legally recognizable facts. Judges are not authorized to "see" or name a generalized state of harm or violence. Nor are they authorized to attribute responsibility for structural harms outside of a specific narrative of cause and effect linked to responsible (state) parties. It is via narratives of cause and effect peopled by legally responsible actors and legally recognized victims that lawyers and judges translate collective and pervasive patterns of violence into justiciable events (Wilson 2011).

And it is through legally authorized reading practices that they establish who is directly or indirectly responsible for those harms.

Making Anti-Roma Racial Discrimination Justiciable at the ECtHR

As an international human rights court, Strasbourg is not tasked with fact finding per se (and does so only on rare occasions). Yet, the Court nonetheless must work with facts as features of arguments and narratives. Judgments tell stories about what human rights violations look like, for whom and how people claim to experience them. They tell stories about what counts as evidence of those harms. And they set parameters for the kinds of information one needs to provide to seek restitution. Sometimes forms of violence are clear: a forced disappearance, torture, or degrading prison conditions. Yet as a *human rights court*, Strasbourg is also called on to assess process via patterns that may seem diffuse at first glance. There is often a gap between the kinds of evidence required to establish the event of a violation from the conditions that shape it at a deeper level. Nowhere is this so clear as in the ECtHR's Article 14 case law on discrimination.

The road to turning facts into evidence in Article 14 cases has been long. Arguably, the most influential cases in racial discrimination have been those concerning state and police violence against Europe's Roma population (Mačkić 2018). These Article 2 and 3 cases often involve brutality in police custody and other forms of direct, racially motivated violence. A turning point was a 2002 case that many consider the Court's greatest failure in adjudicating Article 14–based racial discrimination: *Anguelova v. Bulgaria*. In 2002, the First Section of the European Court of Human Rights held there was a violation of multiple articles (2, 3, 5, and 13) in this case. The applicant was the mother of a seventeen-year-old Roma man who had died in police detention after being severely and repeatedly beaten. She alleged that the Bulgarian police had beaten her son and failed to provide adequate medical treatment. They were thus responsible for her son's death. In addition, she alleged that the authorities did not carry out an effective investigation and that the detention itself was unlawful. Finally, she argued that she did not have recourse to an effective remedy to these violations within the domestic legal system. The Court unanimously found a violation on all these counts. But the applicant had also brought one more claim forward: a breach of Article 14 of the ECHR. All the violations, she argued, were rooted in racial discrimination against her son based on his Roma origin.

In a vote of six to one, the judges found no violation of Article 14. Although there was evidence that police officers had used racial slurs while beating her son to death (*Anguelova*, para. 164), the Court argued that these did not reach the standard of proof for discriminatory intent. Judges cited case law that "proof 'beyond reasonable doubt' may follow from the coexistence of sufficiently strong, clear and concordant inferences or of similar unrebutted presumptions of fact" (*Anguelova*, para. 166). And within this standard of proof, the judgment noted that the "Court must therefore assess all the relevant facts, including any inferences that may be drawn from the general information adduced by the applicant about the alleged existence of discriminatory attitudes" (*Anguelova*, para. 166). Yet while "the applicant's complaints are . . . based on serious arguments," the Court argued it was "unable . . . to reach the conclusion that proof beyond reasonable doubt has been established" (*Anguelova*, para. 166). In one fell swoop, the judgment granted credence to the applicant's linkage of beating, racial slurs, and racial prejudice (her "serious arguments") and dismissed the claim through a combination of hedges ("in this case"), passive voice ("it is unable"), and conjunctions ("however").

The judgment laid the groundwork for judges to make inferences. This is a process of reading between the lines to render subtle forms of power nameable and therefore legally visible. But in the absence of clear doctrinal guidelines, the Court stopped short of drawing inferences to establish intent. The standard of proof also meant that different words were prima facie given different evidential weight. It is the applicant's word (and a lifetime of experience) against the authority of the state. In the process, something painfully obvious to the victim remains invisible before the law.

Yet *Anguelova* was also notable because of the passion and brilliance exhibited in one of the Court's most famous dissents. As the lone dissenter, Judge Giovanni Bonello (Malta) noted:

> Leafing through the annals of the Court, an uninformed observer would be justified to conclude that, for over fifty years democratic Europe has been exempted from any suspicion of racism, intolerance or xenophobia. The Europe projected by the Court's case-law is that of an exemplary haven of ethnic fraternity, in which peoples of the most diverse origin coalesce without distress, prejudice or recrimination. The present case energises that delusion. (*Anguelova*: Bonello dissent, para. 2)

Judge Bonello was particularly disturbed by the absence of Article 14 violations in Article 2 and 3 cases of police violence. Frustrated by the standard of proof and the need to establish evidence of intent, he noted,

"Misfortunes punctually visit disadvantaged minority groups, but only as the result of well-disposed coincidence" (*Anguelova*: Bonello dissent, para. 3–4).

In response, Judge Bonello modelled precisely how the Court might link Article 14 violations to evidence of racial and ethnic discrimination. The dissent is a rhetorical roadmap. It demonstrates how to layer texts and evidence together to invoke and link case context, comparative law, expert research, and third-party documents.[2] In forging connections among different kinds of knowledge, Bonello seeks to authorize more expansive evidentiary standards.

Western ideologies concerning facticity have long privileged witnessing, looking, and vision or seeing in the production of legal truths (Rosen 2006). Beyond the links between seeing and verifying, the scope of judicial interpretive authority rests in legal rules that delimit what judges are authorized to notice. For example, in Article 14 cases, evidential regimes work only if judges are authorized to take "judicial notice" of complex, extralegal aspects of a case in order to name and recognize racism as a justiciable object of intervention. Evidential standards like judicial notice or inference drawing are necessarily linked to but not identical with what one sees through other optic frames that rely on "visualist ideologies of perspective." (Nakassis, forthcoming). Multimodal ways of representing the "nonvisual" and intersectional aspects of discrimination—schooling practices, economic inequality, teacher bias, and failing material infrastructures and healthcare systems—become "seeable" and nameable through shifts in the evidentiary standards for what judges can and cannot use as a proxy for witnessing events of racism.

Bonello's dissent anticipates the necessary shifts for making patterns of violence justiciable by authorizing new ways of "seeing" (which is to say linking) texts. The problem in *Anguelova* was not a lack of information or facts. It was a self-imposed limit in authorized forms of judicial interpretation. It was rooted in a restriction on what judges could focus on as objects of their "professional vision" (Goodwin 1994). "Nowhere," Bonello notes, "does the Convention mandate the 'proof beyond reasonable doubt' standard today required of the victim to convince the Court that death or ill-treatment were induced by ethnic prejudice" (*Anguelova*: Bonello dissent, para. 9). To the contrary, he argues that Article 32 gives the Court discretion and leeway for interpretation of the Convention and indeed urges interpretations and standards that ensure "'universal and effective recognition and observation' of the guarantees enumerated" (*Anguelova*: Bonello dissent, para. 9).

Judge Bonello's dissent reveals something more fundamentally true about how people figure human rights as objects of intervention in and through texts. A skilled and authorized narrator can link different genres and registers of speech together to establish multiple perspectives as reflecting the "same" harm. Bonello voices moral outrage and passionate argumentation, scholarly expertise, and institutional authority. By embedding these texts within doctrinal frameworks, he turns narrative perspectives into evidence. He does so by offering ways to *legally* link and layer texts and contexts—for example, inference or burden of proof—using novel doctrinal frameworks. This weaving of texts, knowledge, and perspectives makes racialized violence "obvious"—so much so that Bonello can point to the farce of *not* seeing such violence as systematic and patterned. Indeed, it is precisely the language of seeing, or vision, with which Bonello closes his call to action, noting: "The Court has often risen to the challenge in spectacularly visionary manners, and ought, in matters of ethnic discrimination, to succumb with pride to its own tradition of trail blazing" (*Anguelova*: Bonello dissent, para.13). Adjudicating racial discrimination in these ways shifts how knowledge is produced and represented and how those interpretations are institutionally authorized.

Litigating *D. H.*: Bringing Evidential Advocacy to Strasbourg

In the years that followed the *Anguelova* case, the Court did indeed begin to shift its evidentiary standards and standard of proof in ways that reflected Bonello's analysis. This was not necessarily a result of the dissent, of course. It was a collaborative effort based in an evolving approach to case law made possible by the Court's "living instrument" approach (see chapter 1). These innovations included linking police violence to anti-Roma racism through judicial inference and shifts in standard of proof. Yet many cases still largely focused on singular events, such as police beatings or deaths in custody. These were more readily observable instances of harm against individuals rather than ongoing patterns of discrimination against racialized communities. Violence was an event, not a process. Yet these cases laid the groundwork for a doctrinal architecture available for future structural racism claims.

Depictions of racism against Roma as epiphenomenal or individual, rather than structural and systemic occur within the law but are not particular to it. Anthropologist Elana Resnick has called this process determined indeterminacy: "a collective, institutionalized method of denying the ubiquitous systemic racism that undergirds social life" (2024, 434). It is in this context in which Roma Rights activists and their allies try to use strategic litigation, alongside new forms of expert knowledge, to create the interpretive context and authority for structural discrimination in a context of white supremacy that works via erasure. Establishing race as an operative framework for anti-Roma discrimination is a challenge made more difficult by the continued perception of "racelessness" in Eastern Europe at both a vernacular and scholarly level (Rucker-Chang and West Ohueri 2021; see also Myslinska 2024). It was in part for this reason that efforts began, experimentally, with new conceptual categories through grounded and civil society directed research efforts. Countering "racelessness" or the individualizing of structural racism required generating categories and perspectives that litigators could move, via case law, into judicial and interpretative practice.

It took shifts in community organizing, litigation approaches, and new kinds of expertise to lay the groundwork for collective, institutional discrimination cases. Advocacy and community organizing supported policy and academic knowledge production. These bodies of expert material in turn gave communities a language to represent racism in new, comparative and contextually nuanced ways. The next step was to figure out how such a body of knowledge could move into law. This entailed bringing strategic cases that could shift the doctrinal categories through which facts and expertise became evidence. This process was messy, collaborative, and experimental, according to interviews I conducted with strategic litigators (also see chapter 5). One key participant in litigation efforts described translating anti-discrimination and anti-racist cause-lawyering models from the North American context to Europe. That work built on community-based efforts to document anti-Roma violence in the 1990s, particularly in Romania and Bulgaria. Much of this work was supported through new funding streams that supported litigation, rule of law, and democratization efforts in formerly socialist Eastern Europe (see chapter 5).

Early on, legal and civil society activists recognized that data was key. Indeed, my interlocutor told me that:

> The challenge . . . in documenting discrimination [is] . . . the cultural aversion in so much of continental Europe among both oppressed and oppressor to ethnic data [data broken down by ethnicity]. Given the history of misuse and abuse, people don't want to hear anything about the data that's needed to actually show that they're suffering disparate treatment.

This "obstacle," in his words, required building a knowledge infrastructure to collect meaningful data. But it also necessitated introducing and socializing the use of statistics at the country level and at the Court. My interlocutor recalled the highly professional way that "the European Roma Rights Center started to do more . . . human rights monitoring and documentation of specific country situations. It was an organization dedicated to generating that kind of information systematically." From the beginning, litigation included new approaches to knowledge production to address the practical difficulty of adjudicating racism within human rights frameworks. The terrain was "so wide open and the practices were so egregious," my interviewee explained. Alongside documentation, civil society groups and a younger generation of advocates began to network and learn from each other (chapter 5). As case law developed, so too did new categories of legal intervention and doctrine.

At this stage, strategic litigators, applicants, and third-party interveners didn't just have to convince the Court that discrimination existed. They had to establish that the respondent state was responsible for these kinds of violations and that a solution fell within the scope of existing Convention rights. Another strategic litigator who had been part of the initial *D. H.* team and then gone on to apply those lessons to gender justice cases explained that "at the time, the European court hadn't ever recognized indirect discrimination—full stop. [And it had] actually rejected the statistics as a way of demonstrating that." With *D. H.*, she and others were able to build new persuasive strategies and standards—in particular, the use of statistical evidence.

This doctrinal infrastructure created room to experiment with other persuasive strategies and arguments that built on indirect discrimination in *D. H.* In subsequent litigation in gender discrimination, she described going before the Court and appealing to "comparative pressure." She told the judges, "This court holds itself out as the best human rights court in the world, and yet you're way behind. You're twenty years behind CEDAW; you're ten years behind the inter-American system. . . . And so, this is your opportunity to trailblaze." Of course, we can't know how influential her testimony was. The case she was referring to did become a landmark violation in gender-based discrimination and positive obligations to protect women victims of domestic violence. The point is that innovations in one case became a baseline for experimentation in intertextual approaches to figuring complex, structural violence and state responsibility.

Anatomy of the *D. H. and Others v. The Czech Republic* Judgment

The Grand Chamber's ruling in *D. H.* established that Roma children received differential treatment; it argued that evidence of that differential treatment (through statistics and other documentary means) is sufficient to shift burden of proof and that it is the government's responsibility to demonstrate the difference is justified once the burden is shifted. Most significantly, it authorized judges to make inferences based on parties' facts and submissions. The judgment notes, "The courts of many countries and the supervisory bodies of the United Nations treaties habitually accept statistics as evidence of indirect discrimination in order to facilitate the victims' task of adducing *prima facie* evidence" (*D. H.*, para. 188). The ruling allows for "statistics which appear on critical examination to be reliable and significant [as] sufficient to constitute the *prima facie* evidence the applicant is required to produce" (*D. H.*, para. 188). And with the establishment of differential treatment, "the burden then shifts to the respondent State, which must show that the difference in treatment is not discriminatory" (*D. H.*, para. 189).

Together, these moves represent *D. H.*'s key contributions to doctrine and evidential standards. The judgment authorizes noneventful and systematic discrimination as *visible before the law*. When situated as a backdrop to applicant narratives, statistics support inference. In addition, the judgment figures violence through voices and perspectives of applicants, authorized by expert knowledge, to paint a picture of institutional and national contexts. Out of this collection of information, details, and perspective, the judgment inductively generates an interpretive frame that authorizes reading new kinds of documentation as evidence via the legal warrant of emergent doctrine.

Like all significant cases, the eighty-nine-page *D. H. and Others* Grand Chamber judgment is a composite of many voices and kinds of texts. Drafting lawyers weave together government and applicant arguments. They engage the work of researchers, human rights analysts, and civil society organizations. And they include legislation and case law from the respondent state, the ECtHR, and comparative international law. Judgments close with a section on the "Court's assessment"—a trace of the confidential, consensus-based judicial deliberation process. Analyzing a judgment is not a straightforward reflection of any one position. It is an archive of negotiations filtered through legal and evidentiary links that judges and drafting lawyers find most persuasive.

D. H. begins with a brief overview of long-standing violence against European Roma populations, including Nazi extermination policies. This sets the tone for sections on the facts of the case, including the disproportionate placement of Roma students in so-called special schools. Throughout its pages, the judgment makes several references to expert research and reports, including those from respected international human rights, Roma rights, and educational organizations, and academic research.[3] Through these layered texts, it builds an authoritative account of the widespread existence of discrimination. These "facts" of the case are then compared to binding legal principles, including domestic and comparative international law and Convention case law. This provides the comparative legal framework. Across this, the judgment stretches a canvas on which to paint the claims and positions of key players and relationships among them. This makes visible subtle power dynamics born out of these interactions.

Together this narrative structure gives the case breadth and depth across a web of interrelated experts and institutional actors. The effect is a comparative perspective that highlights the gaps among what school children experience (via the voicing of applicants) and the rights to which they are entitled within domestic and international law. The scope of the problem is foregrounded against the aggregate and patterned systematicity of numbers (e.g., *D. H.*, para. 18).[4] Indeed this repetition of statistical information operates as a refrain that links the applicant's submissions and the expert reports and ultimately as the basis for the Court's assessment (*D. H.*, para. 82–83, 180, 187).

For example, a series of passages uses comparative data to illustrate that "the Czech Republic ranked *second* highest in terms of placing children with physiological impairments in special schools and in *third* place in the table of countries placing children with learning difficulties in such schools. Further, of the eight countries . . . the Czech Republic was *the only one* to use special schools" (*D. H.*, para. 18; emphasis added). These comparative frameworks (country to country) create the international context for other kinds of comparisons at different orders of scale: comparisons across nations, between institutions, and applicants' experiences as against official reports. Arguing that "they had not been sufficiently informed of the consequences of placement," the applicants explain that testing and placement practices

> had resulted in de facto racial segregation and discrimination that were reflected in the existence of two separately organised educational systems for members of different racial groups . . . [and] that they had received an inadequate education and an affront to their dignity. (*D. H.*, para. 25)

The judgment contrasts Roma applicants' experience of racial prejudice and their calls for dignity with the narrow technical response of educational institutions to student needs. It also invokes the coded (or not so coded) racializing language of the state ministry's response. For example, "the Ministry of Education denied any discrimination and noted a tendency on the part of the parents of Roma children to have a rather negative attitude to school work" (para. 26).

Such local and national dynamics are situated in relationship to international law and other European country contexts. Moving into sections on relevant law, the judgment brings to bear several major relevant conventions, the Court's own case law, and approaches to discrimination from constitutional courts and parliamentary bodies. These range from the U.S. Supreme Court to the House of Lords.[5] The interplay among statistics, social science expertise, and applicant perspectives forms a textual matrix against which the reader can see the limits of existing doctrinal standards. This leads the Court to conclude that establishing proof of discrimination is sufficient, regardless of intent (*D. H.*, para. 132, 179). If Judge Bonello's dissent operated by pointing to the gap between obvious facts and the legal basis for their interpretation and recognition, *D. H.* creates the channels and pathways to make discrimination legally legible. It takes the next step to allow for inferences to be drawn from the complex social picture that it paints.

The section titled "Court's Assessment" is where the judgment formally introduces judicial perspectives. This section begins by noting the "particularly invidious" nature of racial discrimination (*D. H.*, para. 176). Struggling over how to prove something socially entrenched but *noneventful* builds to the judges shifting the burden of proof. Having established differential treatment of Roma students through statistical evidence, the Court notes that "once an applicant has shown a difference in treatment it is for the Government to show that it was justified" (*D. H.*, para. 177). It goes on to state as to

> what constitutes prima facie evidence capable of shifting the burden of proof on to the respondent State, the Court stated in *Nachova and Others* (cited above, § 147) that in proceedings before it there are no procedural barriers to the admissibility of evidence or predetermined formulae for its assessment. The Court adopts the conclusions that in its view, supported by the free evaluation of all evidence, including such inferences as may flow from the facts and the parties' submissions. According to its established case-law, proof may follow from the coexistence of sufficiently strong, clear and concordant inferences or of similar unrebutted presumptions of fact. (*D. H.*, para. 178)

Following the lead of the applicants' litigation team, the judgment zeros in on testing metrics and procedures as both evidence of and the engine for this discriminatory treatment. Discrimination writ large becomes a necessary background to a more narrow definition of harm. This narrowing was key to winning the case. But it had implications for the social justice efforts that followed. The shift in burden of proof and the category of indirect discrimination was supported by a wide-ranging body of knowledge, including statistics, historiography, comparative law, and expert reports. And it was this same body of knowledge through which applicants ultimately asked the judges to use their expanded interpretive power to focus on disproportionate placement and testing methods. Statistical evidence was needed to widen the interpretive scope and shift the burden of proof. But it was also used to define a justiciable harm within the context of that same widespread, systematic discrimination. The resulting judgment is an archive of two ways to figure the problem. And it also served as a resource to chart two very different paths forward with regard to the general measures needed to execute the judgment. The struggle over the direction of interpretation and the kinds of responses data supports are the subjects of the rest of the chapter.

From Discrimination to Inclusive Education:
The Struggle to Define the Scope of Execution

What it takes to win a violation in Strasbourg is not necessarily what it takes to execute that judgment meaningfully. In *D. H.* the applicants used statistical measures to demonstrate the disproportionate placement of Roma students in special education schools. This meant that the argument of the case hinged on linking discrimination to bias in testing procedures. The argument did not directly address whether the system of special schools would perpetuate bias no matter what the placement numbers. Nor did it include a demand for more inclusive education tout court. As a third-party intervener in the case explained to me, "There were lots of discussions that we had about how broadly we should frame the argument and to what extent we should be arguing, in a broader sense . . . that everybody should be mainstreamed and that no separate institutions, no separate classes, no separate schools were permissible." Ultimately the case argued that "you can have whatever institutions and separation you want, but make sure you're not discriminating on the grounds of ethnic or racial origin." That was the "argument that won the day."

The special schools system racialized and segregated Roma students through deficit models. This is evident in the language of the Czech legal code cited in *D. H.* that included notions of social pathology and cultural aversion to education (para. 32). Arguing for better testing mechanisms did not address the intersection of race, disability rights, or the need for inclusive education models. Nor did it address the links between social stereotyping, educational categories, and human rights.[6] Indeed, the litigator quoted above noted:

> To this day, we discuss with our colleagues arguing for persons with disabilities and others the extent to which [the approach in *D. H.*] helped or hurt. . . . Some people [say] it was very helpful notwithstanding. . . . Others [claim] it narrowed the claim too much. It legitimize[d] the fact of separate education for some people, even if not for the people on whose behalf you were advocating.

Given this initial framing, it is not surprising that the early executions process focused on eliminating bias in testing rather than bias in education per se. The judgment was structured to achieve certain persuasive effects. Statistics were an authorized proxy for amorphous relationships among institutions, social categories, and political practices. As the case shifted to the next phase, it ported over this interpretative framework. Czech government representatives set the agenda by focusing their efforts on student placement and testing procedures—at least at first. State representatives argued that the case could be closed once they had addressed these narrow technical issues. Yet, applicants and community organizations wanted more. Thus began a multiyear struggle to redefine the scope of the problem and what would count as evidence of meaningful change.

This gave rise to a different kind of narrative struggle than that of litigation. It involved building a related but more expansive discursive and informational infrastructure. From the beginning of implementation, civil society organizations and Roma rights advocates were highly engaged in trying to frame the process and deliver different perspectives and data to the Committee of Ministers. The goal for applicants was to pinpoint the root causes and means for addressing structural racism within secondary education and within Czech society more generally.

All formal communications in the execution process are publicly accessible in the HUDOC-EXEC platform. The extant record includes over one hundred documents. These constitute an archive of ongoing negotiation over the goals of execution and debates concerning the kind of evidence needed to establish success in achieving these goals. I focus on select, representative documents from an approximately fifteen-year period. These were submitted by multiple actors all responding to each other: state representatives, DEJ lawyers, Committee of Minister diplomats and their staff, civil society organizations and human rights advocates, academic and policy experts, and Roma rights organizations, the applicants, and affected Roma communities. The execution phase led to a range of reports, policies, and new legislation. The process also sparked new institutional initiatives and expert investigations: teacher training, legislative proceedings, education policy committees, academic and NGO-led research initiatives, and community-based organizing and consultation. As might be clear from this list, this constellation of actors had different responses to the question of what would make the judgment practical and effective. It also gave rise to clashes over how to represent genuine change and whose perspective should be centered. As with the litigation of the case itself, execution also rested on persuading others to establish and take up shared evidentiary standards and practices.

Czech Authorities

If the execution process requires "general measures" (see chapters 1 and 3), respondent states must produce regular action plans in which they detail specific efforts to address the core problem of the violation. These are submitted to the lawyers in the Department for the Execution of Judgments (DEJ), who convey them to the Committee of Ministers (CM) for review at their biannual meetings. If implementation is moving forward, the violating state can argue for standard monitoring. This means that implementation is proceeding adequately, and the case does not require additional scrutiny. The goal for state representatives is to have an open case declared closed or fully executed. In *D. H.*, this would mean that the state met its obligations to address the general aspects of the violation (racist practices in Roma education). On the other hand, NGO representatives and the applicants and their lawyers often seek a process of enhanced supervision. This means additional scrutiny of government action plans, including more regular discussions of the case at CM meetings, and requests for detailed information. Enhanced supervision means it is more likely that comments, criticisms, and suggestions concerning government action plans are taken up or at least heard by the CM. While a case is under enhanced review, there is more space for dialogue, lobbying, and persuasion.

In the early 2010s, the Czech government action plans held fast to the most technical definition of the problem in order to close the case quickly. They foregrounded improvements to the testing methodologies that had disproportionately placed Roma students in special schools. These approaches mirrored the judgment. Testing stood for larger issues related to discrimination in the classroom, teacher resistance to integrating Roma students, family distrust of the educational system, and legal frameworks that classed Roma students as mentally deficient because of (implicitly racializing) "social pathology" (as in the 2004 Czech law; see *D. H. and Others*, para. 32). But the Czech communications tried to keep linkages limited and reforms narrow in scope. An early communication to the DEJ demonstrates this narrow, technical reading:

> The Czech authorities consider that the *D. H. and Others* judgment primarily indicates that during the placement of the applicants into special schools there were insufficient guarantees that such placement would not be incorrect and that it would not lead to discrimination. Pursuant to this plan, the Czech authorities aim to implement measures that will effectively prevent possible discrimination in any way and enable stricter control and methodological management at all levels of the consultation, decision-making and executive process. (DH-DD(2012)1074)

The document goes on to explain that while the Czech authorities understood the issue of inclusive education, that goal was too long-term to address. Rather, they "have . . . decided to adopt the more tightly focused, specific measures detailed in the consolidated action plan that will accelerate the execution of the judgment. . . . These measures pertain to questions of correct placement of children in schools" (DH-DD(2012)1074). Action plans in the early years after the judgment focused only on these technical questions of educational testing standards and in tracking changes in statistics in placement.[7]

Applicants and civil society pushed back to argue for a more capacious response centered on the notion of inclusive education. While state representatives continued to argue that goal lay outside the scope of their obligations, the back and forth had some impact. Over time, the Czech communications expanded the scope of their activities to address unequal schooling. Around 2015 state communications mention broader legislative changes intended to supplement the focus on testing metrics and diagnostic procedures (DH-DD(2015)161). Formal Czech communications during this time also include more subtle analyses of the ways that educational and social categories perpetuate bias. These documents tentatively represent Roma students not only as statistical objects but as "full-fledged" persons facing complex social disadvantages. A new education act "does not aim to define obstacles on the part of the pupil but to provide the necessary support whilst recognizing the pupil as a full-fledged person" and will even address "a one-sided view that the majority has about educational needs or social stereotypes" (DH-DD(2015)161, p. 4).

The Czech state documents still largely focus on testing, diagnostic practices, student counseling services, and teacher and administrative training. But the Czech government's responses have grown more expansive over time. For one, the documents begin to move the goal of inclusivity in education from margin to center. As time has gone on and the Committee of Ministers has continued to call for enhanced supervision, the Czech state has proposed new legislative frameworks. By the mid-2010s, state documents also make reference to more consultative processes with stakeholders (cf. DH-DD(2016)161, section G), and state funding for education activities (DH-DD(2016)1040). In 2017 and 2018 the Czech plan incorporated a wider range of legislative measures, funding, stakeholder consultations, and training initiatives as well. As I detail in the final section, by 2024, the Czech state representatives no longer actively argued for closing the case before it was fully implemented through meaningful general measures.

Civil Society

Civil society submissions in *D. H.* are an important part of ongoing negotiations with the Czech state and the CM. These communications demonstrate how legal advocates build on the intertextual, narrative work that made racism legally visible in the judgment. In turn, they slowly introduce alternate ways to center antiracism as a policy and legislative focus. NGOs try to strike a balance between acknowledging the work of Czech state officials, while continuing to apply pressure to keep the implementation process moving forward. They stretch the meaning of execution *and* establish concrete benchmarks for what counts as evidence of successful anti-discrimination initiatives. And they directly challenge the authority of state officials to set the agenda by demanding more community voices and representation. They do so by raising questions about the trust that the CM ought to place in state accounts and Czech political will to implement the case meaningfully.

Civil society and expert submissions keep racism in the forefront by giving it narrative shape (through concrete examples), weight and heft (through a language of statistics), and voice (through the invocation and citation of the applicants and Roma parents and children). In so doing, the civil society documents counter not just the facts provided by state representatives in their action plans and reports. They also create different context through which people might produce authoritative knowledge of the situation on the ground. In addition to raising the question of what constitutes structural racism, the civil society interveners reframe who is authorized to communicate or represent it. One common narrative approach is to invoke community activists. This shift in voicing highlights the importance of local participation and emphasizes local forms of knowledge. It thus questions the legitimacy of the Czech authorities to represent community needs.

A 2012 fifteen-page submission to the CM (DH-DD(2012)1089) demonstrates a number of these strategies. Authored by local and international civil society representatives, the report reiterates the importance of community voices in assessing how and by whom success should be measured. Using the notion of "concrete progress on the ground," the report questions whether the Czech monitoring systems are adequate to really speak to the experience and representation of discrimination (p. 8). In addition to a critical perspective on the limits of state-generated statistics and data (p. 7), the document suggests a range of other local on-the-ground assessment practices. These include non-discriminatory testing, informed parental consent, and proof that legislative changes have taken effect.[8] This notion of "on the ground' echoes and resonates with other civil society documents submitted to the CM, including calls for "field research" in the affected communities.

Such counter-representational strategies appear throughout the archive. These alternative sources of expertise challenge state facts and figures and the top-down approaches to policymaking. The documents also channel applicants' voice and perspective. One, for example, notes that "the original D. H. applicants remain disillusioned that inclusive education will become a reality any time soon" (DH-DD(2012)334). They invoke models of success for implementation based on specific schools and case studies. One example cites "Jachymov, a town of 3,000 people, [in which] the impending closure of a school compelled its new headmaster to reconceptualize the school as the heart of the community, aiming to prevent social exclusion" (DH-DD(2011)1164). And they include reports from local NGOs that serve as evidence of civil society links to communities (DH-DD(2012)579). Within this intertextual matrix, the documents position community voices on equal and in some instances privileged footing for assessing implementation.

Civil society documents also put these voices in direct conversation with Czech state officials to create an imagined dialogue between equals. Another NGO report from 2012 (DH-DD(2012)629) details the conflict that arises when the Czech government tries to co-opt a local NGO forum for community members to speak to state officials. The report notes that while the Czech state claimed to have organized a community roundtable in its action plan report to the CM, the event was in fact organized by the local NGO. The NGO report warns the Committee of Ministers that

> under no circumstances did the ministry contribute toward initiating, convening or coordinating the round tables. The planning and organization of the round tables, the establishment of their aims, and their facilitation were completely managed by the Together to School Coalition. . . . We request that the Government of the Czech Republic correct this point in the report.

This passage, like several others, puts the CM on alert about who to trust and how to read official documents. The NGO report evokes authenticity through various stylistic markers. The account reads like a local community paper report. It is brief, focused on local places and names that only community members and participants might know. It invokes a specific meeting—a time, place, and series of institutional and community actors. This local authenticity stands in stark contrast to the outside government officials who claim to speak for the event. Such examples are part of a web of documents that emphasize the importance of hearing from affected communities in a participatory process in developing inclusive policies. In voicing authentic community styles and locales, the NGO report challenges Czech state representatives' authority and questions their actions and intentions in speaking with and for the community.

At stake is who controls the narrative and who might meaningfully use the language of accountability when writing about Roma constituents and communities affected by state education policies. The politics of evidence in this case is thus fundamentally a politics of representation. It is achieved by alerting the CM to what they ought to consider trustworthy evidence. It attunes readers to different perspectives through shifts in genres, narratives, and voicing of those authorized to speak in the name of Roma communities. In this sense, shifting evidence of implementation requires peopling the archive with a proliferation of registers—and the social roles and forms of personhood for which they stand (Agha 2005).

In arguing that evidence-gathering ought to be participatory, these documents also question the underlying structure of knowledge production and state power within the ECHR system. It is a move that parallels and is supported by shifts in the standard of proof themselves. As many scholars have argued, one of the central limitations of the international human rights system is that it is composed of nation-states as both the perpetrators of rights violations and the arbiters of justice (Çalı and Koch 2014). The presupposition that state representatives' word can be taken at face value means state communications are given prima facie weight and credibility. This evidential bias is built into the very fabric of ECtHR practice and doctrine (Alpes and Baranowska 2024). Shifting the balance of power requires shifting the ways in which words are afforded weight, credibility, and truth value on their face.

The theme of trust resonates with another trope, good will or political will, that appears across the documents. In reallocating trust and credibility from state institutions and representatives, civil society documents make room to privilege other sources of knowledge. For example, an Amnesty International report to the Committee of Ministers (DH-DD(2013)1295) specifically questions the trustworthiness of state documents. It notes that Amnesty is

> submitting these comments to assist the Committee of Ministers in assessing the government's report, as well as the overall progress in the execution of the *D.H.* judgment. In particular, Amnesty International's evidence demonstrates that to date, the government has failed to adopt measures (a) explicitly mandating the desegregation of Czech schools and (b) that would put in place sufficient safeguards against discrimination in access to education.

The rest of the document tracks discrepancies between government action plans and its failure to follow up in policy and data gathering. The analysis monitors state promises and actions over time. In turn, it teaches the CM how to read government documents with skepticism. The request both educates the CM (demonstrating the kinds of knowledge it ought to be asking for) while channeling the power and authority of that body as the official decision-maker and only body formally positioned to issue requests to the Czech state.

By exposing the politics of knowledge underlying evidential regimes, civil society counternarratives offer the CM an expansive diagnosis of power, trust, and representational politics. They materialize amorphous concepts (good will or lack of political will) by linking them explicitly to kinds of evidence (legislation). And they both channel and call on the CM in its authoritative capacity to pressure states to produce more and better knowledge.

This shift in knowledge politics lays the groundwork for the CM to recognize alternative approaches to data and the complex social dynamics such data indexes. For example, a 2015 research report (DH-DD(2015)151) authorized by prominent international and Czech NGOs (COSIV-KLUSÁČEK 2015) provides a robust critique of Czech state statistics submitted to the CM. Recall that the judgment allows for statistics as evidence and that the disproportionate placement of Roma children in special schools was both the justiciable object and evidence of that discrimination. In 2015, the Czech government presented statistical information on the reduction of these numbers, claiming it was evidence of successful implementation. It followed from the most literal reading of the judgment: high placement numbers indicate discrimination and lower placement numbers would indicate effective responses. Yet between 2007 and 2015, a trove of documents in the HUDOC-EXEC archive details civil society pushback both against the meaning of these statistics and the ways in which statistics of student placement narrowed the focus of execution. Civil society interventions build on the bare bones logic of the judgment use legally authorized but sociologically and politically more expansive ways to account for, represent, and respond to structural racism. By 2015, the continued use of statistics to represent successful implementation not only looks paltry and insufficient to "count" (quite literally) as evidence of implementation.

The COSIV group report is effective at building on this shift in what counts as meaningful knowledge. It builds on subtle but persistent ways in which the Czech state's trustworthiness and "good will" has been called into question. The submission critiques the data that supports the New School Act legislation—a response to *D. H.* initiated by the Czech state. At issue was the reintroduction of testing mechanisms for children with "intellectual disabilities" that civil society groups worried would reintroduce precisely the problem of disproportionate placement of Roma children in special schools, but now with a new statutory imprimatur. To challenge this, the report highlighted aspects of state methodologies in testing that consistently reproduced the problem of discrimination through testing mechanisms. It also questioned the intentions of those running such schools in generating a population of students that would keep schools open and in business. The report centers and critically engages official state statistical representations (representations and trends they are increasingly experiencing pressure to produce). It also highlights the ways in which institutional interests were bound up with classifying students as special needs. In turn, the COSIV report makes visible an institutional landscape that produced inequality through tiered educational systems.

As of 2022, NGO groups continued to critique what remains, in their view, an overly narrow focus on testing methods and diagnostics rather than the underlying issues of social, political, economic, and institutional discrimination. A submission from that time makes explicit what the stakes have been all along: "to effectively implement the judgment in the case of *D.H. and Others v. The Czech Republic* and to remedy the situation of Roma children requires applying a broader approach." A submission notes:

> Although the judgment did not directly address the need for adapting the educational system to the principles and features deriving from the right to inclusive education, these are inherent conditions for bringing a real and sustainable change for Roma children. Without them, the segregating practice will transform into its new forms, seemingly falling outside the scope of the judgment but not ending the systemic segregation of Roma children in education. The implementation would then become only formal. (DH-DD(2022)404)

As of 2024, the Committee of Ministers continues to keep the case open under enhanced supervision.

The Afterlife of Legal Problem Spaces

The ongoing story of *D. H.* exemplifies the ways that human rights frameworks narrow and simplify structural issues in order to adjudicate violations. And it also demonstrates how the same legal frameworks provide a language and forum to widen the scope of rights law through execution. The open-endedness of *D. H.* has been disappointing to applicants and the litigators who brought it (Open Society Justice Initiative 2016b). But it is also an effect of an institutional architecture designed to do many things at once: to bring states into compliance with the ECHR, to provide a hearing for individual applicants to gain redress from violations, to encourage states to fix structural causes of human rights violations, and to be both a framework for technical legal and policy reforms and an agent of justice. What the process has enabled has not been execution as such, but perhaps is just as significant.

In 2024, I spoke with someone at the Council of Europe who was familiar with the status of *D. H.*'s execution and the ongoing negotiations among the Committee of Ministers, applicant representatives, state officials, and other stakeholders. The conversation helped me to understand the depth and contours of *D. H.* as a legal problem space. Fifteen years of negotiations about execution generated connection points among applicants, community organizations, litigators, and diplomats. This conversation was anchored in the initial judgment. Yet it also stretched and challenged the limited legal scope of that text. As my interlocutor described it,

> the judgment is a starting point. But you can see that the Committee is quite flexible in its interpretative powers. The execution process is based and framed by the judgment . . . but we take into account the dynamics of the situation. We take into account not only the status at it was, at the time of the facts of the case, but also what happened in the meantime.

It was through this process of contestation and dialogue among many players over many years that the Committee of Ministers had finally come to "the situation where more or less there is a diagnosis of the problem." Of course, the idea of a diagnosis is a dialogic process in and of itself. How respondent state officials made this diagnosis in the beginning and where they were by 2024 were by no means the same. This is evident from my analysis of execution documents and confirmed by my interviewee. He told me that even up through 2018, the "Czech authorities were saying 'it's sorted out.'" But, he noted,

> at this stage, the authorities tell us (e.g., acknowledge) there is a problem, so we don't have to confront pressure from government side to close the case. This is probably a sign of a small change . . . new data appeared, civil society flagged new elements, so it was kept open. And they themselves admitted the problem still exists.

By 2024, the Czech authorities had committed to "a higher level of involvement" and a commitment to a more ongoing and capacious approach to execution. This renewed political will and involvement indicated a real "willingness of authorities to do something," at least for the time being. And yet as a community of interlocutors defined and redefined the problem, they faced new challenges. Government agents, DEJ lawyers, Committee ministers, and community advocates also had to rescope what evidence of actually meaningful change with regard to structural racism meant. As my interlocutor noted, "from the execution point of view, [one] ideal scenario would be to have comparable proportion of Roma kids (in special schools) as their proportion in society. . . . But realistically, with such a long-standing issue . . . this is a process that will still take years and years." Thus, while there are "real changes and action by state authorities." it was difficult "to see . . . tangible results" As a case, it presented "complex issues" that "required time" among "many interlocutors." In this sense, "it is not a simple case, which you can just solve through one set of means and it's done."

A long-standing open case is a double-edged sword. *D. H.* offers an opportunity to meaningfully chart responses to racism as a human rights problem—one grounded in law but also always in excess of it. As such, the case remains a model and it is necessary not to close it too soon. It's not the oldest case on the docket, he reminded me, but it's one of the oldest. And while it wasn't in the interests for the CM to keep it open forever, "the Committee has the responsibility to be sure that the underlying reasons are solved, more or less." This was not only for the well-being of the community involved, but for the ECHR system as a site of hope for meaningful change. He added, "It's a symbolic case. It's also another argument that can be used for keeping it open. . . . In a case like this, you have to be really sure that everything is solved within reasonable grounds . . . because if you close it prematurely, you give a very bad sign to other states."

In the end, the issue in executing *D. H.* points back to a few key lessons. What makes for evidence of the problem within the confines of legal interpretation is simply not adequate to what serves as evidence for a meaningful resolution. The issues at hand are too wide-ranging, socially complex, and long-standing. As such, execution required redefining the scope and origins of the violation and innovating ways to measure and assess change that were distributed across multiple experiences and actors. Lawyers in the execution department struggled with how to generate this information because they were "not on the ground." They could use statistics, Rule 9 submissions, and other information to identify when there were patterns and "deduce problems." But knowing when and how there was meaningful change was a necessarily dialogic process—one made more complicated because that self-same process involved advocacy and persuasion to define and redefine the problem itself. The result was a step-by-step, sometimes-forward-and-sometimes-back process for constituting a conversation—a legal problem space shaped through shared terms of debate. When I asked whether my interlocutor had seen an impact on consciousness around Roma rights through the lens of this case, he reminded me how much the Czech authorities had changed in attitude. With no one pushing to simply close the case, it had come to actually represent hope. "The states are probably full of hope for what this new positive approach of the authorities will bring," he remarked. "It is obvious that the problem is still important . . . is considered as important by the CM, and the CM is full of hope that it will be solved."

As I noted in chapter 5, this long-term process is not without costs. This is especially true for applicants for whom the initial process of bringing a case and waiting for a result and then the slow building of a solution can mean alienation and frustration. After all, the pace of legally driven social change and the rhythms of childhood and early education are fundamentally mismatched. For the applicants who have aged out of the Czech schools and moved on, it not clear whether justice has been achieved. For future generations, at least, it remains an open question.

Moving from Compromise to Complicity

Rule of Law as Fragile and Enduring

FROM JUNE 2021 TO AUGUST 2022, my family and I lived in Strasbourg, France, while I researched and started writing this book. I first began this project in 2016, when I set out to examine the ways in which human rights law shapes a semi-coordinated discursive and epistemic community through which people ask (and respond to) questions about collective European futures. Those questions came out of my first book (Greenberg 2014), which examined the hopes and the disappointments of postsocialist democratization in Serbia. With the turn to judicialization across Eastern Europe, I wanted to examine how people reconciled earlier visions of social change, human rights and institution-driven notions of justice. In charting that balancing act, I hoped to speak to the generative possibilities and the limits of rule of law as a collective social achievement.

These tensions crystallized devastatingly in late February 2022 with Russia's invasion of Ukraine. On Saturday, March 12, 2022, on a walk with my kids, my older son, Gabriel, paused in front of the Agora building, which houses Council of Europe offices. He pointed to the placard listing the basic statistics for Council membership, alongside a map and the flags of every member state (see figure C.1). Sometime in the past few days, someone had taken a black permanent marker and drawn a large, thick X across the number 47 (for forty-seven Council members). In its place they had written 46 in bold block letters. Russia's flag also had a large X through it.

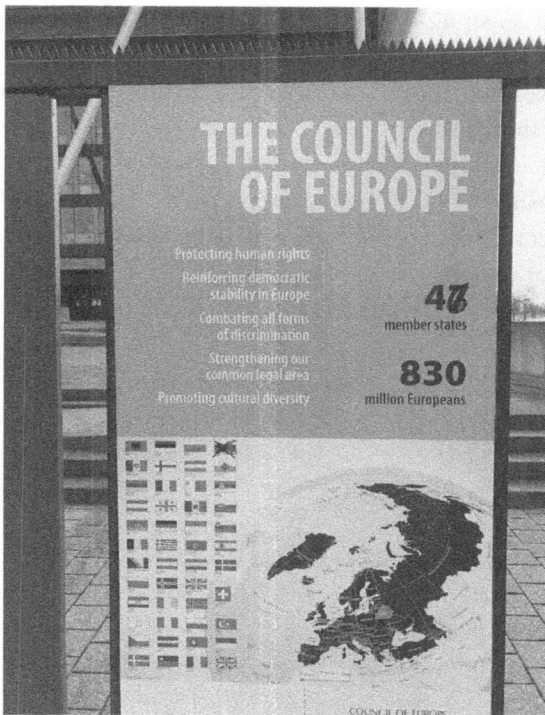

FIGURE C.1.   Council of Europe sign with Russia crossed out, and 47 changed to 46 Member States, after Russia's expulsion from the Council of Europe in March 2022. Source: Photo by author.

Russia had just recently been suspended from the Parliamentary Assembly of the Council of Europe (PACE), the legislative body of the Council. By the following week, it was formally expelled. Russia's expulsion and the war that prompted it raised questions about how to shore up legal and democratic institutions, while also coming face to face with their limits. Most people I spoke with in the Council agreed that the scale of violence, Russia's violation of international legal norms, and the need for urgent solidarity with Ukraine made expulsion inevitable. At the same time, drawing a clear line raised questions about past complicities and future sustainability. In interviews, people wondered whether they had waited too long to sanction Russia. Should they have done so in 2014 after the first war in Ukraine? When was it possible to know if a country had gone too far? And if the Council had taken a stand in this case, what ought it do when other countries refused to comply with the standards and practices that held the system together?

This sense of the fragility of the rule of law was not wholly new, as I've been arguing throughout the book. At the close of the Second World War, European intellectuals and politicians tried to rebuild a devastated Europe by forging new institutions to a secure a lasting peace. But the need for consensus also led to tremendous compromise and multiple exclusions. The resulting vision, simultaneously capacious and technocratic, is exemplified by the dual function of the European Court of Human Rights as the self-proclaimed "conscience of Europe" and a legal institution bound by doctrinal and practical deference to sovereign state power. It is a balance between an internationalist vision of a better world and the compromises of enacting that vision through the building blocks of the nation-state. It is a tension that has defined much of the contemporary pan-European institutional landscape, as well as the backlash against it (Holmes 2001).

People working within the Council were aware of these limits and compromises in granular ways. In chapter 3, I referred to my interview with a former member of the Venice Commission. His observation that "rule of law is not a definition but a process" was central for how I conceptualized this book. At the same time, he attuned me to the dynamics of institutional power within the ECHR system. Such power, he noted, was largely persuasive, based in communication and consensus. It came from the Council's ability to convince states that it's in their interests "to have a system where member states comply" and that "it is better to be in the system than out of it." This vision had its limits, he confided. Indeed, the 2008 economic crisis and COVID brought home the costs of formal democracy and human rights, particularly when "social rights were sidelined." For too many people, he told me, there is a "a feeling that the democratic process leads to nothing." It took those committed to democracy "within this Council framework . . . too much time to realize that democracy needs to provide hope."

Yet compromises within the institution also allowed him and others to forge some paths forward. The question was at what cost? My interlocutor was not alone at the Council in having questions about complicity, compromise, and ethical lines in the sand. With Russia's expulsion, people experienced both an increased sense of urgency about shoring up the system and reflected on the limits of a rule-of-law institution. For example, in 2022 I had the privilege to attend a two-day conference of human rights scholars, lawyers, and advocates from across Europe. On the agenda was a way to improve implementation of ECtHR judgments, particularly in the so-called difficult countries. These are countries that have records of systematic human rights violations and a series of judgments that call for structural, legislative, and policy reform. The violations against these states speak to some of Europe's most egregious instances of state violence. If the Council of Europe could be decisive enough to expel Russia, should it not also sanction other member states whose noncompliance with judgments might make a mockery of the system itself? If so, participants wondered, what kinds of sanctions would actually be effective?

Russia and the Council of Europe

It is deeply destabilizing to see how forms of political and legal engagement that took years to build can shift seemingly overnight. Russia's expulsion came almost exactly twenty-six years after it joined the Council of Europe (1996) and twenty-four years after it became a signatory to the European Convention on Human Rights. The expulsion happened in a matter of days. Russia's integration into the Council had taken years. Russia was woven into the very fabric of Europe's largest human rights body. It was one of the largest financial contributors, had a massive Strasbourg-based staff, and was an influential presence in the Committee of Ministers and the Parliamentary Assembly. Its citizens were some of the most active in bringing cases to the European Court of Human Rights; its civil society organizations were some of the most respected and most engaged in strategic litigation and rights advocacy (Sundstrom et al. 2019). In hindsight, it seems unthinkable that the Council could take any other action but expulsion. But on the cusp of the invasion and in a short period afterwards, this was not taken for granted. This shift from contingency to certainty helps us see how geopolitical shifts are the product of real time and emergent interactions.

It was difficult to imagine Russia's expulsion at the cusp of the invasion for two reasons. First, it was an almost unprecedented sanction: the only other country to be temporarily expelled was Greece under the 1969 military junta. The Council had sanctioned Russia before, following the 2014 invasion of Crimea and in subsequent years for noncompliance with judgments of the European Court of Human Rights. But every time things reached almost a point of no return, Russia came back into the fold. The second, more fundamental reason is that the fragile architecture of rule of law within the Council system is grounded in compromise, negotiation, confidentiality, and soft diplomacy. Expulsion is not only antithetical to the forms of power that shape the ECHR system and the Council. It also stands to make real the limits of an international legal order that is formally binding but ultimately a fragile social achievement. In hindsight, this position might seem at best a naïve and at worst an act of appeasement with historical resonance. Indeed, as I show below, people did revisit these earlier moments of compromise with Russia in precisely this way. Yet, in real time, people had to generate the conditions for a firm stand on the grounds of soft power.

As I argued in chapters 1 and 2, the emergence of consensus-based power is central to the story of the Council of Europe. The ECHR system is innovative because, unlike other standard-setting international institutions (Cowan 2013), it combines binding legal commitments and diplomatic supervision. It offers political persuasion within the ambit of the law. These dual forms of pressure are channeled through multiple institutional opportunities for supervision that result in overall compliance with judgments. Combined with active civil society oversight, it has also produced profound social change on the ground (Hodson 2011). At the same time, the ECHR system is exemplary of a core problem of human rights and rule-of-law systems more generally. They are ultimately fragile and subject to breach when those who participate refuse to be bound by ultimately unenforceable commitments. In this sense, the ECHR system is exemplary of how the rule of law works: it is effective insofar as people believe in it, generate and institutionalize binding commitments, and feel bound by the rules of engagement. Rule of law after all is a practice-based achievement (Cheesman 2018). While this flexibility is what makes it socially generative, it also results in political and ethical murkiness.

As much as people talked about persuasion as central to the effectiveness of the system, it came with potential costs. An institution premised on binding legal authority and soft diplomacy is always haunted by complicity with violence among members within its rank. After all, if the goal is to keep countries "in," at what point does everyone become responsible for the kind of violence committed by member states? I spoke to this issue in chapter 2. The questions of how much violence was too much violence and how much noncompliance among member states was truly threatening to the system were a frequent theme in my research across the years. Such questions can be answered only in real time, within the situation in which one finds oneself and the terms of engagement on offer. Yet, in hindsight or with new contexts and interactions, the reassessment may change drastically. Compromise may suddenly—even overnight—become complicity.

The encounter with an extreme—although not wholly unprecedented—form of military violence during the Russian invasion of Ukraine revealed two key things. First, it demonstrated that member states could engage (and indeed already had engaged) in forms of violence that undercut the European Convention in fundamental ways and still remain in the system. Second, it revealed that the line between compromise (as a necessary feature of rule of law) and complicity was extremely fuzzy. Many people I spoke with expressed that calculus between compromise and complicity in the question: Was "worth it" to keep a noncompliant country in the Council? Right up to the point of Russia's expulsion, this balance was the subject of heated debate in formal meetings and in conversations in halls and offices across Strasbourg. Had access to the European Court of Human Rights for Russian citizens outweighed the negative impact of noncompliance and widescale convention violations?

In interviews I conducted between 2016 and 2022, people struggled with this balance but almost always came to the conclusion that it was "worth it." A 2018 interview with two activists from one of Russia's most respected human rights organizations reveals much of what was at stake when people considered this question. I asked what role the Court and the ECHR had played in Russian human rights activism. My first interlocutor replied that for many people in post-Soviet countries and particularly in Russia, "this court is the only hope. . . . This is really the court that is independent. And more importantly, the decisions of this court are binding. That is why it is really trustworthy—because they have hope, the victims, that the decisions of this court will be executed, and they will receive redress." Yet both women I interviewed were clear that the system wasn't perfect and that it required work, patience, and compromise. In this sense, the question of whether it was "worth it," was always also shaped by disappointments and limits: the calculus of an imperfect response to an imperfect world. Neither was engaging with the Russian state without difficulty (indeed, one of my interviewees had had her life threatened for her activism). But their analysis illustrated the pragmatics of necessity in the context of an imperfect but effective institution that facilitated negotiation and action.

Another interviewee familiar over many years with the work of the Committee of Ministers and its human rights advisory meetings reflected on something similar, a few weeks before Russia's expulsion. He talked eloquently about the often-complicated dynamics of the CM and frankly about the tensions between new and old members. But he also credited the model of soft diplomacy backed by hard law with much more effective human rights results than the Council often gets credit for. Here, as was frequently the case, Russia served as a limit case of both the hardest, most entrenched human rights and political problems as well as a sign of some progress. He noted that when it comes to more technical issues, Russia had implemented many judgments that are not frequently mentioned. He added that there are the positive examples of execution and changes all the time, including with "more difficult countries." We must, he noted, put talk of the lack of effectiveness of the system into perspective.

A great deal was at stake in Russia's expulsion: not only the access of its citizens to the Court, two decades of relationships, and a staff fully integrated into the Council but also the credibility of the institution itself. The shift in perspective was stark and swift in the days leading up to and just after Russia's expulsion. As the scale of the violence became clearer, the Committee of Ministers asked for PACE to advise on the expulsion of Russia from the Council of Europe. The proceedings consisted in hours of PACE member country representatives asserting unanimous support for Russia's expulsion and words of solidarity and support for Ukraine. Interspersed with these comments were devastating reports from Ukrainian representatives, some of whom had traveled with family members to Strasbourg to be heard and were shortly to return to the war. The display of unanimity was remarkable. In seemingly one fell swoop, at least in the publicly mediated platform of the hearings, the many years of posing and answering the question "Is it worth it?" gave way a resounding no: a crystallization of purpose that resulted in formal expulsion. The comments ranged widely in eloquence and power. But few diplomats who spoke failed to mention the need to reaffirm the values that bound the Council as a community. It was time to draw a line in the sand and on the public face of the Council itself. Indeed, many people I talked to were surprised, although pleased, with the speed of the decision. One interviewee working in communications and media relations noted that even his team was surprised to how quickly the CM reacted. The day after invasion they were suspended from PACE. "That is lightning quick for CoE. We just don't move that fast."

It is rare in instances of fieldwork that we experience what Caroline Humphrey has called a "decision event," in which the "multiple strands of personhood achieve unity and singularity," to overturn "accustomed patterns of intelligibility and the advent of a radically new idea" (2008, 357). Yet, what I realized was that expulsion was not the advent of something radically new. It was a crystallization of social relations, discursive expressions, and interactional practices that hardened a long-standing set of distinctions that were foundational to the ECHR system. But they were also distinctions that many people had worked to overcome in practice. People struggled daily to enact a rule-of-law and human rights system that was fair and meaningful, despite multiple contradictions and tensions: those between individual justice and structural change, between efficiency and access, and between national sovereignty and European supervision, to name a few. But for all the flexibility and room for maneuver, the foundational tension of who is and is not "us" remained available as a hard line with which to re-create borders and boundaries at moments of crisis.

The idea of unity both as a staging of a new community and a form of coherent personhood was central to this shift. The line drawn through Russia on the sign on the Council fence had its strong correlate in a sharp and sudden line-drawing in my interviews and conversations. The speed of the expulsion was accompanied by rapid reassessment not only of the Council's relationship to Russia but the history that had preceded it. While not coordinated, people's perspectives moved in remarkable concert, as a new framing of crisis, threat, and rupture replaced that of compromise. And the need to both explain and distance themselves from past cooperation was also striking.

An ambassador I spoke with told me, "More than three weeks ago, you would have heard me speaking words not of optimism, but of no illusions, of the necessity to keep Russia engaged." Russia is not monolithic, she reminded me, and its presence in Strasbourg had given her a vision of a European Russia. It was this Russia, one "turned toward the West," that was and will be again a goal for the European institutions. At the same time, there was a breaking point for her. She reflected on the decision to "give Russia one more chance" in 2019, following the suspension of voting rights from the PACE after the Crimea invasion of 2014 and a building record of noncompliance with Court judgments. While it was a kind of victory of diplomacy and unanimity at the time, she noted,

> now we can say, in these three years, they [Russia] have been a tremendous disappointment in human rights. From 2019 to now, the level of implementation has gone down . . . and also outright opposite legislation. . . . This means the old arguments from three years back that those 140 million Russians need the protection of the Court and Convention are no longer valid.

This real-time reassessment of whether it was "worth it" involved a few moves, exemplary of broader narrative shifts. People often first spoke of the complexity of making a real-time call about keeping Russia in or out of the Council in the face of violence. They narrated the shift in perspective and the realization that compromise had not worked. And they also often reassessed moments when they had believed things had been working, but in hindsight they might not have been. In other words, in conversation, people acknowledged both that perhaps they ought to have taken action years ago and how hard it was to know or see that course of action in real time, within the context of relationships based on consensus and diplomacy.

A legal attaché from the western Balkans told me a couple days before the expulsion: "I was here in 2014 when Crimea happened. We had almost the same conversation in those days." At the time, he told me, his state's position was that they shouldn't throw Russia out, because it was too important for Russian citizens to be protected by the ECtHR. But two days ago, he had received a communication from a network of NGOs representing civil society in Russia, who supported Russia's expulsion. This, he noted, was "quite shocking." He went on to note that things are different now than in 2014 (with Crimea). "If we tolerate one member state engaging in this kind of action, where is the limit?" He went on to note, "It's sad, but this [Russia's expulsion] will happen. The problem is how we will one day get them back." Perhaps, he noted, "in fifteen years someone will say it was a mistake to let them leave [but] on the spot in the moment, you see it's not so easy." He concluded, "if someone would come back to that same moment in time, they would decide the same thing in that moment and under those conditions."

As people made sense of their past actions, these narratives began to harden into a more public-facing set of categories, stances, and timelines that drew clear demarcations between Russia and the rest of the Council. In the face of institutional enmeshment, dialogue and negotiation gave way to calls for a strong ethical stance. This led to a hardening stance about the necessity of expulsion. As one legal attaché told me frankly at the start of our interview, "I'm glad they are gone."

In the period leading up to the invasion, observers, scholars, military experts, and ordinary people participated in trying to understand unintelligible decisions shaped by irrational violence. A headline in a major French magazine that sat on the shelves of a newsstand I passed nearly every day for two weeks posed the unanswerable question "What does Putin want?" Posts and analysts have pointed to Russian imperial traditions, Putin's own madness, and his increasing isolation. Yet the conversation still hinges on the question of the rational and irrational as a terrain in which we might know, decipher, and in turn operationalize diplomatic solutions (or justify military ones). In this case, the idea of intentionality is central to a theory of agency and personhood in which diplomatic relations are grounded. Geopolitical power politics may be brutal, unfair, and a mask for might making right. But people operationalize such power by attempts to uncover intentionality and appeal to the rational self-interest at the heart of liberal personhood. Action without clear reason and rationality were not only unthinkable for many of my interlocutors. They threaten the underlying communicative ideologies around which the fiction of rule of law is generated, sustained, and practiced. "What does Putin want?" is a question that threatens the European project by exposing the limits of rational communication as an infrastructure for political consensus that is at the very heart of democracy, rule of law, and human rights. Even as the line between rationality and irrationality was drawn through the Council via Russia's exclusion, people I spoke with moved to reconsolidate the forms of personhood and communicative practice that make rule of law work as a modality of social interaction

Thus despite the work of "bringing the outside in" that I discussed in chapter 2, the recursive distinctions that formed both the postwar and post–Cold War logics of the ECHR system remained available for reactivation at a moment of crisis. As universalizing logics that organize difference within a comparative and hierarchical framework, they operate as "an assemblage of shifting conjugations that alter the grammars within and through which we find ourselves making claims" (McGranahan and Collins 2018, 3). When the basis of those relationships come under question, difference can once again be foregrounded as the primary axis along which belonging is defined. In other words, at one moment we can see the operations of the ECHR system, the Court, the Committee, and the Parliamentary Assembly as a space for the pragmatic negotiation of difference (East/West, democratic/less democratic). At some points in time shared registers of rights and law withstand challenges, arguments, and differences internal to a community of belonging. In the next moment we can see how difference is reframed as a problem, foregrounded as an external threat rather than an internal resource, in ways that reconsolidate the universalizing project itself.

Conclusion

In the end, it took longer for the Council of Europe to take down the defaced sign than it did to decide on expulsion. Sometime in the last few days of April, it had been taken down, leaving only an absence. At some point, a new sign was posted listing forty-six member states. It signaled a constitutive absence that will continue to shape the experiences and interactions of those who remain. Analyzing the "before" and "after" demonstrates that consensus-based community can be drawn and redrawn to externalize a previously internal point of tension or compromise. Such distinctions rely on a theory of personhood, intentionality, and agency that is consolidated (rather than destabilized) by the crisis posed by extreme state violence and the refusal to abide by the rule of law. It is thus telling that a moment of crisis in the rule of law produced calls for more and better law and a recommitment to international institutions. This is a clue that judicialization is about far more than strategic interests of any one group of stakeholders. It is instead an ethos and a way of understanding and approaching fundamental questions about what holds societies together and what might tear them apart. As I've demonstrated here, it is one grounded in liberal presuppositions about personhood, democratic maturity, and trust. That doesn't mean it is not worth investing in. The question is: Is this version of justice "worth it"? Liberal institutions *both* reproduce the longue-durée project of the West and provide means and mechanism for responding to demands for justice, equity, and social change. They are places to take a stand against the horrific wages of state violence. And they are built on the very same categories that often justify it—rational intentionality, comparative civilizational and political hierarchies, and European "us-ness." This "imperial debris" (Stoler 2013) lives in what is both best and worse in European human rights: a deep commitment to humanism and the sanctity of the person as well as the legacies through which that humanity has always been contingent, differentially allocated, racialized, and policed.

In this spirit, I close by asking, So what? What does it get us and how does it help to offer a critical perspective on normative institutions when people are facing down extreme violence in their everyday lives? In 2004, Bruno Latour posed the question, Has critique run out of steam? He was increasingly worried at how right-wing and climate-denial groups embraced antifoundationalist thought that was resonant with his own intellectual project. Drawing a distinction between matters of fact and matters of concern, Latour asked,

"Can we devise another powerful descriptive tool that deals this time with matters of concern and whose import then will no longer be to debunk but to protect and to care" (232). I agree with my interlocutors over the years that rule of law and democracy are and should be a matter of concern worth not only critiquing but nurturing. The ECHR system does do an excellent if flawed job of creating a forum for activists, diplomats, state officials, and others to generate critical human rights practices. The commitment to democracy is urgent, and institutions that preserve and safeguard democratic rights and freedoms are under brutal attack across the continent and beyond. Having studied democracy from an anthropological perspective for twenty years, I am trying to hold onto these contradictory positions of investment in and critique of the terms of politics on offer.

Our categories come to us as layers upon layers of social relations, semiotic and language ideologies, and deeply held commitments and beliefs. It is difficult to shift them, even as one feels caught between the messiness of experience and the desire for something better or new. This emerging collective humility about the possibility of progress is a crack in the structure of North Atlantic universals (Trouillot 2002). I have hoped to show in these chapters how people committed to human rights and rule of law can harness institutions and work the cracks and fissures in normative forms. What we need most are spaces for more experimental, tentative, and vulnerable forms of imagination, what Maja Petrović-Šteger has called a process of visioning that helps us "to identify the events, processes, and individual and collective conditions that are recognized as capable of making a difference or yielding change" (2020, 9). Whether we can find these within normative institutions like the Council or the Court requires first understanding how certainty is produced and referenced even or especially in the face of uncertainty. People unwittingly participate in the reproduction of categories that have been deployed as forms of domination and exclusion because they feel invested in the best version of those categories and because there often seems to be little other choice. Perhaps it offers the possibility for different and better questions about what social justice looks like in practice. Human rights, rule of law, and democracy are social and discursive achievements somewhere between normativity and imagination. And they are never free from dynamics of power and the historical conditions of possibility that shape their expression.

Legal responses to political problems will always be partial and in many ways unsatisfying. Yet as years of scholarship in socio-legal studies have demonstrated, law does important social, ideological, and affective work. If the rule of law is a social fiction, it is nonetheless a generative one. In a recent piece (Greenberg 2020), I explored alternative ways to think about the social and political work of legal categories and institutional frameworks, beyond normative assessments of success or failure. These concerns were driven not only by scholarly curiosity but the everyday problems people face in making the law stretch to address pressing concerns, while still carefully guarding institutional legitimacy. In the context of lawfare, authoritarianism, and constitutional capture (Scheppele 2018), those engaged in institutions like the Council and Court are asking how flexible systems based on compromise, diplomacy, and goodwill can be before they break. And if the answer is "very flexible," does that mean the institution itself is ethically compromised and politically weak? In an era of juridical politics (Eckert et al. 2012), the stakes in balancing hope in justice with formal institutional mechanisms are high. Those who have used human rights to engage in decades of activism, organizing, and coordination to make the system work must figure out how to adapt to shifting goals and newly drawn lines.

I hope this book is a small contribution to finding collective ways to navigate both the limits and needs for institutions and practices that nurture democracy, rule of law, and human rights—as well as the possible ways that we, as anthropologists and people, can try to build alternatives. Finally, confronting the fragility of the rule of law raises important questions about the role of scholarly critique. Human rights institutions are "not enough" (Moyn 2018). But they can also be socially efficacious and meaningful. Normative institutions and categories can offer important ways to take ethical and political stands against forms of state violence. In the wake of post–Cold War triumphalist narratives, many writing about postsocialist transformations felt intellectually and politically obliged to critique the categories through which emerging democracies were managed and policed.[1] They sought to think beyond East and West and pose critical questions about the exclusions of liberalism. In recent years, with what political scientists would label "democratic backsliding," illiberal politics, and neofascism, it has been more difficult to know how those critiques will circulate and land in the context of people's advocacy and struggles. These realities necessitate multiple and alternative approaches to institutions—ones that ask what they do within and potentially beyond the formal categories through which they operate. Anthropologists in and of Europe might take this moment to ask how to both support calls for democracy among our activist interlocutors and still think critically about the terms of ethics and politics on offer. Pluralizing justice, human rights, and the rule of law means both understanding institutions and thinking with and beyond them.

Notes

Preface

1. Lily Lynch (@lilyslynch), https://x.com/lilyslynch/status/1783776462576714097.

Introduction

1. See, for example, *Al Skeini and Others v. The United Kingdom* (2011).

2. The Court issues an extensive overview of these criteria available on their website: https://www.echr.coe.int/documents/d/echr/admissibility_guide_eng.

3. One major gap is that I did not speak with applicants directly. This was both a practical decision, given the difficulty of accessing applicants and the confidentiality that bound their legal representatives, and an ethical decision. I did not feel that I could do justice to applicant experiences in the length and depth they would deserve. Nor did I wish to put applicants in positions of reliving traumatic and painful experiences. I hope that the analysis here is useful for litigators and applicants in the future in that it attempts to make more accessible the complex workings of an institutions that many often find alienating and difficult to engage.

4. I recorded interviews when given permission or kept careful notes, also with permission, if people preferred me not to record.

5. My coursework included foundations courses, including criminal law, legal writing, and specialized courses in administrative law, international humanitarian and human rights law, and comparative criminal procedure (with a European focus), among others. In addition, I completed an MA thesis comparing freedom of expression case law at the ECtHR and in the United States. Parts of that thesis were published in Stanislaw Gozdz Roszkowski and Gianluca Pontrandolfo (see Greenberg 2021b) and are also cited to in chapter 2.

6. This often went hand in hand with a sense of vulnerability in the face of the seemingly uncheckable power of state violence and a rising trend of militarized anti-

democratic authoritarianism (Darian-Smith 2022) and fascist politics (Holmes 2019).

7. As Susan Coutin and Barbara Yngvesson have argued, "Law and ethnography are bounded in that, as technologies, each closes off other ways of knowing or revealing. They are limitless in that their potential for revealing truth can be directed toward a seemingly endless array of problems and practices. Further, the truths that they reveal are both already there—merely uncovered or made visible by particularly techniques—and also new creations, brought into being through technology itself" (2008, 2).

Chapter 1

1. For example, Article 10 of the ECHR reads as follows:

Everyone has the right to freedom of expression. This right shall include freedom to hold opinions and to receive and impart information and ideas without interference by public authority and regardless of frontiers;

The exercise of these freedoms, since it carries with it duties and responsibilities, may be subject to such formalities, conditions, restrictions or penalties as are prescribed by law and are necessary in a democratic society, in the interests of national security, territorial integrity or public safety, for the prevention of disorder or crime, for the protection of health or morals, for the protection of the reputation or rights of others, for preventing the disclosure of information received in confidence, or for maintaining the authority and impartiality of the judiciary.

2. For a parallel shift, see Pavone's (2022) account of an emerging consciousness of European legal systems among strategic litigators at the International Court of Justice.

3. Representative Mr. Ungoed-Thomas, UK.

4. The drafting committee ultimately argued between two alternatives, which they dubbed A and B. Plan A would be an enumeration of general principles, and B would be a listing of precise definitions.

5. See *Tyrer v. United Kingdom* (1978).

6. See Greenberg 2021b, which examines this case in similar ways in relationship to how courts "teach" domestic member states to attune to the appropriate scope for context in different cases involving margin of appreciation doctrine.

7. For a recent overview, see ECtHR, *Guide on the Case Law of the European Convention on Human Rights: Rights of LGBTI Persons*, updated 31 August 2024, https:// echr.coe.int/Documents/Guide_LGBTI_rights_ENG.pdf. For a comprehensive sociolegal analysis of this case law, see Johnson 2013.

8. See, for example, the work of ILGA Europe in strategic litigation, https://www .ilga-europe.org/.

9. Including positive obligations to promote tolerance (see *Identoba and Others v. Georgia*, 2015, § 100, and *Association ACCEPT and Others v. Romania*, 2021, § 146,)

10. Anushka Asthana and Rowena Mason, "UK Must Leave European Convention on Human Rights, Says Theresa May, *The Guardian*, 25 April 2016, https://www.the guardian.com/politics/2016/apr/25/uk-must-leave-european-convention-on-human -rights-theresa-may-eu-referendum.

11. The video can be found at https://www.youtube.com/watch?v=ptfmAY6M6aA.

Chapter 2

1. This took the form of massive investment in civil society promotion and rule of law and democracy programming (Hann and Dunn 1996; Wedel 2001; Carothers 2006); new hierarchies of knowledge production (Boyer 2005); and shifts in economic ordering of value, labor, and property (Verdery 2003).

2. European Court of Human Rights, *Overview 1959–2020*, Council of Europe report, p. 4 https://www.echr.coe.int/documents/d/echr/Overview_19592020_ENG.

3. European Court of Human Rights, *Overview 1959–2020*, Council of Europe report, https://www.echr.coe.int/documents/d/echr/Overview_19592020_ENG.

4. See *Broniowski v. Poland* (2004).

5. See *Ibrahim and Others v. The United Kingdom* (2016).

Chapter 3

1. See Council of Europe, "Rule of Law," Venice Commission, https://www.venice.coe.int/WebForms/pages/?p=02_Rule_of_law&lang=EN.

2. *Vavřička and Others v. The Czech Republic* (2021).

3. This was the second time a female judge told me that in the face of horrible and overwhelming human rights violations, they "couldn't cry" but had to maintain professional distance. The gendered nature of this insistence on professional distance in shared terms is a potentially interesting avenue to explore, although it is difficult to generalize from only two examples.

4. Basak Çalı, "Farewell to Marckx and All That or How I Received 'The Letter' (From the Registry of the European Court of Human Rights)," *Strasbourg Observers*, 20 January 2017, https://strasbourgobservers.com/2016/01/20/farewell-to-marckx-and-all-that-or-how-i-received-the-letter-from-the-registry-of-the-european-court-of-human-rights/.

5. Helena De Vylder, "Stensholt v. Norway: Why Single Judge Decisions Undermine the Court's Legitimacy," Strasbourg Observers, May 28, 2014, https://strasbourgobservers.com/2014/05/28/stensholt-v-norway-why-single-judge-decisions-undermine-the-courts-legitimacy-2/.

6. "A Section is an administrative entity and a Chamber is a judicial formation of the Court within a given Section. The Court has 5 Sections in which Chambers and Committees are formed." "Composition of the Court," European Court of Human Rights, n.d., https://www.echr.coe.int/composition-of-the-court.

Chapter 4

1. Haider (2013) traces the emergence of the pilot judgment procedure to the Court's earlier handling of repetitive cases. It was a way to formalize a method of accounting that stemmed both from managerial need and registry lawyers' experience that there was resonance across cases in some instances.

Chapter 5

1. Different qualities of time—the rhythms of cases and the relationships and professional networks through which they are enacted—also shape people's sense of themselves as legal subjects, lawyers, judges, applicants, or advocates. Indeed, there is no workable, living system of institutional organization without the ability to manage, harness, and comment on different experiences and uses of time (Munn 1992).

2. Sarat and Scheingold (2001) argue that "the objective of the attorneys that we characterize as cause lawyers is to deploy their legal skills to challenge prevailing distributions of political, social, economic, and/or legal values and resources. Cause lawyers choose clients and cases in order to pursue their own ideological and redistributive projects" (13). In her extensive study on litigation and civil society mobilization in the EU, Cichowski notes that a key condition of social change litigation is that it impacts institutional frameworks and has a feedback effect on governance that may provide opportunities for future mobilization (2007, 9–11).

3. The event was public recorded and was not under Chatham House rules.

4. I owe a great debt in my thinking on the meaning of strategic litigation and how it's changed to an opportunity to support this project in small volunteer ways. This analysis benefited from the vision of human rights litigators and EIN staff in understanding how cases might support and sustain more robust opportunities for change.

Chapter 6

1. See for example, *Opuz v. Turkey* as one example interviewees cited as directly influenced by the *D. H.* experience. Beyond this, the case is routinely cited in case law on Article 14 violations.

2. For example, the dissent cites extensive empirical research: Amnesty International reports on brutal and systematic anti-Roma police violence in Bulgaria; findings by the United Nations Special Rapporteur on Extrajudicial, Summary or Arbitrary Executions to the United Nations Commission on Human Rights; the Council of Europe's Commissioner for Human Rights; and research and publications by the European Roma Rights Centre, the Human Rights Project, the Bulgaria Helsinki Committee, and Human Rights Watch.

3. These include ECRI, the Human Rights Commissioner, educational institutions (Global Alliance for the Education of Young Children [para. 43]), and international children's rights organizations (UNICEF). Major international human rights and advocacy organizations also weighed in, such as, Amnesty International, the European Roma Rights Center, Interrights, Human Rights Watch, Minority Rights Group International, the European Network Against Racism, and the European Roma Information Office, International Step by Step Association, the Roma Education Fund, the European Early Childhood Education Research Association.

4. According to data supplied by the applicants, which was obtained through questionnaires sent in 1999 to the head teachers of the eight special schools and sixty-nine primary schools in the town of Ostrava, the total number of pupils placed in special schools in Ostrava came to 1,360, of whom 762 (56%) were Roma. Conversely, Roma represented only 2.26% of the total of 33,372 primary-school pupils in Ostrava. Further, although only 1.8% of non-Roma pupils were placed in special schools, in Ostrava the proportion of Roma pupils assigned to such schools was 50.3%. Accordingly, a Roma child in Ostrava was twenty-seven times more likely to be placed in a special school than a non-Roma child (*D. H. and Others*, para. 18).

5. And through the direct commentary of major institutions such as the Parliamentary Assembly of the Council of Europe, the European Commission Against Racism and Intolerance (ECRI), the Commission for Human Rights, European Monitoring

Centre on Racism and Xenophobia (now the European Union Agency for Fundamental Rights), and other constitutional courts.

6. The intersection of human rights and stereotyping has subsequently been developed in case law. See Timmer 2011.

7. See for example a focus on changes in numbers in a 2014 document "First and foremost, results of the Czech School Inspectorate survey carried out in autumn 2013 have shown one important fact, namely the increasing number of pupils with a mild mental disability who are educated in mainstream classes following individual integration: since 2009 their number has increased by more than 66%. On the contrary, the number of pupils in special classes has decreased by more than one quarter (please see the Table below). These data show that integration of disadvantaged pupils into mainstream schools and classes takes place in the Czech education system on an ongoing basis" (DH-DD(2014)541). This focus on the raw numbers is something the NGOs will later take issue with as a mischaracterization, It focuses on absolute numbers and not on underlying practices through which the production of numbers retains and reinforces discrimination at other levels, categories, testing procedures, and interactional contexts.

8. In countering government reports and accounts of implementation as accurate, the civil society submissions not only shift what counts as meaningful data, but they also offer alternative participatory frameworks for knowledge production and who has the authority to speak as to what counts as implementation. Thus DH-DD (2012) 1089 notes that "in order to assess the implementation of the D. H. judgment on the ground—and whether these safeguards are in fact working—Amnesty International and ERRC conducted field research is Ostrava (the region in which the D. H. case originated)."

Conclusion

1. For an excellent overview of this critical project, see Dace Dzenovska and Larisa Kurtović, eds., 2018, "Lessons for Liberalism from the 'Illiberal East," Hot Spot series, *Fieldsights*, https://culanth.org/fieldsights/series/lessons-for-liberalism-from-the-illiberal-east.

Bibliography

Achiume, E. Tendayi and Asli Bali. 2021. "Race and Empire: Legal Theory within, through, and across National Borders." *UCLA Law Review* 67(6; April): 1386–1431.

Agha, Asif. 2005. "Voice, Footing, Enregisterment." *Journal of Linguistic Anthropology* 15(1): 38–59.

Ahmann, Chloe. 2018. "It's Exhausting to Create an Event Out of Nothing": Slow Violence and the Manipulation of Time." *Cultural Anthropology* 33(1): 142–171.

Ahmed, Sarah. 2012. *On Being Included: Racism and Diversity in Institutional Life.* Duke University Press.

Allen, Lori. 2009. "Martyr Bodies in the Media: Human Rights, Aesthetics and the Politics of Immediation in the Palestinian Intifada." *American Ethnologist.* 36(1): 161–180.

———. 2013. *The Rise and Fall of Human Rights: Cynicism and Politics in Occupied Palestine.* Stanford University Press.

Alpes, M. J, and G. Baranowska. 2024. "The Politics of Legal Facts: The Erasure of Pushback Evidence from the European Court of Human Rights." *Law and Social Inquiry.* 1–24.

Alter, Karen J. 2001. *Establishing the Supremacy of European Law: The Making of an International Rule of Law in Europe.* Oxford University Press.

Alter, Karen J., Laurence R. Helfer, and Mikael Rask Madsen. 2018. *International Court Authority.* Oxford University Press.

Anderson, Benedict. 1983. *Imagined Communities: Reflections on the Origin and Spread of Nationalism.* Verso Press.

Anderson, Perry. 2023. "The Standard of Civilization." *New Left Review* 143: 5–29.

Anders, G. 2008. "The Normativity of Numbers: World Bank and IMF Conditionality." *PoLAR: Political and Legal Anthropology Review* 31(2): 187–202.

Anghie, Antony. 2005. *Imperialism, Sovereignty, and the Making of International Law.* Cambridge University Press.

———. 2009. "Rethinking Sovereignty in International Law." *Annual Review of Law and Social Science* 5: 291–310.

———. 2023. "Rethinking International Law: A TWAIL Retrospective." *European Journal of International Law* 34(1): 7–112.

Asad, Talal. James W. Fernandez, Michael Herzfeld, Andrew Lass, Susan Carol Rogers, Jane Schneider, and Katherine Verdery. 1997. "Provocations of European Ethnology." *American Anthropologist* 99 (4): 713–730.

Babul, Elif. 2017. *Bureaucratic Intimacies: Translating Human Rights in Turkey.* Stanford University Press.

Bakhtin Mikhail M. 1982. "Forms of Time and Chronotope in the Novel." In *The Dialogic Imagination*, edited by Michael Holquist. University of Texas Press.

Ballestero, Andrea. 2015. "The Ethics of a Formula: Calculating a Financial-Humanitarian Price for Water." *American Ethnologist* 42(2): 262–278.

Bass, Gary. 2000. *Stay the Hand of Vengeance: The Politics of War Crimes Tribunals.* Princeton University Press.

Bates, Ed. 2011. *The Evolution of the European Convention on Human Rights from Its Inception to the Creation of a Permanent Court of Human Rights.* Oxford University Press.

Bauman, R., and C. L. Briggs. 2003. *Voices of Modernity: Language Ideologies and the Politics of Inequality.* Cambridge University Press.

Baumgärtel, Moritz. 2019. *Demanding Rights: Europe's Supranational Courts and the Dilemma of Migrant Vulnerability.* Cambridge University Press.

Baxi, Pratiksa. 2014. *Public Secrets of Law: Rape Trials in India.* Oxford University Press.

Bear, Laura. 2014. "Doubt, Conflict, Mediation: The Anthropology of Modern Time." *Journal of the Royal Anthropological Institute* 20(1): 3–30.

Bens, Jonas. 2022. *The Sentimental Court: The Affective Life of International Criminal Justice.* Cambridge University Press.

Berdahl, Daphne. 2001. "'Go Trabi Go': Reflections on a Car and Its Symbolization over Time." *Anthropology and Humanism* 25(2): 131–141.

Berlant, Lauren. 2016. "The Commons: Infrastructures for Troubling Times." *Environment and Planning D: Society and Space* 34(3): 393–419.

Bernstein, Anya. 2017. "Bureaucratic Speech: Language Choice and Democratic Identity in a Taipei Bureaucracy." *PoLAR* 40(1): 28–51.

Besson, Samantha. 2017. "Legal Human Rights Theory." In *A Companion to Applied Philosophy*, edited by Kasper Lippert-Rasmussen, Kimberley Brownlee, and David Coady. John Wiley & Sons.

Billaud, Julie, and Jane K. Cowan. 2020. "The Bureaucratisation of Utopia: Ethics, Affects and Subjectivities in International Governance Processes." *Social Anthropology* 28(1): 6–16.

Bishara, Amahl. 2013. *U.S. News Production and Palestinian Politics.* Stanford University Press.

Böröcz, József. 2006. Goodness Is Elsewhere: The Rule of European Difference. *Comparative Studies in Society and History* 48(1): 110–138.

Boyer, Dominic. 2005. "The Corporeality of Expertise." *Ethnos* 70(2): 243–266.

Brems, Eva. 2021. "Hidden Under Headscarves? Women and Religion in the Case Law of the European Court of Human Rights." *Religion and Human Rights* 16(2–3): 173–200.

Brković, Čarna. 2016, "Scaling Humanitarianism: Humanitarian Actions in a Bosnian Town." *Ethnos* 81(1): 99–124.

———. 2024. "Socialist Modernist Worldmaking: Yugoslav Interventions in the International Humanitarian Debates in the 1970s." *Humanity: An International Journal of Human Rights, Humanitarianism, and Development* 15(1): 18-40.

Bruce-Jones, Eddie. 2016. *Race in the Shadow of Law: Contemporary Violence in Europe.* London: Routledge.

Burton, Orisanmi. 2023. *Tip of the Spear: Black Radicalism, Prison Repression, and the Long Attica Revolt.* University of California Press.

Buyse, Antoine, Katharine Fortin, Brianne McGonigle Leyh, and Julie Fraser. 2021."The Rule of Law from Below—A Concept under Development." *Utrecht Law Review* 17(2): 1–7.

Bryant, Rebecca, and Mete Hatay. 2020. *Sovereignty Suspended: Building the So-called State.* University of Pennsylvania Press.

Cabatingan, Lee. 2023. *A Region Among States: Law and Non-sovereignty in the Caribbean.* University of Chicago Press.

Cabot, Heath. 2014. *On the Doorstep of Europe: Asylum and Citizenship in Greece.* University of Pennsylvania Press.

Çalı, Başak. 2007. "Balancing Human Rights? Methodological Problems with Weights, Scales and Proportions." *Human Rights Quarterly* 29(1): 251–270.

Çalı, Başak, and Anne Koch. 2014. "Foxes Guarding the Foxes? The Peer Review of Human Rights Judgments by the Committee of Ministers of the Council of Europe." *Human Rights Law Review* 14(2): 301–325.

Çalı, Başak, Anne Koch, and Nicola Bruch. 2013. "The Legitimacy of Human Rights Courts: A Grounded Interpretivist Analysis of the European Court of Human Rights." *Human Rights Quarterly* 35(4): 955–984.

Candea, Matei. 2021. "'When I See What Democracy Is . . .': Bleak Liberalism in a French Court." *Social Anthropology.* 29(2): 453–470.

Canfield, Matthew. 2022. *Translating Food Sovereignty.* Stanford University Press.

Canfield, Matthew, Julia Dehm, and Marisa Fassi. 2021. "Translocal Legalities: Local Encounters with Transnational Law." *Transnational Legal Theory* 12(3): 335–359.

Carothers, Thomas, ed. 2006. *Promoting the Rule of Law Abroad: In Search of Knowledge.* Carnegie Endowment for International Peace.

Carr, Summerson, and Michael Lempert. 2016. "Introduction: Pragmatics of Scale." In *Scale: Discourses and Dimensions of Social Life,* edited by Summerson Carr and Michael Lempert. University of California Press.

Cavanaugh, Jillian R., and Shalini Shankar. 2017. "Toward a Theory of Language Materiality: An Introduction." In *Language and Materiality: Ethnographic and Theoretical Explorations,* edited by Jillian R. Cavanaugh and Shalini Shankar. Cambridge University Press.

Chakrabarty, Dipesh. 2000. *Provincializing Europe: Postcolonial Thought and Historical Difference.* Princeton University Press.

Channell-Justice, Emily. 2022. *Without the State: Self-Organization and Political Activism in Ukraine*. University of Toronto Press.

Cheesman, Nick. 2018. "Rule-of-Law Ethnography." *Annual Review of Law and Social Science* 14: 167–184.

Chua, Lynette. 2018. *The Politics of Love in Myanmar*. Stanford University Press.

Cichowski, Rachel. 2007. *The European Court and Civil Society: Litigation, Mobilization and Governance*. Cambridge University Press.

Clarke, Kamari M. 2009. *Fictions of Justice: The International Criminal Court and the Challenge of Legal Pluralism in Sub-Saharan Africa*. Cambridge University Press.

———. 2019. *Affective Justice: The International Criminal Court and the Pan-African Pushback*. Duke University Press.

Cody, Francis. 2023. *The News Event: Popular Sovereignty in the Age of Deep Mediatization*. University of Chicago Press.

Cohen, Mathilde. 2014. "Ex Ante versus Ex Post Deliberations: Two Models of Judicial Deliberations in Courts of Last Resort." *The American Journal of Comparative Law* 62: 401–458.

Council of Europe. 1975–1985. 8 vols. *Collected Edition of the "Travaux Préparatoires" of the European Convention on Human Rights*. Martinus Nijhoff.

———. 1975. *Preparatory Commission of the Council of Europe, Committee of Ministers, Consultative Assembly 11 May–8 September 1949*. Vol. 1 of *Collected Edition of the "Travaux Préparatoires."* Martinus Nijhoff.

———. 1976. *Committee of Experts 2 February–10 March 1950*. Vol. 3 of *Collected Edition of the "Travaux Préparatoires."* Martinus Nijhoff.

Council of Europe, ECtHR. 1977. "Preparatory Work on Article 1 of the European Convention on Human Rights," 31 March 1977. https://www.echr.coe.int/docu ments/d/echr/echrtravaux-art1-cour-77-9-en1290551.

Christoffersen, Jonas, and Mikael Rask Madsen. 2011. *The European Court of Human Rights Between Law and Politics*. Oxford University Press.

Constable, Marianne. 2014. *Our Word Is Our Bond: How Legal Speech Acts*. Stanford University Press.

Cooper, Jessica. 2018. "Unruly Affects: Attempts at Control and All That Escapes from an American Mental Health Court." *Cultural Anthropology* 33(1): 85–108.

Coutin, Susan, and Barbara Yngvesson. 2008. "Technologies of Knowledge Production: Law, Ethnography and the Limits of Explanation." *PoLAR* 31(1): 1–7.

Cowan, Jane. 2013. "Before Audit Culture: A Genealogy of International Oversight of Rights." In *The Gloss of Harmony: the Politics of Policy Making in Multilateral Organizations*, edited by Birgit Muller. Pluto Press.

Cowan, Jane K., Marie-Benedicte Dembour, and Richard Wilson. 2001. *Culture and Rights: Anthropological Perspectives*. Cambridge University Press.

Crenshaw, Kimberlé. 1989. "Demarginalizing the Intersection of Race and Sex: A Black Feminist Critique of Antidiscrimination Doctrine, Feminist Theory and Antiracist Politics." *University of Chicago Legal Forum* 1989(1): Article 8.

Darian-Smith, Eve. 2022. *Global Burning: Rising Antidemocracy and the Climate Crisis*. Stanford University Press.

Das, Veena. 2019. "A Child Disappears: Law in the Courts, Law in the Interstices of Everyday Life." *Contributions to Indian Sociology* 53(1): 97–132.

De Genova, Nicholas. 2017. *The Borders of "Europe": Autonomy of Migration, Tactics of Bordering*. Duke University Press.

Dembour, Marie-Benedicte. 2006. *Who Believes in Human Rights?* Cambridge University Press.

———. 2015. *When Humans Become Migrants*. Oxford University Press.

———. 2023. "The Evidentiary System of the European Court of Human Rights in Critical Perspective." *European Convention on Human Rights Law Review* 4(4): 363–374.

Dezalay, Yves, and Bryant G. Garth. 2012. "Introduction: Constructing Transnational Justice." In *Lawyers and the Construction of Transnational Justice*, edited by Yves Dezalay and Bryant G. Garth. Routledge.

Drzemczewski, Andrew. 2017. "Human Rights in Europe: An Insider's View." *European Human Rights Law Review* 2: 134–144.

Dunn, Elizabeth. 2004. *Privatizing Poland: Baby Food, Big Business, and the Remaking of Labor*. Cornell University Press.

Duranti, Marco. 2017. *The Conservative Human Rights Revolution: European Identity, Transnational Politics, and the Origins of the European Convention*. Oxford University Press.

Dzenovska, Dace. 2018. *School of Europeanness: Tolerance and Other Lessons in Political Liberalism*. Cornell University Press.

Dzehtsiarou, Kanstantsin. 2019. "European Consensus and the Evolutive Interpretation of the European Convention on European Rights." *German Law Journal* 12(10): 1730–1745.

Eckert, Julia, Brian Donahoe, Christian Strumpell, and Zerrin Ozlem Biner. 2012. *Law Against the State: Ethnographic Forays into Law's Transformations*. Cambridge University Press.

Edwards, Terra. 2024. *Going Tactile: Life at the Limits of Language*. Oxford University Press.

Eltringham, Nigel. 2012 "Spectators to the Spectacle of Law: The Formation of a 'Validating Public' at the International Criminal Tribunal for Rwanda." *Ethnos* 77(3): 425–445.

Espeland, Wendy, and Mitchell Stevens. 1998. "Commensuration as a Social Process." *Annual Review of Sociology* 24: 313–343.

Espeland, Wendy, and Berit Irene Vannebo. 2007. "Accountability, Quantification, and Law." *Annual Review of Law and Social Science* 3: 21–43.

Fechter, Anne Meike. 2023. "'Every Person Counts': The Problem of Scale in Everyday Humanitarianism." *Social Anthropology* 31(1): 14–29.

Fedirko, Taras. 2021. "Liberalism in Fragments: Oligarchy and the Liberal Subject in Ukrainian News Journalism." *Social Anthropology* 29(2): 471–489.

Fedirko, Taras, Farhan Samanani, and Hugh F. Williamson. 2021. "Grammars of Liberalism." *Social Anthropology* 29(2): 373–386.

Fernando, Mayanthi. 2014. *The Republic Unsettled: Muslim French and the Contradictions of Secularism*. Duke University Press.

Fraser, Nancy. 1990. Rethinking the Public Sphere: A Contribution to the Critique of Actually Existing Democracy. Social Text 25/26: 56–80.

Fuchs, Sandhya. 2024. *Fragile Hope: Seeking Justice for Hate Crimes in India*. Stanford University Press.

Fudge, Judy. 2011. "Constitutionalizing Labour Rights in Europe." In *The Legal Protection of Human Rights: Sceptical Essays*, edited by Tom Campbell, Keith Ewing, and Adam Tompkins. Oxford University Press.

Gal, Susan. 2006. "Contradictions of Standard Language in Europe." *Social Anthropology*. 14(2): 163–181.

Gal, Susan, and Judith T. Irvine. 2019. *Signs of Difference: Language and Ideology in Social Life.* Cambridge University Press.

Gal, Susan, and Gail Kligman. 2000. *The Politics of Gender after Socialism.* Princeton University Press.

Gal, Susan, and Kathryn Woolard. 2001. *Languages and Publics. The Making of Authority.* St. Jerome's.

Gellner, Ernest. 1983. *Nations and Nationalism.* Cornell University Press.

Gershon, Ilana. 2011. "Studying Cultural Pluralism in Courts versus Legislatures." *PoLAR* 34(1): 155–174.

Getachew, Adom. 2019. *Worldmaking After Empire: The Rise and Fall of Self-Determination.* Princeton University Press.

Giannoulopoulos, Dimitrios. 2016. "Strasbourg Jurisprudence, Law Reform and Comparative Law: A Tale of the Right to Custodial Legal Assistance in Five Countries." *Human Rights Law Review* 16(1): 103–129.

Gille, Zsuzsa. 2016. *Paprika, Foie Gras, and Red Mud: The Politics of Materiality in the European Union.* Indiana University Press.

Goodale, Mark. 2006. "Ethical Theory as Social Practice." *American Anthropologist* 108(1): 25–37.

———. 2009. *Surrendering to Utopia: An Anthropology of Human Rights.* Stanford University Press.

———. 2019. *A Revolution in Fragments: Traversing Scales of Justice, Ideology and Practice in Bolivia.* Duke University Press.

Goodman, Jane, Matt Tomlinson, and Justin B. Richland. 2014. "Citational Practices: Knowledge, Personhood and Subjectivity." *Annual Review of Anthropology* 43: 449–463.

Goodwin, Charles. 1994. "Professional Vision." *American Anthropologist* 96(3): 606–633.

Graan, Andrew. 2016. "Strategic Publicity: On International Intervention and the Performativity of Public Communication in Postconflict Macedonia." *HAU: Journal of Ethnographic Theory* 6(3): 277–303.

Greenberg, Jessica. 2014. *After the Revolution: Youth, Democracy and the Politics of Disappointment in Postsocialist Serbia.* Stanford University Press.

———. 2020. "Law, Politics, and Efficacy at the European Court of Human Rights." *American Ethnologist* 47(4): 417–431.

———. 2021a. "Counterpedagogy, Sovereignty, and Migration at the European Court of Human Rights." *Law and Social Inquiry* 46(2): 518–539.

———. 2021b. "Pedagogies of Context: Language Ideology and Expression Rights at the European Court of Human Rights." In *Law, Language and the Courtroom: Legal Linguistics and the Discourse of Judges*, edited by Stanislaw Gozdz Roszkowski, and Gianluca Pontrandolfo. Routledge.

———. 2024. "Justice Suspended: Rethinking Institutions, Regimentation, and Channels from a Human Rights Law Perspective." *Journal of Linguistic Anthropology* 34(1): 45–65.

Guilhot, Nicolas. 2005. *The Democracy Maker: Human Rights and the Politics of Global Order.* Columbia University Press.

Hann, C. M., and Elizabeth Dunn. 1996. *Civil Society: Challenging Western Models.* Routledge.

Haas, Peter M. 1992. "Introduction: Epistemic Communities and International Policy Coordination." *International Organization* 46(1): 1–35.

Haider, Dominik. 2013. *The Pilot-Judgment Procedure of the European Court of Human Rights.* Martinus Nijhoff Press.

Habermas. Jurgen. 1992. *The Structural Transformation of the Public Sphere.* MIT Press.

Hampson, Françoise, Claudia Martin, and Frans Viljoen. 2018. "Inaccessible Apexes: Comparing Access to Regional Human Rights Courts and Commissions in Europe, the Americas, and Africa." *International Journal of Constitutional Law* 16(1; January): 161–186.

Handman, Courtney. 2025. *Circulations: Modernist Imaginaries of Colonialism and Decolonization in Papua New Guinea.* University of California Press.

Hathaway, Oona. 2022. "A Crime in Search of a Court." *Foreign Affairs*, May 19. https://www.foreignaffairs.com/articles/ukraine/2022-05-19/crime-search-court.

Helfer, Laurence. 2008. "Redesigning the European Court of Human Rights: Embeddedness as a Deep Structural Principle of the European Rights Regime." *The European Journal of International Law* 19(1): 125–159.

Heri, Corina. 2024. "Deference, Dignity and 'Theoretical Crisis, Justifying ECtHR Rights between Prudence and Protection." *Human Rights Law Review* 24: 1–19.

Hetherington, Kregg. 2011. *Guerrilla Auditors: The Politics of Transparency in Neoliberal Paraguay.* Duke University Press.

Hillebrandt, Maarten, and Stephanie Novak. 2016. 'Integration without Transparency'? Reliance on the Space to Think in the European Council and Council." *Journal of European Integration* 38(5): 527–540.

Hindess, Barry. 2008. "Political Theory and 'Actually Existing Liberalism.'" *Critical Review of International Social and Political Philosophy* 11(3): 347–352.

Hirschl, Ran. 2004. *Towards Juristocracy: The Origins and Consequences of the New Constitutionalism.* Harvard University Press.

Hlavka, Heather, and Sameena Mulla. 2021. *Bodies in Evidence: Race, Gender and Science in Sexual Assault Adjudication.* NYU Press.

Hodson, Loveday. 2011. *NGOs and the Struggle for Human Rights in Europe.* Hart Publishing.

Holmes, Douglas R. 2001. *Integral Europe: Fast-Capitalism, Multiculturalism, and Neofascism.* Princeton University Press.

———. 2019. "Fascism at Eye Level: The Anthropological Conundrum." *Focaal* no. 84: 62–90.

Hull, Matthew. 2003. "The File: Agency, Authority, and Autography in an Islamabad Bureaucracy." *Language & Communication* 23: 287–314.

———. 2012. *Government of Paper. The Materiality of Bureaucracy in Urban Pakistan.* University of California Press.

Huneeus, Alexandra, Javier Couso, and Rachel Sieder. 2010. *Cultures of Legality, Judicialization, and Political Activism in Latin America.* Cambridge University Press.

Inoue, Miyako. 2003. *Vicarious Language: Gender and Linguistic Modernity in Japan.* University of California Press.

Jamison, Kelda. 2016. "Hefty Dictionaries in Incomprehensible Tongues: Commensurating Code and Language Community in Turkey." *Anthropological Quarterly* 89(1): 31–62.

Johnson, Paul. 2013. *Homosexuality and the European Court of Human Rights.* Routledge.

Judt, Tony. 2011. *A Grand Illusion.* New York University Press.

Kahn, Jeffrey. 2019. *Islands of Sovereignty: Haitian Migration and the Borders of Empire.* University of Chicago Press.

Karakasidou, Anastasia N. 1997. *Fields of Wheat, Hills of Blood: Passages to Nationhood in Greek Macedonia, 1870–1990.* University of Chicago Press.

Keane, Webb. 2018. "On Semiotic Ideology." *Signs and Society* 6(1): 64-87.

Keller, Helen, and Alec Stone Sweet, eds. 2008. *A Europe of Rights: The Impact of the ECHR on National Legal Systems.* Oxford University Press.

Kindt, Eline. 2018. "Giving Up on Individual Justice? The Effect of State Non-execution of a Pilot Judgment on Victims." *Netherlands Quarterly of Human Rights* 36(3): 173–188.

Kleinfeld, Rachel. 2006. "Competing Definitions of the Rule of Law." In *Promoting the Rule of Law Abroad: In Search of Knowledge*, edited by Thomas Carothers. Carnegie Endowment for International Peace.

Koga, Yukiko. 2013. "Accounting for Silence: Inheritance, Debt, and the Moral Economy of Legal Redress in China and Japan." *American Ethnologist* 40(3): 494–507.

Koselleck, Reinhart. 2004. *Futures Past: On the Semantics of Historical Time.* Columbia University Press.

Krastev, Ivan, and Stephen Holmes. 2019. *The Light That Failed: A Reckoning.* Simon & Schuster.

Krygier, Martin. 2016. "The Rule of Law: Pasts, Presents, and Two Possible Futures." *Annual Review of Law and Social Science* 12(1): 199–229.

———. 2019. "What's the Point of the Rule of Law?" *Buffalo Law Review* 67(3): 743–791.

Kubal, Agnieszka. 2023. "The Women's Complaint: Sociolegal Mobilization against Authoritarian Backsliding following the 2020 Abortion Law in Poland. *Journal of Contemporary Central and Eastern Europe* 31(3): 585–605.

Kurban, Dilek. 2016. "Forsaking Individual Justice: The Implications of the European Court of Human Rights' Pilot Judgment Procedure for Victims of Gross and Systematic Violations." *Human Rights Law Review* 16(4; December): 731–769.

———. 2020. *Limits of Supranational Justice: The European Court of Human Rights and Turkey's Kurdish Conflict.* Cambridge University Press.

Kurtović, Larisa, and Azra Hromadžić. 2017. "Cannibal States, Empty Bellies: Protest, History and Political Imagination in Post-Dayton Bosnia." *Critique of Anthropology* 37(3): 262–296,

Lacey, Nicola. 2019. "Populism and Rule of Law." *Annual Review of Law and Social Science* 15: 79–96.

Langford, Malcolm. 2018. "Critiques of Human Rights." *Annual Review of Law and Social Science* 14: 69–89.

Latour, Bruno. 2004. "Has Critique Run Out of Steam? From Matters of Fact to Matters of Concern." *Critical Inquiry* 30: 225–238.

———. 2009. *The Making of Law: An Ethnography of the Conseil d'Etat.* Polity Press.

Leach, Philip, and Alice Donald. 2016. *Parliaments and the European Court of Human Rights.* Oxford University Press.

Lloyd, David, and Paul Thomas. 1998. *Culture and the State.* Routledge Press.

Luxemburg, Rosa. 1900 (2004). "Social Reform or Revolution?" (Sozialreform oder Revolution?). Translated by Dick Howard. In *Rosa Luxemburg Reader,* edited by Peter Hudis and Kevin Anderson. Monthly Review Press.

Mačkić, Jasmina. 2018. *Proving Discriminatory Violence at the European Court of Human Rights.* Brill Press.

Macpherson, C. B. 1962. *The Political Theory of Possessive Individualism: Hobbes to Locke.* Oxford University Press.

Madsen, Mikael Rask. 2004. "France, the UK, and the 'Boomerang' of the Internationalization of Human Rights (1945–2000)." In *Human Rights Brought Home: Socio-Legal Perspectives on Human Rights in the National Context,* edited by Simon Halliday and Patrick Schmidt. Hart Publishing.

———. 2007. "From Cold War Instrument to Supreme European Court: The European Court of Human Rights at the Crossroads of International and National Law and Politics." *Law & Social Inquiry* 32(1): 137–159.

———. 2018. "The European Court of Human Rights: From the Cold War to the Brighton Declaration and Backlash." In *International Court Authority,* edited by Karen J. Alter, Laurence R. Helfer, and Mikael Rask Madsen. Oxford University Press.

Makaremi, Chowra, and Pardis Shafafi. 2019. "Introduction to Symposium: Desire for Justice, Desire for Law: An Ethnography of People's Tribunals." *Political and Legal Anthropology Review* 42(2): 181–190.

Marshall, Anna-Marie, and Daniel Crocker Hale. 2014. "Cause Lawyering." *Annual Review of Law and Social Science* 10: 301–320.

Mathur, Nayanika. 2016. *Paper Tiger: Law, Bureaucracy and the Developmental State in Himalayan India.* Cambridge University Press.

Mattei, Ugo, and Laura Nader. 2008. *Plunder: When the Rule of Law Is Illegal.* Blackwell Publishing.

Mattioli, Fabio. 2020. *Dark Finance: Illiquidity and Authoritarianism at the Margins of Europe.* Stanford University Press.

Mazzarella, William. 2019. "The Anthropology of Populism: Beyond the Liberal Settlement." *Annual Review of Anthropology* 48: 45–60.

McGranahan, Carole, and John F. Collins. 2018. "Introduction: Ethnography and U.S. Empire." In *Ethnographies of U.S. Empire,* edited by Carole McGranahan and John F. Collins, Duke University Press.

Merry, Sally Engle. 2006a. *Human Rights and Gender Violence: Translating International Law into Local Justice.* University of Chicago Press.

———. 2006b. "Transnational Human Rights and Local Activism: Mapping the Middle." *American Anthropologist* 108(1): 38–51.

———. 2016. *The Seductions of Quantification: Measuring Human Rights, Gender Violence and Sex Trafficking.* University of Chicago Press.

Mertz, Elizabeth. 2007. *The Language of Law School: Learning to Think Like a Lawyer.* Oxford University Press.

Messer, Ellen. 2002. "Anthropologists in a World with or without Human Rights." In *Exotic No More: Anthropology on the Front Lines*, edited by Jeffrey MacClancy. University of Chicago Press.

Mills, Charles W. 1999. *The Racial Contract.* Cornell University Press.

Mol, Annemarie. 2003. *The Body Multiple: Ontology in Medical Practice.* Duke University Press.

Moor, Louise, and A. W. Brian Simpson. 2005. "Ghosts of Colonialism in the European Convention on Human Rights." *British Yearbook of International Law* 76(1): 121–194.

Mora, Agathe. 2023. "Property Rights Are Human Rights: Bureaucratization and the Logics of Rule of Law Interventionism in Postwar Kosovo." *PoLAR: Political and Legal Anthropology Review* 46(1): 82–96.

Mowbray, Alastair. 2005. "The Creativity of the European Court of Human Rights." *Human Rights Law Review* 5(1): 57–80.

Moyn, Samuel. 2010. *The Last Utopia: Human Rights in History.* Harvard University Press.

———. 2014. "From Communist to Muslim: European Human Rights, the Cold War and Religious Liberty." *South Atlantic Quarterly* 133(1): 63–86.

———. 2018. *Not Enough: Human Rights in an Unequal World.* Harvard University Press.

Muehlebach, Andrea. 2023. *A Vital Frontier: Water Insurgencies in Europe.* Duke University Press.

Muir, Sarah. 2021. *Routine Crisis: An Ethnography of Disillusion.* University of Chicago Press.

Muir, Sarah, and Akhil Gupta. 2018. "Rethinking the Anthropology of Corruption." *Current Anthropology* 59(Supplement 18): S4–S15.

Muller, Birgit. 2013. "Lifting the Veil of Harmony: Anthropologists approach international Organizations." In *The Gloss of Harmony: The Politics of Policy Making in Multilateral Organizations*, edited by Birgit Muller. Pluto Press.

Munn, Nancy D. 1992. "The Cultural Anthropology of Time: A Critical Essay." *Annual Review of Anthropology* 21: 93–123.

Myslinska, Rita Dagmar. 2024. *Law, Migration, and the Construction of Whiteness: Mobility within the European Union.* Routledge Press.

Nader, Laura. 1972. "Up the Anthropologist: Perspectives Gained from 'Studying Up." In *Reinventing Anthropology*, edited by D. Hyms. Random House.

———. 2011. "Ethnography as Theory." *HAU: Journal of Ethnographic Theory* 1(1): 211–219.

Nakassis, Constantine V. Forthcoming. "Voicing, Looking, Perspective." *Current Anthropology.*

Navaro-Yashin, Yael. 2012. *The Make-Believe Space: Affective Geography in a Postwar Polity.* Duke University Press.

Nelson, Diane. 2015. *Who Counts: The Mathematics of Life and Death after Genocide.* Duke University Press.

Newfield, Christopher, Anna Alexandrova, and Stephen John, eds. 2022. *Limits of the Numerical: The Abuses and Uses of Quantification.* University of Chicago Press.

Niezen, Ronald. 2010. *Public Justice and the Anthropology of Law.* Cambridge University Press.

Niezen, Ronald, and Maria Sapignoli. 2017. *Palaces of Hope: The Anthropology of Global Organizations.* Cambridge University Press.

Open Society Justice Initiative. 2016a. *Strategic Litigation Impacts: Insights from Global Experience.* Open Society Foundations. https://www.justiceinitiative.org/publica tions/strategic-litigation-impacts-insights-global-experience.

———. 2016b. *Strategic Litigation Impacts: Roma School Desegregation.* Open Society Foundations. https://www.justiceinitiative.org/publications/strategic-litigation-im pacts-roma-school-desegregation.

Osanloo, Arzoo. 2020. *Forgiveness Work: Mercy, Law, and Victims' Rights.* Princeton University Press.

Özyürek, Esra. 2006. *Nostalgia for the Modern: State Secularism and Everyday Politics in Turkey.* Duke University Press.

Paley, Julia. 2008. *Democracy: Anthropological Approaches.* SAR Press.

Pavone, Tommaso. 2022. *The Ghostwriters: Lawyers and the Politics behind the Judicial Construction of Europe.* Cambridge University Press.

Paz, Alejandro. 2018. *Latinos in Israel: Language and Unexpected Citizenship.* Indiana University Press.

Petrović-Šteger, Maja. 2020. "On the Side of Predictable: Visioning the Future in Serbia." *Etnološka tribina* 43(50): 3–31.

Poovey, Mary. 1998. *A History of the Modern Fact: Problems of Knowledge in the Sciences of Wealth and Society.* University of Chicago Press.

Philips, Susan U. 2016. "Balancing the Scales of Justice in Tonga." In *Scale: Discourse and Dimensions of Social Life*, edited by S. Carr and M. Lempert. University of California Press.

Prasse-Freeman, Elliot. 2023. *Rights Refused: Grassroots Activism and State Violence in Myanmar.* Stanford University Press.

Rajah, Jothie. 2012. *Authoritarian Rule of Law: Legislation, Discourse and Legitimacy in Singapore.* Cambridge University Press.

———. 2015. "'Rule of Law' as Transnational Legal Order." In *Transnational Legal Orders*, edited by Terence C. Halliday and Gregory Shaffer. Cambridge Studies in Law and Society. Cambridge University Press.

———. 2023. *Discounting Life: Necropolitical Law, Culture and the Long War on Terror.* Cambridge University Press.

Ramsay, Georgina. 2020. "Time and the Other in Crisis: How Anthropology Makes Its Displaced Object." *Anthropological Theory* 20(4): 385–413.

Reichel, David, Maarten Vink, and Jonas Grimheden. 2020. "Regional Diffusion, EU Conditionality and Council of Europe Treaty Ratification 1949–2016." *Journal of European Public Policy* 27(10): 1565–1584.

Resnick, Elana. 2024. "The Determined Indeterminacy of White Supremacy: Strategies of Racial Disavowal in Bulgaria." *American Ethnologist* 51: 433–447.

Richland, Justin. 2021. *Cooperation without Submission: Indigenous Jurisdictions in Native Nation–US Engagements*. University of Chicago Press.

Riles, Annelise. 2000. *The Network Inside Out*. University of Michigan Press.

———. 2006. "Anthropology, Human Rights and Legal Knowledge: Culture in the Iron Cage." *American Anthropologist* 108(1): 52–65.

Robbins, Joel. 2004. *Becoming Sinners: Christianity and Moral Torment in Papua New Guinean Society*. University of California Press.

Roitman, Janet. 2013. *Anti-Crisis*. Duke University Press.

Rosen, Lawrence. 2006. *Law as Culture: An Invitation*. Princeton University Press.

Rosenblatt, Adam. 2015. *Digging for the Disappeared: Forensic Science After Atrocity*. Stanford University Press.

Rucker-Chang, Sunni, and Chelsea West Ohueri. 2021. "A Moment of Reckoning: Transcending Bias, Engaging Race and Racial Formations in Slavic and East European Studies." *Slavic Review* 80(2): 216–223.

Sapignoli, Maria. 2017. "'Bushmen' in the Law: Evidence and Identity in Botswana's High Court." *Political and Legal Anthropology Review* 40(2): 210–225.

Sarat, Austin, and Roger Berkowitz. 1998. "Disorderly Difference: Recognition, Accommodation and American Law." In *Ethnography and Democracy*, edited by Carol Greenhouse. SUNY Press.

Sarat, Austin, and Stuart Scheingold. 2001. *Cause Lawyering and the State in a Global Era*. Oxford University Press.

Scheppele, Kim Lane. 2018. "Autocratic Legalism." *University of Chicago Law Review* 85: 545–583.

Scott, David. 1999. *Refashioning Futures: Criticism After Postcoloniality*. Princeton University Press.

———. 2004. *Conscripts of Modernity*. Duke University Press.

Shaffer, Gregory, Tom Ginsburg, and Terence C. Halliday. 2019. *Constitution Making and Transnational Legal Order*. Cambridge University Press.

Sharpe, Christina. 2016. *In the Wake: On Blackness and Being*. Duke University Press.

Silverstein, Paul. 2005. "Immigrant Racialization and the New Savage Slot: Race, Migration and Immigration in the New Europe." *Annual Review of Anthropology* 34: 363–384.

Sikkink, Kathryn. 2018. *Evidence for Hope: Making Human Rights Work in the 21st Century*. Princeton University Press.

Skocpol, Theda. 1979. *States and Social Revolutions*. Cambridge University Press.

Slotta, James. 2023. *Anarchy and the Art of Listening: The Politics and Pragmatics of Reception in Papua New Guinea*. Cornell University Press.

Spano, Robert. 2014. "Universality or Diversity of Human Rights? Strasbourg in the Age of Subsidiarity." *Human Rights Law Review* 14: 487–502.

Speck, Anne-Katrin. n.d. "The Evidentiary Practice of the European Court of Human Rights." PhD dissertation, University of Ghent. https://research.ugent.be/web/person/anne-katrin-speck-o/en.

Sperling, Stefan. 2011. "The Politics of Transparency and Surveillance in Post-Reunification Germany." *Surveillance and Society* 8(4): 396–412.

Stoler, Ann, ed. 2013. *Imperial Debris: On Ruins and Ruination*. Duke University Press.

Stone Sweet, Alec. 2000. *Governing with Judges: Constitutional Politics in Europe*. Oxford University Press.

———. 2004. *The Judicial Construction of Europe*. Oxford University Press.

———. 2009. "On the Constitutionalisation of the Convention: The European Court of Human Rights as a Constitutional Court." *Revue trimestrielle des droits de l'homme* 80: 923–944.

Stone Sweet, Alec, Wayne Sandholtz, and Mads Andenas. 2022. "The Failure to Destroy the Authority of the European Court of Human Rights: 2010–2018." *The Law and Practice of International Courts and Tribunals* 21: 244–277.

Sundstrom, Lisa, Valerie Sperling, and Melike Sayoglu. 2019. *Courting Gender Justice: Russia, Turkey, and the European Court of Human Rights*. Oxford University Press.

Teitel, Ruti. 2011. *Humanity's Law*. Oxford University Press.

———. 2014. *Globalizing Transitional Justice*. Oxford University Press.

Timmer, A. 2011. "Toward an Anti-stereotyping Approach for the European Court of Human Rights." *Human Rights Law Review* 11: 707–738.

Trouillot, Michel-Rolph. 2002. "North Atlantic Universals: Analytic Fictions 1492–1945." *South Atlantic Quarterly* 101(4): 839–858.

———. 2003. *Global Transformations: Anthropology and the Modern World*. Palgrave.

Tsampi, Aikaterini. 2021. "The Role of Civil Society in Monitoring the Executive in the Case-Law of the European Court of Human Rights: Recasting the Rule of Law." *Utrecht Law Review* 17(2): 102–115.

Wedeen, Lisa. 1998. "Acting 'As If': Symbolic Politics and Social Control in Syria." *Comparative Studies in Society and History* 40(3): 503–523.

Weizman, Eyal. 2017. *Forensic Architecture: Violence at the Threshold of Detectability*. Zone Books.

Wekker, Gloria. 2016. *White Innocence: Paradoxes of Colonialism and Race*. Duke University Press.

Wheatley, Natasha. 2023. *The Life and Death of States*. Princeton University Press.

Wildhaber, Luzius. 2011. "Rethinking the European Court of Human Rights." In *The European Court of Human Rights between Law and Politics*, edited by Jonas Christoffersen and Mikael Rask Madsen. Oxford University Press.

Wilson, Richard. 2001. *The Politics of Truth and Reconciliation in South Africa: Legitimizing the Post-Apartheid State*. Cambridge University Press.

———. 2011. *Writing History in International Criminal Trials*. Cambridge University Press.

Urciuoli, Bonnie. 2008. "Skills and Selves in the New Workplace." *American Ethnologist* 35(2): 211–228.

———. 2009. "Talking/Not Talking about Race: The Enregisterments of Culture in Higher Education Discourses." *Journal of Linguistic Anthropology* 19(1): 21–39.

———. 2010. "Entextualizing Diversity: Semiotic Incoherence in Institutional Discourse." *Language & Communication* 30: 48–57.

Valverde, Marianne. 2015. *Chronotopes of Law: Jurisdiction, Scale and Governance*. Routledge.

Vauchez, Antoine. 2012. "The Force of a Weak Field: Law and Lawyers in the Government of Europe." In *Lawyers and the Construction of Transnational Justice*, edited by Yves Dezalay and Bryant G. Garth. Routledge.

Vetters, Larissa, and Alice Margaria. 2024. "'Law and Anthropology' as Interdisciplinary Encounter: Towards Multi-sited, Situated Knowledge Production." In *Leading Works in Law and Anthropology*, edited by Larissa Vetters and Alice Margaria. Routledge Press.

Verdery, Katherine. 1996. *What Was Socialism and What Comes Next?* Princeton University Press.

———. 2003. *The Vanishing Hectare: Property and Value in Postsocialist Transylvania.* Cornell University Press.

Wedel, Janine. 2001. *Collision and Collusion: The Strange Case of Western Aid to Eastern Europe.* St. Martins Press.

Wolfson, Sam. 2022. "It's a Slam Dunk: Philippe Sands on the Case against Putin for the Crime of Aggression." *The Guardian*, March 31. https://www.theguardian.com/law/2022/mar/30/vladimir-putin-ukraine-crime-aggression-philippe-sands.

Zenker, Olaf. 2021. "Anthropology and the Postliberal Challenge." *Social Anthropology* 29(2): 370–372.

Ziegler, Mary. 2020. *Abortion and the Law in America: Roe v Wade to the Present.* Cambridge University Press.

Zigon, Jared. 2013. "Human Rights as Moral Progress, a Critique." *Cultural Anthropology* 28(4): 716–736.

ECtHR Cases

Association ACCEPT and Others v. Romania (Application no. 19237/16) (1 June 2021)

Al Skeini and Others v. The United Kingdom (Application no. 55721/07) (7 July 2011)

Anguelova v. Bulgaria (Application no. 38361/97) (13 June 2002)

Broniowski v. Poland (Application no. 31443/96) (22 June 2004)

Burmych and Others v. Ukraine (striking out) [GC] (Application nos. 46852/13, 47786/13, 54125/13 et al.) (12 October 2017)

Christine Goodwin v. The United Kingdom (Application no. 28957/95) (11 July 2002)

D. H. and Others v. The Czech Republic (Application no. 57325/00) (13 November 2007)

Dudgeon v. The United Kingdom (Application no. 7525/76) (22 October 1981)

Handyside v. The United Kingdom (Application no. 5493/72) (7 December 1976)

Hirsi Jamaa and Others v. Italy (Application no. 27765/09) (23 February 2012)

Hirst v. The United Kingdom (no. 2) (Application no. 74025/01) (6 October 2005)

Ibrahim and Others v. The United Kingdom (Application nos. 50541/08, 50571/08, 50573/08 and 40351/09) (13 September 2016)

Identoba and Others v. Georgia (Application no. 73235/12) (12 May 2015)

Opuz v. Turkey (Application no. 33401/02) (9 June 2009)

Rees v. The United Kingdom (Application no. 9532/81) (17 October 1986)

Salduz v. Turkey (Application no. 36391/02) (27 November 2008)

S.A.S. v. France (Application no. 43835/11) (2014)

Tyrer v. The United Kingdom (Application no. 5856/72) (25 April 1978)

Vavřička and Others v. The Czech Republic (Applications nos. 47621/13 and 5 others) (8 April 2021)

Index

Note: Page numbers in *italics* refer to illustrations.

Stanford Studies in Human Rights
Mark Goodale, editor

Editorial Board

Alison Brysk

Gráinne de Búrca

Louise Chappell

Rosemary Coombe

Amal Hassan Fadlalla

Audrey Macklin

Virginia Mantouvalou

Ronald Niezen

Laurence Ralph

Sridhar Venkatapuram

Richard A. Wilson

The Subject of Human Rights
Edited by Danielle Celermajer and Alexandre Lefebvre
2020

#HumanRights: The Technologies and Politics of Justice Claims in Practice
Ronald Niezen
2020

The Grip of Sexual Violence in Conflict:
Feminist Interventions in International Law
Karen Engle
2020

When Misfortune Becomes Injustice: Evolving Human
Rights Struggles for Health and Social Equality
Alicia Ely Yamin
2020

The Politics of Love in Myanmar: LGBT Mobilization
and Human Rights as a Way of Life
Lynette J. Chua
2018

Branding Humanity: Competing Narratives of
Rights, Violence, and Global Citizenship
Amal Hassan Fadlalla
2018

Remote Freedoms: Politics, Personhood and Human
Rights in Aboriginal Central Australia
Sarah E. Holcombe
2018

Letters to the Contrary: A Curated History of
the UNESCO Human Rights Survey
Edited and Introduced by Mark Goodale
2018

For a complete listing of available titles in this series, visit
the Stanford University Press website, www.sup.org.